WHAT'S DIFFERENT ABOUT TEACHING READING TO STUDENTS LEARNING ENGLISH?

STUDY GUIDE

Dorothy Kauffman
Center for Applied Linguistics, Washington, DC

Copyright © 2007 by Center for Applied Linguistics

All rights reserved. No part of this publication may be reproduced or transmitted in any form or by any means, electronic or mechanical, including photocopying, recording, or any information storage and retrieval system, without permission in writing from the publisher.

Requests for permission to make copies of any part of the work should be sent to:

PERMISSIONS
CENTER FOR APPLIED LINGUISTICS (CAL)
4646 40th Street, NW
Washington, DC 20016-1859
permissions@cal.org
www.cal.org/about/permissions.html

Editorial/Production Supervision: Jeanne Rennie
Editors: Joy Kreeft Peyton, Betty Ansin Smallwood
Document Management: Sarah Young
Copyediting: EEI Communications
Proofreading: Amy Fitch
Interior Design/Production: Linda Bruell
Cover: Damon Taylor

ISBN–10: 1-932748-58-X
ISBN–13: 978-193748-58-1

*For JoAnn (Jodi) Crandall, who opened CAL's door to me,
and for all the wonderful friends and colleagues that CAL
has brought and continues to bring into my life.*

TABLE OF CONTENTS

INTRODUCTION   Professional Development for Teaching Reading to English Language Learners—Program Overview

CHAPTER 1   The Nature of Reading

Table of Contents

CHAPTER 2   Comprehension

CHAPTER 3   Vocabulary Development

Table of Contents

CHAPTER 4   Beginning Reading

Table of Contents

CHAPTER 5   Reading Fluency

Table of Contents

CHAPTER 6   Content Area Reading and Study Skills

CHAPTER 7　　Putting It All Together

Foreword

What's Different About Teaching Reading to Students Learning English? is a practical resource for trainers to provide professional development for teachers who work with elementary grade and middle school English language learners. The materials focus on developing students' reading skills. These materials are not designed to give trainers or teachers a "magic bullet" or definitive answers. Instead, the Trainer's Manual, the *Why Reading Is Hard* video, and the Study Guide offer useful information—summaries of research on teaching native English speakers and English language learners to read, classroom–based lesson plans, video clips of students' reading experiences, and interactive workshop activities and simulations. They also offer instructional suggestions for teachers to help all of their students, especially English language learners, to learn to read.

The organizational framework for these materials is aligned with reports of the National Reading Panel (2000) and the National Literacy Panel (August & Shanahan, 2006). For each component of reading addressed, key findings from the work of those two panels are summarized and relevant research cited. Moreover, these materials build on a significant finding of the National Literacy Panel—that the development of oral language skills and vocabulary knowledge, and opportunities for meaningful learning experiences, are key to developing the literacy skills of English language learners. These findings play a central role in the materials presented here.

In each section of the training materials, the information presented and activities suggested are designed to help teachers make applications from research findings to practice in their classrooms. Both during and following the workshops, these training materials guide teachers, working individually and in collaborative groups, to think about their own reading curriculum and materials and to determine how they can apply the information and activities provided in their own instruction. Following implementation, teachers are encouraged to reflect on which applications were successful and which were not, based on their students' performance.

Professional developers, teacher trainers, and teacher mentors will find these materials to be comprehensive, practical, and flexible for use in preservice and inservice professional development settings.

Diane August, Principal Investigator
National Literacy Panel on Language Minority Children and Youth

Acknowledgments

The idea for the publication of the first edition of *What's Different About Teaching Reading to Students Learning English?* emerged from the experiences of its co–authors, Linda Franco and Dorothy Kauffman, in preparing teachers to teach reading to English language learners. We recognized that many mainstream teachers had training in reading instruction but not in second language acquisition and that many English as a second language (ESL) teachers had knowledge of second language acquisition but not reading instruction. We also recognized that there are many overlapping aspects of effective reading instruction for native English speakers and English language learners, but the instructional needs of second language readers are complex. Our goal for that first edition was to identify and describe the components of effective reading instruction for both native English speakers and English language learners.

This second edition of the publication carries the same goals as those of the first edition. This edition includes summaries of more recent research, additional activities suggested by the research, a study guide, and activities based on the video, *Why Reading Is Hard* (Center for Applied Linguistics, 2002). The study guide and video–based activities give trainers and teachers opportunities to think about and apply their learning immediately. The study guide also serves as a resource for teachers as they go about teaching reading to the English language learners in their classes.

I am grateful to a number of people for their significant contributions to the development of this edition. Judy Jameson, a colleague from the Center for Applied Linguistics (CAL), gave me the vision, text concept, and organizational framework for developing these professional development materials. Joy Kreeft Peyton and Betty Ansin Smallwood managed the project and edited the text; patiently and carefully guided me through its completion; reviewed multiple drafts; made contributions to the content; and made sure the work was clean, concise, and coherent. Sarah Young took my various texts and integrated them into the new products. Jeannette Roy acted as an efficient and supportive research assistant. Inge Siggelkow developed a comprehensive reference list and a set of correct Internet links. Jeanne Rennie provided guidance and coordination on editing. Grace Burkart read and critiqued the materials, and she and Dora Johnson wrote the contrastive analyses of English/Spanish and English/Arabic in Chapter 1.

I am especially grateful for the contributions of the teachers who gave me permission to include their lesson plans in the study guide. These teachers created the lessons using the strategies and techniques presented during workshops and then used them in their instruction. These lesson plans and the teachers' reflections on their instruction supply sample real–classroom applications of the recommended strategies and techniques. Specifically, I thank Carolyn Patton, Wake County Public School System, Raleigh, North Carolina, and the following teachers in Massachusetts: Nancy Veaudry, Kingston Intermediate School; Rebecca Zieminski and Danielle Rivet, Marlborough Intermediate Elementary School; Lois Mason, Mill Pond Intermediate School, Westborough; Harriet R. Griffin and Diane Fuimara, Medford Public Schools; Ana Oveido Healey, Mulchaey Middle School, Taunton; and Lori Viet, North Attleborough Middle School.

The suggestions and insights of the following reviewers contributed significantly to the quality of the content: Diane August, National Literacy Panel on Minority Children and Youth; Donna Christian, Center for Applied Linguistics; Laura Golden, independent consultant; Candace Harper, University of Florida; Judith O'Loughlin, ESL consultant; Carolyn Patton, Wake County (NC) Public School System; and Holly Stein, independent consultant. I thank them for their thoughtful and helpful comments.

I also thank the staff of EEI Communications for their careful attention to the task of copyediting, Amy Fitch for proofreading the manuscript, and Delta Systems for turning the manuscript into a beautiful and useful training package.

Dorothy Kauffman
Center for Applied Linguistics, Washington, DC

What's Different About Teaching Reading to Students Learning English?
Study Guide

INTRODUCTION
Professional Development for Teaching Reading to English Language Learners—Program Overview

Purpose and Goals of the Program

The purpose of these materials is to help workshop participants achieve the following:

◆ Develop an understanding of how learning to read in English differs for native English speakers and English language learners.

◆ Understand five components of reading that are the foundation of successful reading programs: phonemic awareness, phonics, vocabulary development, reading fluency, and reading comprehension.

◆ Identify effective strategies and techniques to improve reading instruction for native English speakers and English language learners in elementary and middle school classrooms.

Major Topics and Goals

Chapter 1   The Nature of Reading

Goal: To develop an understanding of how learning to read differs for native English speakers and English language learners

Chapter 2   Comprehension

Goal: To understand that reading comprehension is a complex process that involves a reader's knowledge of how English syntax, grammar, and vocabulary work; the ways that spoken English is represented in print; and connections between background knowledge and experiences and printed text

Chapter 3   Vocabulary Development

Goal: To understand the role of word roots and affixes and of vocabulary development in learning to read; to understand the characteristics of effective instructional strategies to teach vocabulary

Chapter 4   Beginning Reading

Goal: To develop an understanding of the basic components of learning to read in English for native English speakers and English language learners

---

Chapter 5   Reading Fluency

Goal: To understand the role that reading fluency plays in reading comprehension

Chapter 6   Content Area Reading and Study Skills

Goal: To understand that reading to learn is a complex process that involves a reader's knowledge of how English works, how content is represented in print, and how to select and employ appropriate reading strategies and study skills to meet specific purposes

Chapter 7   Putting It All Together

Goal: To reflect on the basic components of learning to read and consider what is the same and what is different about teaching reading to native English speakers and English language learners

~

Four Principles of Instruction

These professional development materials are organized around four principles of second language acquisition that are used to adapt instruction for English language learners. The four principles state that when planning lessons to include English language learners, teachers should take steps to do the following:

- *Principle 1.* Increase comprehension: Make meaning clear through visuals, demonstrations, and other means.

- *Principle 2.* Increase student–to–student interaction: Engage students in using English to accomplish academic tasks.

- *Principle 3.* Increase higher order thinking and the use of learning strategies: Explicitly teach thinking skills and learning strategies to develop English language learners as effective, independent learners.

- *Principle 4.* Make connections to students' background knowledge: Explicitly plan and incorporate ways to engage students in thinking about and drawing from their life experiences and prior knowledge.

In these professional development sessions, participants learn about and apply a variety of instructional strategies to put these four principles into practice in their classes. The research supporting these principles follows.

Principle 1: Increase Comprehension

Comprehensible input (language that is understandable to the learner) is a prerequisite for language acquisition (Krashen, 1985). Learners must understand the meaning of new language through nonverbal clues or through language that they already understand. Comprehension of academic content is increased through a variety of means, such as the use of demonstrations, visual aids, hands–on activities, and modified (sheltered) English, and the clarification of key concepts in the learner's native language (Krashen, 1981; Krashen & Terrell, 1983; Rigg & Enright, 1986; Short, 1991b). Comprehension is also increased by building on learners' prior knowledge and language through discussion, brainstorming, use of graphic organizers, and other prereading and prewriting strategies (Crandall, 1993; Crandall, Jaramillo, Olsen, & Peyton, 2001, 2002; Olsen & Gee, 1991; Short, 1991a, 1991b).

Principle 2: Increase Student–to–Student Interaction

Receptive skills (listening and reading) are necessary but not sufficient for success in school. Students must explain their reasoning, justify answers, and write essays and lab reports; in other words, they must produce language by speaking and writing (Ellis, 1997; Swain, 1995). To produce language proficiently, students must practice using language during instruction (Freeman & Freeman, 1998–1999). In fact, increased student participation in peer interaction has been shown to enhance students' language acquisition more than teacher–directed activities (Doughty & Pica, 1986; Long, 1983; Long & Porter, 1985). The use of instructional conversations in which teachers guide students to higher levels of comprehension of text through discussion has proven valuable to English language learners (Goldenberg, 1992–1993). Techniques such as cooperative learning ensure that all students are engaged and on task, and are using the academic language of the content area (Holt, 1993; Holt, Chips, & Wallace, 1991; Kagan, 1986). Long and Porter (1985) examined English language learners working in small groups and found that group work increased learners' language practice opportunities, improved the quality of student talk, helped individualize instruction, promoted a positive learning climate, and motivated learners. Cooperative learning is one of nine instructional strategies that promises to affect student achievement across all content areas and grade levels (Marzano, Pickering, & Pollack, 2001); it is also one of five practices identified as effective for teaching Hispanic students (Padrón, Waxman, & Rivera, 2002). Jacob (1999) found cooperative learning particularly effective in heterogeneous classes with native English speakers and English language learners.

Principle 3: Increase Higher Order Thinking and the Use of Learning Strategies

Academic language or CALP (cognitive academic language proficiency) (Cummins, 1981) involves more than knowledge of academic vocabulary, syntax, and rhetorical style. It is also the ability to use language for higher–order thinking and communicating: to analyze and summarize cognitively demanding material, to argue a position, and to accomplish other complex tasks (Echevarria, Vogt, & Short, 2000). Research demonstrates the importance of these skills for success in school. Collier (1995a) found that effective programs for students learning English explicitly

Introduction

teach learning strategies, thinking skills, and problem solving. Chamot and O'Malley (1986, 1994) developed the Cognitive Academic Language Learning Approach (CALLA), which integrates learning strategies and language development. The CALLA work was the focus of later research on learning strategies (Chamot, Barnhardt, El–Dinary, & Robbins, 1999). In that study, the authors provide an extensive discussion of the theoretical background for and research on learning strategies, with an emphasis on English language learners. They conclude that good language learners use a variety of learning strategies (pp. 163–167) and that instruction in learning strategies leads to increased use of those strategies, increased learner motivation, and improved performance on a variety of language learning tasks (pp. 167–178). Marzano, Pickering, & Pollack (2001) identified learning strategies that are most likely to improve all students' achievement. Montes (2002) demonstrated that students instructed in the use of learning strategies perform significantly better on state standardized tests, with the strongest effects for English language learners and at–risk students in school. The national ESL Standards for PreK–12 Students (Teachers of English to Speakers of Other Languages, 1997) acknowledge the importance of learning strategies by making them the focus of three of the nine standards for English language learners.

Principle 4: Make Connections to Students' Background Knowledge

Teachers at every grade level find a wide range of diversity among their students—physical, emotional, and intellectual. In addition, in the ever–changing classrooms of the 21st century, there is an increasing range of cultural differences as more and more students from other countries enter U.S. schools. Every child born, raised, and socialized in the culture of a group of people learns what that group of people knows and believes, what they do, and what they make and use (Peregoy & Boyle, 2000). The child uses this accumulated knowledge to make sense of the world. Cross–cultural research reveals there are characteristics of culture that make one culture different from another (Richard–Amato & Snow, 1992). Both teachers and students need to be aware of these cultural differences and to recognize that not everyone is "just like me" (Richard–Amato & Snow, 1992, p. 77). In terms of comprehending text, it is important that students are able to see themselves when they read and to make connections with the content, because the text relates to what they know (Cloud, Genesee, & Hamayan, 2000; Larrick, 1969).

Additional Considerations for Instruction

In addition to applying these four principles in instruction, teachers must also use appropriate assessments and track the progress and needs of individual students. In terms of assessment, mainstream teachers need to find out which content objectives English language learners have achieved, but they must also use measures that are aligned with students' language proficiency levels. For example, assessments for beginning students should not depend heavily on their reading extended texts in English or using complex responses in English to demonstrate learning. Performance assessment, portfolio assessment, student self–assessment, and modified traditional assessments are recommended (O'Malley & Valdez Pierce, 1996; Teachers of English to Speakers of Other Languages, 1997, 2000a). Awareness of students' cultural backgrounds is also important in curriculum and instruction (Menkart, 1993) and in parent and community involvement (Teachers of English to Speakers of Other Languages, 2000b; Violand–Sanchez, Sutton, & Ware, 1991). A school's respect for students' home languages and cultures and the creation of an explicitly welcoming climate in school contribute significantly to student success (Collier, 1995a, 1995b).

~

Background of the Program

Reading First

This manual is compatible with new requirements put in place by the Reading First Initiative, part of the 2001 reauthorization of the Elementary and Secondary Education Act (known as No Child Left Behind). Schools must show that the reading programs that they use are research based and that they include instruction in five components of reading (U.S. Department of Education, 2002):

- Phonemic awareness—the understanding that spoken words may be broken into smaller parts such as syllables and individual sounds

- Phonics—an approach to reading instruction that emphasizes the matching between individual sounds and their spellings

- Vocabulary—learning new words with their meanings and how they are used in sentences, as well as strategies for building vocabulary

- Fluency—reading connected text with speed, ease, and understanding

- Reading comprehension—constructing meaning from the text and integrating it with background knowledge and experience

Introduction

Research About the Teaching of Reading

The title of this manual is *What's Different About Teaching Reading to Students Learning English?* Research on the teaching of reading in a second language has increased in recent years, but there are still many gaps. Nevertheless, there are discussions throughout the manual of the important differences between teaching reading to native English speakers and to students learning English as a second language.

Some of the important things that we know about learning to read in a second language are summarized here (based on work by August & Shanahan, 2006; Bialystok, 1997; Burns, Griffin, & Snow, 1999; Burt, Peyton, & Adams, 2003; Snow, 2002).

Children who grow up in a rich language environment, no matter what their native language, are building strong foundations for literacy. Oral proficiency in a language, whether the native language or English, helps children become sensitive to both the sounds and the meanings of words. Awareness of sounds is the foundation for phonological awareness. A large vocabulary increases the chances that the child will recognize and understand the words in early reading materials. Children whose families have provided them with many varied experiences and have talked with them about daily routines and events have the advantage of a relatively large body of knowledge about the world around them. Although the transition from speaking to reading is much more difficult if children have to learn the spoken language at the same time that they are learning to read, if they have a good foundation of world knowledge, they will be better able to make sense of the second language as they learn it.

Many children begin school already knowing a lot about literacy. As their parents read storybooks to them, they begin to notice the difference between printed text and pictures. They learn to sing alphabet songs and play games that involve the letters of the alphabet. They learn to recognize common brand names. They may pretend to write by making scribbles. They may recognize and even learn to write their own name. Of course, not all children come to school having had these experiences even in their native language. However, those who have such experiences benefit even when the home language and school language are different. Children are prepared to understand that written text carries meaning.

Acquiring initial literacy in a second language is harder than learning to read in a second language after having become literate in the first language. If the first language uses an alphabetic writing system, the student has already learned the alphabetic principle—that spoken sounds are represented by written letters—and this knowledge transfers to reading in the second language. If the first and second languages are both written with the Roman alphabet, the shapes of most letters will already be familiar and even some of the correspondences between sounds and letters will be similar.

Initial teaching of correspondences between sounds and spellings is much easier if it is done in the context of meaningful words and texts. This is difficult to do if students have a limited vocabulary, and English language learners usually have much smaller English vocabularies than their monolingual English–speaking peers. English language learners may also require explicit instruction about some English vocabulary so that they can comprehend texts. Moreover, students need to have enough oral proficiency in English to learn the matching of sounds to spelling through phonics instruction. Most reading curricula are designed with the oral language skills of the native English speaker as the point of departure.

All students bring certain strengths and weaknesses to the task of learning to read. In the case of English language learners, they may not have the same background experiences or knowledge as their peers who are native English speakers and thus may have different concepts for the same word.

The disparity in oral English proficiency of native English speakers and English language learners leads many researchers to conclude that English language learners will benefit from reading instruction in their native language, if possible. If this is not possible, the oral language proficiency of English language learners should be developed as they develop literacy skills.

Speakers of two languages sometimes have an advantage over monolinguals in the acquisition of literacy. One underlying principle of literacy that students must grasp is that the written word carries meaning and that the same written form is consistently used to represent a given meaning. For example, the letters c–a–t are used to represent a spoken word that has a particular meaning. The meaning carried by c–a–t doesn't change merely because the word is mistakenly placed on a label next to a picture of a dog. Young bilinguals appear to grasp this principle more readily than monolinguals do.

The ability to use cognates—words in two related languages that are similar in their meanings and in their pronunciations or spellings—to build vocabulary and aid reading comprehension is another advantage that some bilinguals have over monolinguals. Cognates become more important as students move into the upper elementary grades. Sometimes the spelling of the cognate in English is identical with or closely similar to the spelling in the student's native language—for example, English *conversation*, French *conversation*, and Spanish *conversación*. Other times the connection is less transparent—for example, English *liberty*, French *liberté*, and Spanish *libertad*. Students who know Spanish or French can find cognates to be very helpful in learning to read in English.

Study Guide Scavenger Hunt

Directions: Work with a partner. Use the Study Guide to find the answers.

1. How many goals are there for the program? _____

2. How many chapters are in the study guide? _____

3. Which chapters address how English works? _____

    _____

4. How does each chapter begin? _____

    _____

5. How does each chapter end? _____

    _____

6. In what chapter is Predictors of Success in Learning to Read? _____

7. On what page are Stages of Second Language Acquisition? _____

8. Who wrote From One Teacher's Perspective in Chapter 3? _____

9. How many pages are devoted to Activities for Vocabulary Development? _____

10. On what pages are activities for teaching phonemic awareness? _____

11. On what pages are Preparing English Learners to Read Academic Content? _____

12. Who planned and taught *April Morning*? _____

CHAPTER 1
The Nature of Reading

Goal and Objectives

Goal
Participants will achieve the following:

- Develop an understanding of how learning to read differs for native English speakers and English language learners.

Objectives
Participants will be able to do the following:

- Describe what readers do when they read.

- Identify the major principles of second language acquisition and describe how they affect learning to read in English.

- Give some reasons why learning to read in English is hard.

- Identify five components of successful reading programs.

- Identify and describe how readers use four cueing systems as they read.

The Nature of Reading

What Is the Nature of Reading?

Directions: Make a list of what readers do when they read.

_____

_____

_____

_____

_____

_____

_____

_____

_____

_____

_____

_____

_____

_____

_____

_____

_____

_____

_____

_____

_____

What's Different About Teaching Reading to Students Learning English?
Study Guide

Catching Spies

Directions: Read the article below. As you read it, pay particular attention to what you do. Then revise your list on page 2 of what readers do when they read, if desired.

Spies spill their secrets in a cookbook that tells how these clandestine agents serve up such gourmet delicacies as Rocky Mountain Oysters* and delightful desserts to soften up their sources. Now, you can discover some secrets of spy catching while cooking up a pot of dongo–dongo soup, an African recipe that can be made with fish or meat but must always include okra and garlic.

Recently, the Brig'emin Detective Agency (BDA), a private service that specializes in burglar busting and spotting spies, began selling gimmick products to change its bungling image. The cookbook, *More Than Soups for Snoops*, explains how secret agents use sumptuous meals and draconian drinks in their intelligence work.

BDA critics point to the agency's chequered history of blunders as proof that there's good reason to change its image. One cooking anecdote reports that a secret agent, while testing a recipe, watched helplessly as his miniature tape recorder containing six months of surveillance tapes fell from his pocket into the bubbling broth. Another reveals that an agent failed to heed the instructions when making a Scottish haggis, and his overstuffed sheep stomach exploded like a bazooka.

*A dish made from beef, pork, or mutton testicles.

Reading Experts Describe Reading

Directions: Reading experts do not always agree on what's involved in or what's most important about reading in one's native language or in a second language. However, there is evidence that common agreement can be identified. What elements of agreement do you notice in these statements by reading experts?

For many people, reading means moving the eyes across and down a page and understanding the message of the text with little or no effort. As such, reading seems to be an unconscious process, but it is really a very complex process that requires precise knowledge and numerous processing strategies. The knowledge base has two parts: 1) knowledge of the world and its people, places, events, and activities and 2) knowledge of how language(s) work (i.e., the sounds of the language are represented by letters [or symbols], letters comprise words, words are joined together to form phrases, etc.). The knowledge base itself is not sufficient for reading, because it cannot interact with the text. A processing mechanism and strategies (involving language processing and thinking strategies) are also required for the reader to make sense of the squiggles on the page (Birch, 2002).

1. Skilled readers read quickly and automatically, unaware of the underlying processes. They read, but they cannot watch how their minds make sense of print. They link sounds and symbols unconsciously. The speech sounds, syllables, and meaningful parts of words are automatically matched with the written forms, because their attention is given to comprehending the meaning (Moats, 1999).

2. Readers use six types of information when they read:
   • Letter/sound knowledge
   • Semantics or word meanings and associations
   • Lexical or word knowledge
   • Schematic or prior knowledge
   • Syntactic or word order knowledge
   • Pragmatic or practical knowledge (adapted from Rumelhart, 1976, cited in Keene & Zimmerman, 1997)

3. If you read a great poem aloud—for example, "To a Skylark" by Percy Bysshe Shelley—and read it the way he set it up and punctuated it, what you are doing is breathing his inspired breath at the moment he wrote that poem. That breath was so powerful it still can be awakened in us more than 150 years later. Taking it on is very exhilarating. This is why it is good to remember: If you want to get high, don't drink whiskey; read Shakespeare, Tennyson, Keats, Neruda, Hopkins, Millay, and Whitman aloud and let your body sing (Goldberg, 1986, p. 51).

4. "Reading is like driving a car: Whether you learn to drive with a stick shift or automatic transmission, you know the basic rules of driving and can switch to the other type fairly easily" (Vogt, 2000, as cited in Rasmussen, 2000, p. 1).

Describing Reading

Directions: Drawing on your own experiences as a reader, do you agree or disagree with the experts? Briefly describe your thoughts.

_____

_____

_____

_____

_____

_____

_____

_____

_____

_____

_____

_____

_____

_____

_____

_____

Principles of Second Language Acquisition

Language Acquisition Matching

> **Directions:** Match the statements in Part A with the explanations in Part B. Write the letters beside the numbers.

Part A	Part B
____ 1. Language is functional.	A. Research in language acquisition reveals language is learned most effectively when it is used in meaningful ways. Language learning occurs most readily when learners can accomplish their social and academic purposes rather than through rote learning of vocabulary and grammar.
____ 2. Language varies.	
____ 3. Language learning includes cultural learning.	B. Language learning teaches the learner about the culture of the language as well as the language itself. Nonverbal behaviors, such as body and facial movements and speaking distances, are also learned through language instruction.
____ 4. Language acquisition is a long–term process.	C. Language comes in different varieties, and each is influenced by the context in which it is used. The language of the classroom is different from the language of the street. Each variety has a set of structural and functional characteristics that constitute an authentic form of communication.
____ 5. Language acquisition occurs through meaningful use and interaction.	D. An individual who acquires another language has cognitive and linguistic advantages over monolingual speakers. Second language acquisition also benefits society because the individual is able to communicate more readily with people from other linguistic backgrounds.
	E. Language acquisition takes a long time. Research shows that the acquisition of academic language required to be successful in the classroom can take from 5–7 years.
____ 6. Language processes develop interdependently.	F. Language learners acquire the four processes of language (listening, speaking, reading, and writing) in an overlapping fashion.
____ 7. Native language proficiency contributes to second language acquisition.	G. Research shows students who are proficient in their native language can transfer their linguistic skills to a second language more easily and quickly than students who are not proficient in their native language. Thus, if teachers have the opportunity to help students develop oral, reading, and writing skills in their native language, they should do so.
____ 8. Bilingualism is an individual and societal asset.	H. Whether oral or written, language is a means of communication. Language learning should be useful, focusing on the learner's ability to communicate with others. What is most useful for language learners is to continue to acquire the new language while learning challenging academic content.

Source: Teachers of English to Speakers of Other Languages. (1997). *ESL Standards for PreK–12 Students* (pp. 6–8). Alexandria, VA: Author. Adapted with permission.

TESOL's PreK–12 English Language Proficiency Goals and Standards

Teachers of English to Speakers of Other Languages (TESOL, 1997, 2006) has published a set of goals and standards for English language learners that include personal, social, and academic uses of English with tables of indicators of success at five English proficiency levels. The goals and standards follow:

Goal 1: To use English to communicate in social settings.
Goal 2: To use English to achieve academically in all content areas.
Goal 3: To use English in socially and culturally appropriate ways.

Standard 1: English language learners **communicate** for **social, intercultural, and instructional purposes** within the school setting.
Standard 2: English language learners **communicate** information, ideas, and concepts necessary for academic success in the area of **language arts**.
Standard 3: English language learners **communicate** information, ideas, and concepts necessary for academic success in the area of **mathematics**.
Standard 4: English language learners **communicate** information, ideas, and concepts necessary for academic success in the area of **science**.
Standard 5: English language learners **communicate** information, ideas, and concepts necessary for academic success in the area of **social studies**.

The first standard refers to basic interpersonal communication skills (BICS) and to cognitive academic language proficiency (CALP) (Cummins, 1979, 1981). Having BICS means having the ability to use everyday language and behaviors (e.g., gestures, facial expressions) to interact successfully with others. This means that English language learners are able to talk with their peers, hold informal conversations, read simple narratives, or write informal notes or letters (Crandall, 1987).

CALP is the ability to successfully understand and use the kind of language required in academic settings, classrooms, and texts. This means that English language learners can read the abstract language of textbooks, take notes during lectures, take tests, or engage in discussions of science or mathematics (Crandall, 1987). Cummins (1991) proposes that BICS may require from 1 to 2 years to acquire, but CALP may require from 5 to 7 years or more (Thomas & Collier, 2002).

The remaining four standards focus on the skills needed for students to be successful in each of the four academic areas of the school curriculum. Each of the five standards addresses the four language domains of listening, speaking, reading, and writing. In addition, five levels of language proficiency are described within each standard: Level 1—Starting, Level 2—Emerging, Level 3—Developing, Level 4—Expanding, and Level 5—Bridging. These new standards also ground instruction in students' first languages and cultures, and reflect an organizational structure that is in keeping with current federal legislation.

Contextual Factors in Second Language Acquisition

Aída Walqui, West Ed, San Francisco, California
September 2000

> **Directions:** This article addresses three factors in second language acquisition. Read the article and reflect on its meaning by drawing on your experiences with learning a second language or working with students who are learning a second language.

While many discussions about learning a second language focus on teaching methodologies, little emphasis is given to the contextual factors—individual, social, and societal—that affect students' learning. These contextual factors can be considered from the perspective of the language, the learner, and the learning process. This digest discusses these perspectives as they relate to learning any second language, with a particular focus on how they affect adolescent learners of English as a second language.

The Language

Several factors related to students' first and second languages shape their second language learning. These factors include the linguistic distance between the two languages, students' level of proficiency in the native language and their knowledge of the second language, the dialect of the native language spoken by the students (i.e., whether it is standard or nonstandard), the relative status of the students' language in the community, and societal attitudes toward the students' native language.

Language distance

Specific languages can be more or less difficult to learn, depending on how different from or similar they are to the languages the learner already knows. At the Defense Language Institute in Monterey, California, for example, languages are placed in four categories depending on their average learning difficulty from the perspective of a native English speaker. The basic intensive language course, which brings a student to an intermediate level, can be as short as 24 weeks for languages such as Dutch or Spanish, which are Indo–European languages and use the same writing system as English, or as long as 65 weeks for languages such as Arabic, Korean, or Vietnamese, which are members of other language families and use different writing systems.

Native language proficiency

The student's level of proficiency in the native language—including not only oral language and literacy, but also metalinguistic development, training in formal and academic features of language use, and knowledge of rhetorical patterns and variations in genre and style—affects acquisition of a second language. The more academically sophisticated the student's native language knowledge and abilities, the easier it will be for that student to learn a second language. This helps explain why foreign exchange students tend to be successful in American high school classes: They already have high school level proficiency in their native language.

Knowledge of the second language

Students' prior knowledge of the second language is of course a significant factor in their current learning. High school students learning English as a second language in a U.S. classroom may possess skills ranging from conversational fluency acquired from contacts with the English–speaking world to formal knowledge obtained in English as a foreign language classes in their countries of origin. The extent and type of prior knowledge is an essential consideration in planning instruction. For example, a student with informal conversational English skills may have little understanding of English grammatical systems and may need specific instruction in English grammar.

Dialect and register

Learners may need to learn a dialect and a formal register in school that are different from those they encounter in their daily lives. This involves acquiring speech patterns that may differ significantly from those they are familiar with and value as members of a particular social group or speech community.

Language status

Consideration of dialects and registers of a language and of the relationships between two languages includes the relative prestige of different languages and dialects and of the cultures and ethnic groups associated with them. Students whose first language has a low status vis–à–vis the second may lose their first language, perhaps feeling they have to give up their own linguistic and cultural background to join the more prestigious society associated with the target language.

Language attitudes

Language attitudes in the learner, the peer group, the school, the neighborhood, and society at large can have an enormous effect on the second language learning process, both positive and negative. It is vital that teachers and students examine and understand these attitudes. In particular, they need to understand that learning a second language does not mean giving up one's first language or dialect. Rather, it involves adding a new language or dialect to one's repertoire.

This is true even for students engaged in formal study of their first language. For example, students in Spanish for native speakers classes may feel bad when teachers tell them that the ways they speak Spanish are not right. Clearly, this is an issue of dialect difference. School (in this case, classroom Spanish) requires formal registers and standard dialects, while conversation with friends and relatives may call for informal registers and nonstandard dialects. If their ways of talking outside of school are valued when used in appropriate contexts, students are more likely to be open to learning a new language or dialect, knowing that the new discourses will expand their communicative repertoires rather than displace their familiar ways of communicating.

The Learner

Students come from diverse backgrounds and have diverse needs and goals. With adolescent language learners, factors such as peer pressure, the presence of role models, and the level of home support can strongly affect the desire and ability to learn a second language.

Chapter 1

Diverse needs

A basic educational principle is that new learning should be based on prior experiences and existing skills. Although this principle is known and generally agreed upon by educators, in practice it is often overshadowed by the administrative convenience of the linear curriculum and the single textbook. Homogeneous curricula and materials are problematic enough if all learners are from a single language and cultural background, but they are indefensible given the great diversity in today's classrooms. Such diversity requires a different conception of curricula and a different approach to materials. Differentiation and individualization are not a luxury in this context: They are a necessity.

Diverse goals

Learners' goals may determine how they use the language being learned, how native–like their pronunciation will be, how lexically elaborate and grammatically accurate their utterances will be, and how much energy they will expend to understand messages in the target language. Learners' goals can vary from wholly integrative—the desire to assimilate and become a full member of the English–speaking world—to primarily instrumental—oriented toward specific goals such as academic or professional success (Gardner, 1989). Educators working with English language learners must also consider whether the communities in which their students live, work, and study accept them, support their efforts, and offer them genuine English–learning opportunities.

Peer groups

Teenagers tend to be heavily influenced by their peer groups. In second language learning, peer pressure often undermines the goals set by parents and teachers. Peer pressure often reduces the desire of the student to work toward native pronunciation, because the sounds of the target language may be regarded as strange. For learners of English as a second language, speaking like a native speaker may unconsciously be regarded as a sign of no longer belonging to their native–language peer group. In working with secondary school students, it is important to keep these peer influences in mind and to foster a positive image for proficiency in a second language.

Role models

Students need to have positive and realistic role models who demonstrate the value of being proficient in more than one language. It is also helpful for students to read literature about the personal experiences of people from diverse language and dialect backgrounds. Through discussions of the challenges experienced by others, students can develop a better understanding of their own challenges.

Home support

Support from home is very important for successful second language learning. Some educators believe that parents of English language learners should speak only English in the home (see, e.g., recommendations made in Rodriguez, 1982). However, far more important than speaking English is that parents value both the native language and English, communicate with their children in whichever language is most comfortable, and show support for and interest in their children's progress.

The Learning Process

When we think of second language development as a learning process, we need to remember that different students have different learning styles, that intrinsic motivation aids learning, and that the quality of classroom interaction matters a great deal.

Learning styles

Research has shown that individuals vary greatly in the ways they learn a second language (Skehan, 1989). Some learners are more analytically oriented and thrive on picking apart words and sentences. Others are more globally oriented, needing to experience overall patterns of language in meaningful contexts before making sense of the linguistic parts and forms. Some learners are more visually oriented, others more geared to sounds.

Motivation

According to Deci and Ryan (1985), intrinsic motivation is related to basic human needs for competence, autonomy, and relatedness. Intrinsically motivated activities are those that the learner engages in for their own sake because of their value, interest, and challenge. Such activities present the best possible opportunities for learning.

Classroom interaction

Language learning does not occur as a result of the transmission of facts about language or from a succession of rote memorization drills. It is the result of opportunities for meaningful interaction with others in the target language. Therefore, lecturing and recitation are not the most appropriate modes of language use in the second language classroom. Teachers need to move toward more richly interactive language use, such as that found in instructional conversations (Tharp & Gallimore, 1988) and collaborative classroom work (Adger, Kalyanpur, Peterson, & Bridger, 1995).

Conclusion

While this digest has focused on the second language acquisition process from the perspective of the language, the learner, and the learning process, it is important to point out that the larger social and cultural contexts of second language development have a tremendous impact on second language learning, especially for immigrant students. The status of students' ethnic groups in relation to the larger culture can help or hinder the acquisition of the language of mainstream society.

Source: Walqui, A. (2000). *Access and Engagement: Program Design and Instructional Approaches for Immigrant Students in Secondary Schools.* ERIC Digest. Washington, DC: Center for Applied Linguistics.

Contextual Factors in Second Language Acquisition

Directions: Describe your conclusions about the three factors and how they may affect your students' acquisition of English.

The Language:

_____

_____

_____

_____

_____

_____

The Learner:

_____

_____

_____

_____

_____

_____

_____

The Learning Process:

_____

_____

_____

_____

_____

_____

_____

Predictors of Success in Learning to Read

Anticipation Guide

Directions: Read each statement. Based on your knowledge and experience, decide whether you agree or disagree with it. Place an **A** (Agree) or **D** (Disagree) in the blank. Finally, discuss the items you feel least certain about with the people around you.

My Choices	Group Consensus		Page with Answer
_____	_____	1. If native English speakers and beginning English language learners have good letter recognition, they will be able to learn to read.	_____
_____	_____	2. Native English speakers and English language learners can develop reading and oral proficiency skills simultaneously, if they are given a sound instructional program.	_____
_____	_____	3. English language learners must be able to correctly pronounce English words before they can learn to read.	_____
_____	_____	4. The development of phonemic awareness is crucial for English language learners to learn to read in English with comprehension.	_____
_____	_____	5. English language learners with little knowledge of concepts of print in their native language will most likely experience challenges learning concepts of print in English.	_____

Predictors of Success in Learning to Read

Directions: Read the following article with the statements on the Anticipation Guide in mind. After reading it, revise your responses to the statements on the guide, if you wish.

"What is the best way to teach reading?" This question surfaces and resurfaces time after time (Adler, 2001; Chall, 1967). Reading experts, researchers, educators, publishers, parents, and even readers themselves all have different responses. Today, with more and more students who need to learn to read in English entering American schools, this question becomes even more complex because these students are faced with the dual challenge of learning to understand, speak, read, write, and spell in English as they simultaneously learn academic content.

Predictors of success in learning to read

Which students will learn to read successfully, and which ones will not? While there is no definitive answer to these question, students' performance in some skills areas can give indications of how successful they may be in learning to read. In this article we focus on five categories: letter recognition, oral language proficiency, pronunciation, phonemic awareness, and concepts of print. For each category we review what the research says regarding native English speakers and English language learners.

Letter recognition

Letter recognition refers to the ability to identify and name the letters of the alphabet. This ability enables readers to unlock the print–sound code of written text. This skill is critical for learning to read and write alphabetic languages.

Native English Speakers

Traditionally, reading readiness evaluations include such measures as repeating sentences, retelling stories, and recognizing letters. Of these, letter recognition, the ability to identify and name the squiggles on the page, appears to be the strongest predictor of reading success (Adams, 1990; Chall, 1967; Durrell, 1958; Snow, Burns, & Griffin, 1998). Children are generally able to remember the sounds of letters, because the names of the letters are closely related to their sounds. In other words, the children have grasped the underlying principle of the alphabetic system: that written words stand for the sounds of spoken words (Birch, 2002).

For older, skillful readers, good letter recognition means they are able to easily recognize letter patterns in words and process and remember the meaning of what they read (Adams, 1990). This means these readers have "ready knowledge of words—their spellings, meanings, and pronunciation—and [the] considerations of the contexts in which they occur" (Adams, 1990, pp. 409–410). As these readers fixate on words, they recognize the letters almost instantly and without effort, associate the letters with familiar spelling patterns, and use the print to obtain information (Adams, 1990).

English Language Learners

Recognizing the relationships between the sounds and symbols of a language, that is, the fact that print is speech written down, is a critical skill for learning to read not only English, but any written language (Birch, 2002).

Learning to read English can be a challenge for English language learners. Unlike Spanish and other languages in which words are spelled as they sound, English does not have a one–to–one letter–sound correspondence; one letter can spell more than one sound.

For example, the letter *g* can represent the sounds of /g/ in *goat* and *gem*. Some letters in English words do not represent sounds at all, such as the *gh* in *night*. To complicate matters even more, in English the same sound can be spelled in different ways, as the sounds of /ou/ and /au/ in *bought* and *caught*, the sound of /o/, /ew/, and /ow/ in *so*, *sew*, and *sow*, and the sound of /ight/ and /ite/ in *sight* and *site*.

In Spanish, on the other hand, with few exceptions, a given sound is usually spelled in one way. For example, the letter *ñ* is pronounced /ny–/ as in *señor* and *señorita*; the letter *h* is always silent, as in *hasta luego* (goodbye), *hombre* (man), *hoy* (today), and *tengo hambre* (I am hungry). As a result, when Spanish readers encounter words with the letter *h*, they expect it to serve as a place holder and not to represent a speech sound.

What this means for English language learners is that learning the variety of ways English sounds can be spelled is especially problematic for those who expect one letter to always represent one sound; they do not find what they expect.

Oral language proficiency

Oral language proficiency refers to the ability to use the vocabulary and grammar of English to produce oral messages. This ability is critical for effective oral communication, reading texts, and writing. As English language learners' ability to understand the new language that they hear and their receptive vocabulary increase, they begin to speak (Levine, 1995).

Native English Speakers

From infancy through about age 8, children's oral language proficiency precedes their reading development. Children who have large oral vocabularies know many words and are thus able to sound out, read, and understand them when they appear in early reading materials (National Reading Panel, 2000). But when they reach about age 8, the language in the materials they read is more advanced than their oral proficiency. This being the case, the materials they read then begin to contribute to their oral language proficiency (Chall, 1996). As their vocabularies increase, so does their world knowledge, which results in improved reading comprehension and better overall school performance (Lehr, Osborn, & Heibert, 2004). This situation is sometimes referred to as the "Matthew Effect" (Stanovich, 1986) or "The rich get richer and the poor get poorer."

English Language Learners

English as a second language (ESL) researchers and reading experts agree that it is advantageous for English language learners to develop oral language skills and learn to read in their native language before or at the same time as they learn to read in English (International Reading Association, 1998; Snow, Burns, & Griffin, 1998). Since beginning English language learners are more proficient in their native language than in English, native language development and the ability to identify words in their native language is a better predictor of their ability to read in the second language than is their oral proficiency in the second language (Durgunoglu, Nagy, & Hancin–Bhatt, 1993).

Unfortunately, in many educational settings it is not possible to develop students' native language oral and reading skills. In such cases, then, instructional programs should focus on developing some oral proficiency in English before beginning formal reading instruction (Snow, Burns, & Griffin, 1998). Research by Snow, Burns, and Griffin (1998) reveals that hurrying young English language learners into reading without developing a sound speaking and listening base proves to be detrimental. While these children may in fact learn to skillfully decode words, their comprehension suffers because the reading materials are outside their limited knowledge of English.

What is an adequate level of oral English proficiency? Experts do not agree on an answer to this question. Some experts (Goodman, Goodman, & Flores, 1979) point out it is not unusual for English language learners to understand what they have heard read aloud but not be able to retell or produce the oral English language needed to explain what they understand. They are able to understand more than they can say. What this means for teachers teaching them to read is that oral language development and reading instruction in English can occur simultaneously (Heibert, Pearson, Taylor, Richardson, & Paris, 1998).

Pronunciation

Pronunciation refers to the ability to say or utter a word or words aloud. Most languages have and accept some variations in pronunciation.

Native English Speakers

From birth, infants who are able to speak can produce the sounds of all languages. They are also able to perceive differences between the sounds of the language that they hear and that is directed to them. As they listen to and begin to produce their native language, they become less and less able to discriminate between the sounds that are not associated with this language. Generally, young native English–speaking children understand spoken English before they can produce all of its sounds. For example, native English–speaking children frequently are not able to produce the sounds of /r/, /y/, and /l/ until they are 6 or 7 years of age (Birch, 2002).

English Language Learners

Success in learning to read English is more dependent on the ability to discriminate the sounds of English than the ability to pronounce words correctly (Birch, 2002). This means that English language learners do not need to be able to pronounce the words they read like a native English speaker does in order to understand what they are reading (Hudelson, 1984).

For English language learners, the accuracy of their English pronunciation seems to be closely related to the age at which they learn English. The earlier a child learns English, the more accurate is the child's pronunciation (Celce–Murcia & Goodwin, 1991).

Phonemic awareness

Phonemic awareness refers to the ability to hear, identify, and manipulate the individual sounds in spoken words (Adler, 2001). Phonemic awareness is an important skill that aids word recognition in all alphabetic languages (Francis, 2005, as cited in Vela, 2005).

Native English Speakers

Following their review of studies of reading research, the National Reading Panel (Adler, 2001) reported that teaching native English–speaking children phonemic awareness improves their ability to manipulate the sounds of English speech. This ability then helps them learn to read and spell.

English Language Learners

For English language learners, teaching phonemic awareness in English may create some difficulty in their learning to read. For example, students who are not literate in their native language may have difficulty recognizing and separating spoken words in print (Antunez, 2002). Children who are literate in a language that uses letters to represent sounds that are different from those of English need to learn the sound/letter correspondences of English. Children who are literate in nonalphabetic languages such as Chinese or Japanese have learned a different symbol system and need to learn the symbol system of written English (Burt, Peyton, & Adams, 2003; Peregoy & Boyle, 2000, as cited in Antunez, 2002).

Children who speak Spanish may have an easier time with phonemic awareness in English, because a number of the letters in Spanish (e.g., b, c, d, f, l, m, n, p, q, s, and t) represent sounds that are similar to those of English (Peregoy & Boyle, 2000, as cited in Antunez, 2002). As a result, these children may be able to transfer what they know about the sounds and letters of Spanish to English (Peregoy & Boyle, 2000, cited in Antunez, 2002).

Concepts of print

Concepts of print refers to the ability to recognize that print carries meaning and to use the conventions and mechanics of printed or written English words, sentences, and texts to access this meaning, moving from left to right and from top to bottom.

Native English Speakers and English Language Learners

The process of drawing meaning from printed or written symbols is similar across languages and contexts (Buck, 1979, cited in Birch, 2002). People acquire knowledge about the world and how it works through their experiences. They also learn how their native language works and are able to use this knowledge to communicate with others. When reading, readers draw upon both these sets of knowledge to recognize the words and grasp the meaning of the text (Birch, 2002). Whether reading Chinese, in which each character stands for a word or part of a word, or in the syllabic writing systems of Japanese, in which each symbol represents the sound of a syllable, the concepts of print remain the same. Symbols represent speech and are used in regulated ways (Birch, 2002).

Numerous studies reveal there is a positive correlation between native language literacy and learning English (Clay, 1993; New York State Education Department, 2000, as cited in Antunez, 2002). Literacy in the native language provides a knowledge, concept, and skills base that transfers from first language reading to second language reading (Collier & Thomas, 1992, as cited in Antunez, 2002; Thomas & Collier, 2002). Children who have learned concepts of print in their native language know that symbols on the page work in certain ways and can use this knowledge as they learn to read in the second language. In fact, research in bilingual education indicates that learning to read in one's native language can lead to superior achievement in the second language (Legarreta, 1979, as cited in Snow, Burns, & Griffin, 1998).

Summary

Consistently, letter knowledge and phonological awareness are the two strongest predictors of students' success in learning to read (Adams, 1990; Bond & Dykstra, 1967; Whitehurst & Lonigan, 2001). The size of students' oral vocabulary is another predictor of later reading success (Snow, Burns, & Griffin, 1998; Snow, Tabors, Nicholson, & Kurland, 1995). Concepts of print can also serve as a predictor of students' later success in learning to read (Snow, Burns & Griffin, 1998). Pronunciation, on the other hand, is not a significant predictor of success in learning to read (Birch, 2002; Hudelson, 1984).

There is one requirement that plays a significant role in all instruction for all learners, including English language learners. This requirement is that instruction be meaningful (Antunez, 2002). In terms of reading instruction, this means that the English words and letters students are learning need to be familiar to them. By using letters and words that students know, teachers can begin to teach phonemic awareness, vocabulary words and their meanings, and pronunciation simultaneously. Native English speakers and English language learners who build large English vocabularies improve their listening and reading comprehension at the same time as they increase their knowledge. Combined, these skills contribute to their ease of learning to read in English (Tankersley, 2005).

18

Features of Arabic That May Influence Learning to Read in English

Sounds and spellings

- Arabic uses a non–Roman alphabet and is written from right to left.

- Arabic writing does not distinguish between upper– and lowercase letters.

- On the whole, Arabic spelling is far more regular than is English spelling. Letter/sound representations are generally predictable. As a result, Arabic speakers may pronounce silent letters in English and overemphasize double consonants (e.g., in a word like *singer*, they may pronounce the /g/).

- Arabic does not have the sounds /p/ and /v/, so a reader may pronounce word pairs such as *pill* and *bill* as *bill* and *few* and *view* as *few*.

- There are few consonant clusters in the initial position in Arabic. Where they do exist, they are largely composed of two consonants, unlike in English where there may be three or four (e.g., *straight*). An Arabic speaker may thus add a vowel either before the consonant cluster or right after it (e.g., *steal* is likely to be pronounced *esteal*; *first* may be pronounced *firest*).

- Arabic has three vowels (a, i, u). They have both long and short forms, and they are pronounced without a glide. Therefore, words such as *caught* and *coat*, *sit* and *seat* may not be distinguished. The /e/ sound does not exist in Arabic. Hence, Arabic speakers may not differentiate words such as *pen* and *pan* and *bed* and *bad*.

- The short vowels in Arabic are normally not written. The context provides the reader with the information needed to comprehend the text. Thus when the students read aloud, they may not pay attention to pronouncing the proper short vowel sounds and occasionally the long vowels.

- Stress is predictable in Arabic, and long vowels are always stressed. Therefore in English, *Saturday* may be pronounced *SaturDAY*. Words such as *PERmit* (noun) and *perMIT* (verb) may be confusing.

Vocabulary

- There are a fair number of Arabic loan words in English—*algebra, caramel, amalgam*, and *sugar*, to name a few. However, the pronunciations of the corresponding words are different, so Arabic speakers may not recognize the English word.

- Most Arabic words are based on a root composed of three consonants, such as *k–t–b*, meaning "write." These roots can be combined with different vowels to produce a whole family of words (derivatives) that share a common meaning, such as *kitaab*, meaning "book." In contrast, English forms its derived words by adding prefixes and suffixes, so an Arabic speaker may find learning English word families difficult at first.

- In English, verbs and nouns often have the same form (e.g., *permit* and *permit*). In Arabic, verbs and nouns have distinct forms.

Grammar

- Sentences in formal Arabic (Classical or Modern Standard) have the following word order: verb–subject–object. However, colloquial Arabic uses the word order subject–verb–object, just as English does. Therefore, Arabic–speaking students may not encounter difficulty with basic sentence structures in English. However, they may reverse word order when reading aloud (e.g., *Knows she your cousin* instead of *She knows your cousin*).

- Simple tenses in English, present and past, are often easy for Arabic speakers. However, Arabic does not have forms to distinguish simple present from present progressive and simple past from present perfect when there are no stated time expressions to highlight the difference. Thus, the student may have some difficulty understanding the difference between *I play tennis* and *I am playing tennis*. Similarly, Arabic speakers may not recognize the difference between *I lived in Washington for 10 years* and *I have lived in Washington for 10 years*.

- Verb auxiliaries are understood in Arabic through the context of a sentence. Therefore, Arabic–speaking students may have trouble understanding the concept of verb auxiliaries and may not be able to see the difference between such sentences as *They are going to school now* and *They going to school now*; or, *We will leave him behind unless he comes now* and *We leave him behind unless he comes now*.

Features of Spanish That May Influence Learning to Read in English

Sounds and spellings

- On the whole, spelling in Spanish is far more regular than it is in English, particularly with regard to the spelling of vowel sounds. However, the conventions for the spelling of consonant sounds in the two languages can cause confusion for a Spanish speaker trying to read or spell English words.

- In Spanish *b* and *v* are both used to spell /b/.

- Spanish /d/ between vowels sounds very much like English voiced *th* /th/ as in *the* or *other*, so English /d/ and /th/ may be confused. In English /t/ is pronounced like a /d/ sound in words like *better* and *meeting*; thus, *mudder*, *mother*, and *mutter* could be confused.

- In Spanish, *g* before *a*, *o*, and *u* always spells a "hard" *g* sound as in *gave*, *get*, *give*, *go*, or *gum*, never a "soft" *g* as in *gem*. However, Spanish *g* before *e* or *i* is pronounced with an /h/ sound with a lot of friction, so when trying to read an English word like *gem*, the Spanish speaker might produce something that sounds more like *hem*.

- American dialects of Spanish don't have a voiceless *th* sound like the English /th/ in *thing*; as a result, pairs of English words such as *thing/sing* and *math/mass* may be confused.

- The English /s/ and /z/ sounds may be confused, because in American dialects of Spanish, *s* and *z* stand for the same sound. This sound is usually /s/, but before a voiced consonant (for example, *mismo*, *desgracia*) it may sound more like /z/.

- The only nasal sound that occurs at the end of words in Spanish is /n/. Therefore, the three English nasal sounds may be confused (for example, *some*, *son*, and *sung*.)

- English vowels are challenging for two reasons: the inconsistencies of English spelling and the lack of similar sounds across the two languages. Spanish speakers commonly confuse the vowel sounds in pairs of words like *seat/sit*, *get/gate*, *hat/hot*, *not/nut*, *luck/look*, *pull/pool*, and *cot/caught*.

Vocabulary

- Spanish–English cognates are usually helpful when it comes to guessing the meaning of new words, but sometimes they can cause confusion. The cognate relationship may be disguised by spelling differences: *sección/section*, *énfasis/emphasis*. There may be a style difference: Spanish *edificio* doesn't necessarily mean "edifice," as the cognate would suggest; it may mean simply "building." And of course, there are the "false friends"—cognate words that have come to have quite different meanings in the two languages. Spanish *lectura* means "reading," not "lecture." Spanish *embarazar* may mean "to embarrass," but it is more likely to mean "to make pregnant."

- The fact that English can use a word as a noun or verb without changing the form of the word (e.g., *play*) can cause confusion for a Spanish speaker, because in Spanish nouns and verbs have different sets of endings (inflections) that usually make them look quite different from each other.

- Compound nouns are much less common in Spanish than in English. In English, while the parts of a compound may be understandable, the meaning of the compound as a whole may not be obvious. Pairs such as *lamp table* and *table lamp*, or *wind mill* and *coffee mill*, may be confusing.

Grammar

- In English sentences containing an indirect object, there are often two ways to indicate the indirect object:

> Sue showed the picture to Tom.
>
> *or*
>
> Sue showed Tom the picture.

For a Spanish speaker the second version of the sentence (which uses what is sometimes called the "unmarked" indirect object) could be hard to interpret, because in Spanish the indirect object is marked by a pronoun preceding the verb and a preposition before the noun:

> Susana le mostró a Tomás la pintura.
>
> (literally: Sue him showed to Tom the painting.)

- The time reference of English compound tenses can be difficult to pin down, for example, the difference in meaning and use of *studies* versus *is studying*, or *studied* versus *has studied* versus *had studied*. Spanish has similar compound tenses, but their uses do not exactly parallel the corresponding English tenses.

- English modals can also be a problem, especially when occurring as part of more complex verb forms. The meaning and use of forms such as the following are difficult to sort out: *would study, would have studied, should study, should have studied, could study, could have studied, may study, may have studied, might study, might have studied*, not to mention forms such as *should be studying, should have been studying*, and the like. Corresponding forms in Spanish are expressed by full–fledged inflected verbs.

- There are parallels between Spanish and English with regard to noun clauses, but one feature of English might interfere with reading comprehension for a Spanish speaker. In English, *that* introducing a noun clause may be omitted in sentences such as *I thought (that) Pete was going to the movies*. In such cases in Spanish, the corresponding conjunction is required.

Why Reading Is Hard: Reading Words

What Makes Reading English Easy/Hard for Students Learning to Read in English?

Directions: Identify the characteristics of reading that can make reading English difficult for English language learners. Record these responses in the *Hard* column. Next identify the characteristics of reading that make the task easier for these students. Record these responses in the *Easy* column.

EASY	HARD

Chapter 1

Why Reading Is Hard

Arabic texts

Directions: Use Study Guide pages 24–32 as you view the video clip.

Source: AP/Wide World Photo. Used by permission.

كلينتون ويلتسن يطويان صفحة كوسوفو

The Arabic Alphabet

Name of Letter	Final	Medial	Initial	Standing Alone
'Alif	هنا	تاب	أخ	ا
Baa'	كوب	لبن	بارع	ب
Taa'	تحت	كتب	تراب	ت
Thaa'	مثلث	مثال	ثلج	ث
Jiim	خليج	نجح	جيش	ج
H'aa'	ملح	بحر	حبل	ح
Khaa'	مناخ	شخص	خرج	خ
Daal	سد	مدرس	دين	د
Thaal	بذ	هذا	ذاكرة	ذ
Raa'	بئر	ثري	رأي	ر
Zaay	طرز	تزوج	زيت	ز
Siin	شمس	مسجد	سمع	س
Shiin	مشمش	مشرق	شجرة	ش
Saad	لص	مصر	صمم	ص
Daad	نبض	فضل	ضغط	ض
Taa'	ربط	محطة	طعام	ط

Name of Letter	Final	Medial	Initial	Standing Alone
Dh:aa'	محافظ	مظلة	ظريف	ظ
'Ayn	بجع	بعيد	عجل	ع
Ghayn	بلغ	ببغاء	غواصة	غ
Faa'	سقف	شفيق	فأر	ف
Qaaf	سبق	مقدمة	قارب	ق
Kaaf	سمك	سكر	كبير	ك
Laam	رمل	كلمة	لص	ل
Miim	علم	شمعة	مكان	م
Nuun	سمين	منبر	نحلة	ن
Haa'	سمعه	مهاجر	هبط	ه
Waaw	قبو	موت	وردة	و
Yaa'	يبكي	كبير	يد	ي

What's Different About Teaching Reading to Students Learning English?
Study Guide

kaaf	ك
laam	ل
miim	م
nuun	ن
qaaf	ق

Kaaf

ك   كان كيس سكين شوكة سمك شباك   كو يكو يك

final   medial   initial

Laam

ل   لين ليرا لوز لوج كيلو نيل قول   لو يلو يل

Nuun

ن   نيل نير نور تنس كنغر بنت مين فرن   نو ينو ين

Qaaf

ق   قام قول قربان رقاقات نقانق ورق   قو يقو يق

What's Different About Teaching Reading to Students Learning English?
Study Guide

إن التعليم متاح لكل شخص في الولايات المتحدة بغض النظر عن عمر الشخص أو عرقه أو دينه أو طبقته الاجتماعية. التعليم العام مجاني ويفرضه القانون على جميع الأطفال بين عمر **6** و **16** وقد يكون متاحا للأطفال بعمر أصغر أو أكبر حسب أنظمة المنطقة التعليمية المحلية. وللأبوين خيار آخر وهو تسجيل أبنائهم في مدارس خاصة وللكثير من هذه المدارس ارتباطات دينية إلا أن أجور التعليم فيها غالبا ما تكون باهظة. ويمكن أن يكون التعليم لما بعد المرحلة الإعدادية باهظا جدا.

In the United States, education is accessible for everyone, regardless of a person's age, race, religion, or social class. Public education is free and required by law for all children ages 6 to 16, and may also be available for children older or younger, depending on local school district regulations. Alternatively, parents may enroll children in private schools, many of which have religious affiliations, but tuition at these schools is often expensive. Beyond high school, education can be quite expensive.

Source: Center for Applied Linguistics. (1996). *Welcome to the United States: A Guidebook for Refugees.* Washington, DC: Author.

إن التعليم متاح لكل شخص في الولايات

المتحدة بغض النظر عن عمر الشخص أو عرقه

أو دينه أو طبقته الاجتماعية. التعليم العام

مجاني ويفرضه القانون على جميع الأطفال بين

عمر 6 و 16 وقد يكون متاحا للأطفال بعمر

أصغر أو أكبر حسب أنظمة المنطقة التعليمية

المحلية. وللأبوين خيار آخر وهو تسجيل أبنائهم

في مدارس خاصة وللكثير من هذه المدارس

ارتباطات دينية إلا أن أجور التعليم فيها غالبا

ما تكون باهظة. ويمكن أن يكون التعليم لما

بعد المرحلة الإعدادية باهظا جدا.

ليمون   كوالا   بالون   امريكا

____   ____   ____   ____

Arabic texts: Reading words. Follow–up questions

Directions: In light of your experience with reading Arabic, read and answer the following questions.

1. Sometimes readers feel so frustrated that they simply give up. What are some reasons why they feel so frustrated?

   _____

   _____

   _____

   _____

2. Readers read to get meaning. What meaning did you get from reading the Arabic text? Why?

   _____

   _____

   _____

   _____

3. Good readers use pictures to help them understand what they read. How useful was the picture to you? Why?

   _____

   _____

   _____

   _____

4. What could Dr. Snow have done to make your learning to read Arabic easier?

   _____

   _____

   _____

   _____

The Four Cueing Systems Readers Use

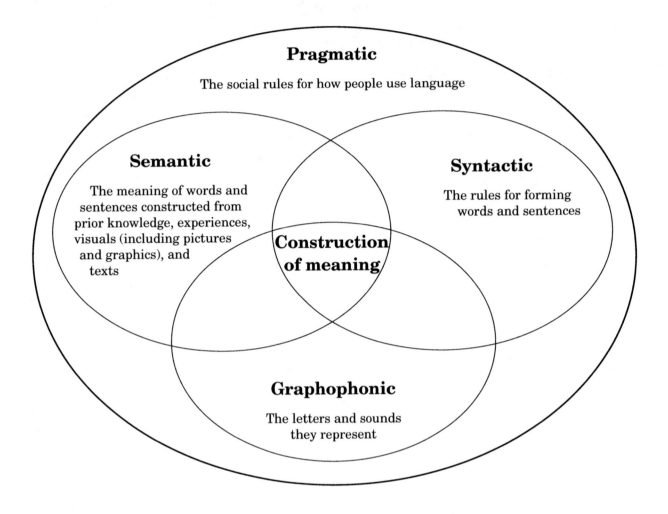

The Pragmatic System	
What It Is	*Examples*
Using language to accomplish a variety of functions such as to inform, to imagine, or to direct	• Wontons are similar to ravioli. • An apartment building is a filing cabinet of lives. • Turn right at the end of the ramp.
Adapting language to meet the requirements of a situation or a listener's needs	• Ladies and gentlemen, the President of the United States. • Go for it, Aaron! • Mr. Park has internal hemorrhaging, or severe bleeding. • Longer ago than you are old…

The Semantic System

What It Is	*Examples*
Making sense by connecting what is known with the words and sentences that are spoken, heard, read, or written	• $E = MC^2$ formed the foundation for the development of nuclear energy. • Proper etiquette requires that one introduce a younger person to an older person. • Ms. Lee's class eagerly awaited the arrival of the latest Harry Potter title.
Making sense of symbols by connecting what is known with visual representations, pictures, and the language of genres	• ♥ ♠ ♣ ♦ • • Longer ago than you are old…
Recognizing the ways words can be related to other words such as synonyms, antonyms, part–whole, and multiple meanings	• enormous – huge • minute – tiny • pitcher – handle • run – verb = 28 meanings; noun = 33 meanings

The Syntactic System

What It Is	*Examples*
The ways we use oral language to form phrases, clauses, and sentences; used in conversations and discourse (including the language of the individual's community)	• Billy's experiences with blocks and counting sometimes end up in a jumble of blocks and boy. • "I just ain't a gonna' do it."
The ways we interpret written language to make sense of the sentences, paragraphs, and complete texts that we read or write	• Preheat the oven to 350°. Butter a 9–inch spring–form pan. Combine graham cracker crumbs, sugar, and mace. Add melted butter and mix thoroughly.
The rules for forming words	• Regular past tense verbs end in –ed.
The rules of grammar	• A singular subject requires a singular verb.
The rules for forming sentences	• The brown big rubber raft…

The Graphophonic System

What It Is	*Examples*
Recognizing the ways letters and words appear	• catalog, *catalog*, **catalog** • turn, turned, returning
Knowing and using the sounds the letters and letter combinations represent	• i–c–e = *ice* c before *e, i,* or *y* = /s/ • /f/ = *f, ph, gh*

Sources: Hirsch, Jr., 2006; Smith, 1978.

What Every Kindergarten Through Grade 3 Reading Program Should Include

Components Every Kindergarten Through Grade 3 Reading Program Should Include

Directions: Underline the five major components that you think every kindergarten through Grade 3 reading program should include.

- Auditory and visual discrimination

- Reading predictable texts

- Oral language development

- Repeated reading of the same text

- Phonemic awareness

- Rhyming

- Phonics

- Vocabulary development

- Free or independent reading

- Reading fluency

- Reading comprehension strategies

The Essential Components of Reading Instruction According to Reading First

> ◆ *phonemic awareness*
> ◆ *phonics*
> ◆ *vocabulary development*
> ◆ *reading fluency*
> ◆ *text comprehension strategies*

Terms	Definitions
phonemic awareness	the ability to hear, identify, think about, and manipulate the sounds, or phonemes, in spoken words Example: 　　What is left if we take away the sound of /s/ in *sink*?　　*ink*
phonics	the understanding that there is a predictable relationship between the sounds of a spoken language and the written symbols (the letters and letter groups) that represent those sounds Examples: 　　/f/ = <u>f</u>ix, <u>ph</u>one, lau<u>gh</u>, o<u>ff</u>–center
vocabulary development	the words people use to communicate with each other Examples: 　　*Receptive vocabulary*—the words we use to understand what we hear and read 　　*Productive vocabulary*—the words we use to speak and write
reading fluency	the ability to recognize words automatically, accurately, and effortlessly while simultaneously making connections between what is known and the meaning of the text Example: 　　I love you, I love you, I love you divine. 　　Please give me your bubble gum, you're sitting on mine! 　　—*Anonymous*
text comprehension strategies	the ability to construct meaning drawn from text and personal knowledge simultaneously Example: 　　The starfish is a spiny–skinned salt water animal that has thick arm–like appendages on its body.

Learning Language: Making Meaning

"We have learned language by using language, by speaking it, reading it, and making sense of it. What we know about language is largely implicit, just like our knowledge of cats and dogs" (Smith, 1978, pp. 87–88).

"…everything we are taught must be related to what we already know if it is to make sense" (Smith, 1978, p. 88).

Using Multiple Methods of Beginning Reading Instruction: A Position Statement of the International Reading Association

According to the International Reading Association (1999)—

There is no one single method or single combination of methods that can successfully teach all children to read. Therefore, teachers must have a strong knowledge of multiple methods for teaching reading and a strong knowledge of the children in their care so they can create the appropriate balance of methods needed for the children they teach.

Reading is a complex system of deriving meaning from print that requires all of the following:
- the development and maintenance of a motivation to read
- the development of appropriate active strategies to construct meaning from print
- sufficient background information and vocabulary to foster reading comprehension
- the ability to read fluently
- the ability to decode unfamiliar words
- the skills and knowledge to understand how phonemes or speech sounds are connected to print (pp. 2–3).

Source: International Reading Association. (1999). *Using Multiple Methods of Beginning Reading Instruction: A Position Statement of the International Reading Association.* Newark, DE: Author. Reprinted with permission.

Second Language Literacy Instruction:
A Position Statement of the International Reading Association

According to the International Reading Association (2001)—

Literacy learning is easiest when schools provide initial literacy instruction in a child's home language. Such instruction is consistent with building on children's strengths and with connecting unfamiliar material to the familiar to maximize learning efficiency. Literacy skills developed in the home language can then be applied to learning to read and write in a second language, which results in students who have become literate and gained proficiency in two (or perhaps more) languages. …[T]he position of the International Reading Association is that proficiency in the dominant language is the goal of language and literacy instruction; bilingualism or multilingualism is desirable; and where possible, families have the right to decide whether initial literacy instruction is delivered in the dominant language or the home language. (p. 1)

Source: International Reading Association. (2001). *Second Language Literacy Instruction: A Position Statement of the International Reading Association.* (2001). Newark: DE: Author. Reprinted with permission.

Models of Reading

Bottom–Up Reading

> **Directions:** Read the passage and answer the questions below.

O–n–c–e–T–r–i–g–b–u–r–b–l–e–d,

T–h–e–g–n–e–e–s–f–r–o–p–e–d

a–n–d–t–h–e–n–P–h–a–n–e–n–r–e–d.

C–h–e–n–a–n–d–Z–i–o–n–f–a–l–t–o–a–n–e–d.

Comprehension questions

1. What happened and to whom?

_____

2. What did Chen do?

_____

Reading task questions

1. Did you recognize the key features of each letter?

_____

2. Could you pronounce the sounds of the letters?

_____

3. Could you recognize all the words?

_____

4. Could you decode the unfamiliar words?

_____

5. How did these limitations affect your understanding of the text?

_____

Top–Down Reading

> **Directions:** Read the passage and answer the questions below.

Trig, Phan, and Chen

Trig and Phan are mights.

Chen is a bledge.

Most mights become bledges when they burble.

But Trig and Phan didn't burble. They ylanted instead.

Chen zelknewed outside Trig's and Phan's gnot.

Zion, Trig, and Phan's cevica, plorried Chen and said,

"Cease zelknewing. Trig and Phan will burble wrently."

Then Chen mneulied pneumiously.

Comprehension questions

1. What do you know about Trig, Phan, Chen, and Zion?

_____

2. What didn't happen, and what will happen?

_____

3. How did Chen feel at the beginning and at the end?

_____

Reading task question

1. How did your prior knowledge help you decode the message and get meaning from it?

_____

What Is Required for Skilled Reading?

Skilled reading clearly requires skill in both decoding and comprehension…. A child who cannot decode cannot read; a child who cannot comprehend cannot read either. Literacy—reading ability—can be found only in the presence of both decoding and comprehension. Both skills are necessary; neither alone is sufficient (Gough, Hoover, & Peterson, 1996, as cited in Grabe & Stoller, 2002).

From One Teacher's Perspective

Everyday Expressions and School Vocabulary: A Prereading Lesson

This lesson was created and taught by Nancy Veaudry, Kingston Intermediate School, Silver Lake School District, Kingston, Massachusetts, and is used with permission.

Student information

one fifth–grade student

English Proficiency Level – Beginning

English Reading Level – Prereading

The student does not understand any English, nor does anyone in his family. Portuguese is spoken at home.

Language objectives

Key Vocabulary

School–related vocabulary

Raise your hand.   *Take out your book.*

Sit in your chair.   *Open your book.*

Close your book.   *Take out your pencil.*

Everyday expressions

How are you?   *Good morning.*

See you later.

Antonyms

short – tall   *beautiful – ugly*

tall – short   *thin – fat*

Alphabet

Write the letters of the alphabet and say the names of the letters.

Short /a/ words

hat, cat, fat, rat, mat, cap

Write short /a/ words and phrases, and eventually write sentences.

Comprehension objectives

My first objective is to teach the student common phrases that are used around the school (social conversation) and simple commands. These relate to basic needs and safety within the school environment.

My second objective is for the student to be able to identify pictures of common objects and to match cards to demonstrate that he understands the concept of opposites. This activity uses pictures, pantomime, and body language in order for him to comprehend this concept.

My third objective is for the student to begin to learn the English alphabet and several short a words. He demonstrates his comprehension by matching words to pictures, spelling words with magnetic letters, and matching sentences with pictures. He also draws pictures of words and phrases dictated in English. We use these pictures as a beginning to create language experience stories. We are using easy picture books as a way to begin learning English.

Before Reading

I try to make connections between the student and the topic. Because the student doesn't speak any English and I don't speak Portuguese, I use a whole–body approach to try to engage him and to aid his understanding. I rely on pictures, drawings, gestures, and demonstrations. He enjoys the magnetic letters. If I show him a picture and then say and spell the English word, he appears to understand and repeats the English words. We have used the opposite cards to create a book about his family and to label family members.

I limit the amount of material presented and use frequent practice and review. I use a multimodal approach and slow down the instruction to allow him time to process the information. I speak clearly and slowly and have him repeat frequently. I use pictures that I find on the Internet or that I scan from my computer at home to increase his vocabulary. We use the vocabulary he has learned to create sentences and stories. He is creating a visual dictionary. I tend to use a theme approach when introducing vocabulary. For example, one day I'll present all animals, the next day vegetables, and so on.

During Reading

I use very simple texts. The amount of text is limited, and the structure is modified to make sure it is simple. He is learning the English alphabet and the sounds of the letters. We use the magnetic letters to manipulate sounds, changing the *f* in fat to an *r* and making *rat*, then finding the matching pictures for *fat* and *rat*.

A Language Experience Approach is used to develop phrases, sentences, and stories for rereading. Picture drawing aids his comprehension of the reading and vocabulary and enhances his learning. I also read to him and then we read together.

After Reading

If the student can match words, phrases, and sentences to draw his own pictures, then I feel sure that he understands what we are doing. Likewise, if he can follow a command such as "Open your book," then I am reassured of his comprehension of the information. I often model a command for him and then have him demonstrate his understanding and have him repeat the command.

Lesson sequence

The sequence of the lesson reflects a number of standards and generally proceeds as follows.

Students will comprehend and communicate orally, using spoken English for personal and social purposes.

"Hello, (student's name)."

"Good morning."

"How are you?"

"It is cold/hot/rainy, etc."

Students will comprehend and communicate orally, using English for academic school–related purposes.

"Raise your hand."

"Open your book."

"Show me where the bathroom is."

"Find the nurse."

Students will comprehend and communicate orally, using spoken English to participate in academic settings.

"Circle the word."

"Spell and write the word."

"Repeat the word."

Students will acquire English vocabulary and apply knowledge of correct syntax to comprehend written text.

"Match the words with the pictures."

"Use the magnetic letters to spell *father*."

"Draw a picture of your family and write their names."

Students will understand the nature of written English and the relationship of letters and spelling patterns to the sounds of speech.

Students will write words that have personal meaning and draw pictures and/or use letters to spell words that give other information.

The student selects the needed letters of the English alphabet, using magnetic letters, to spell familiar words.

"Pick up the *t*, the *e*, the *a*, etc."

The student prints the letters of the alphabet.

The teacher and student manipulate letters to demonstrate how different short /a/ words can be made.

The student matches words with pictures.

The student pronounces, spells, and writes the words that go with the pictures.

The student matches sentences with pictures.

The teacher and student read a short story together.

The student creates a short story of his own using the target words.

Social conversation ends the lesson: "Good–bye. See you tomorrow."

Reflections on Instruction

The prereading lesson was one part of an assignment for teachers attending a reading workshop. The second part of the assignment was to reflect on how the instruction had gone. The following comments (parts A, B, and C below) were made by the teacher who planned and taught the prereading lesson.

A. What reading strategies did you use?

> Select simple, limited texts
> Multimodal instruction
> Slower pace, repetition, and reinforcement
> Pictures and drawings
> Pantomime and gestures
> The Language Experience Approach
> Repeated oral reading

B. What strategy worked best?

If I had to choose the single most effective strategy, it would be the use of pictures (visuals). The student had no oral English skills when I started to work with him. With pictures, I was able to gain his understanding. I think all the strategies that I used are beneficial and that a combination of many strategies is probably what has enabled him to begin to understand and speak English.

C. What do these experiences tell you about teaching reading to students learning English?

First of all, I found that there is an overwhelming amount of research in *What's Different About Teaching Reading to Students Learning English?* that supports my selection of the strategies that I used. For example, the goal of phonics instruction should be to teach children only the most important and regular of the letter–sound relationships because this sort of instruction will most directly reveal the alphabetic principle. Knowledge of the sounds of a few consonants and vowels may provide a sufficient foundation on which to build phonemic awareness and initial word reading instruction.

In addition, teachers can help students learn by using objects, pictures, manipulatives, and meaningful experiences to make the task of language learning easier. Teachers also need to identify the keywords that are critical to understanding the content of the reading material. Teachers should plan how to define the meanings of words or demonstrate how they are used in the text and provide students with multiple experiences with them.

Finally, teachers should read aloud daily to provide models of fluent reading and to expand students' knowledge of the world, vocabulary, and the way English works.

Chapter Summary and Beyond The Workshop

Chapter 1: The Nature of Reading
What's Different About Teaching Reading to Students Learning English?

Some native English speakers may
- have developed an intuitive notion about how the English language works; and
- need to learn the language of schooling that is different from the language they hear and use at home and in the community (Walqui, 2000).

Some English language learners may
- understand more than they can say in English (Goodman, Goodman, & Flores, 1979; Walqui, 2000);
- acquire listening, speaking, reading, and writing skills in English in a nonlinear fashion (TESOL, 1997);
- require 1 to 2 years to acquire basic interpersonal communication skills (BICS) in English (Cummins, 1981);
- require 5 to 7 or more years to acquire cognitive academic language proficiency in English (CALP) (Thomas & Collier, 2002);
- be at one or more levels of English proficiency:
    Level 1—Starting level
    Level 2—Emerging level
    Level 3—Developing level
    Level 4—Expanding level
    Level 5—Bridging level (TESOL, 2006);
- have learned a nonalphabetic writing system and need to learn the English writing system and alphabetic principles (Birch, 2002; Snow, Burns, & Griffin, 1998); and
- find learning English somewhat easier if their native language uses a Roman alphabet and they have strong oral language and reading skills in their native language (Snow, Burns, & Griffin, 1998; Walqui, 2000).

Beyond the Workshop

1. Outside reading

Read *Put Reading First: The Research Building Blocks for Teaching Children to Read*, a description of the findings of the National Reading Panel Report. This summary includes an analysis and discussion about five areas of reading instruction: phonemic awareness, phonics, fluency, vocabulary, and text comprehension. Each area includes a definition of the component, evidence from the research, suggestions for classroom implementation, descriptions of proven instructional strategies, and answers to some frequently asked questions. Read the article and respond by completing one of the following activities.

    A. Identify and describe two or three suggestions or strategies that you believe are appropriate for teaching reading to English language learners and explain the reasons for your choices.

    B. Reflect on your experiences with learning to read Arabic. Identify and describe two or three suggestions or strategies you believe would have helped you be more successful with learning to read Arabic.

The guide is available at www.nifl.gov.

2. Interviews

Interview four students from the same grade level(s) but with different reading abilities, two native English speakers and two English language learners, and ask the following questions.

- What do you think reading is?
- What do you do when you read?
- Do you know someone who is a good reader? And, do you know someone who is not a good reader? How do you know the difference?
- Are you a good reader? Why do you think this is so?

Then, briefly describe how the students' answers reflect the five components of successful reading programs.

3. Five components and kids in classrooms

Collect two examples of students' dictations, language–experience stories, or writing. How does the material reflect the students' knowledge of and current level(s) of ability in the five components? What are the implications for planning instruction for them?

4. Reading with a student

Ask a student to read aloud a text (a book or a section of text). Record your observations and then answer these questions.

- What did you observe the student doing during the reading?
- What did you do to support the student?
- What is this student ready to learn next?
- What would you plan to do if you had a follow–up session with this student?

Share your notes on the experience in the next session.

CHAPTER 2
Comprehension

Goal and Objectives

Goal

Participants will achieve the following:

- Understand that reading comprehension is a complex process that involves a reader's knowledge of how English syntax, grammar, and vocabulary work; the ways that spoken English is represented in print; and connections between background knowledge and experiences and printed text.

Objectives

Participants will be able to do the following:

- Define comprehension and identify effective techniques and reading strategies to develop reading comprehension with native English–speaking readers and English language learners.

- Identify ways to help English language learners make connections between their background knowledge and experiences and new knowledge.

- Describe ways to help native English speakers and English language learners build on and use their knowledge of how English syntax, grammar, and vocabulary work so they can read texts effectively and efficiently.

- Describe the reading behaviors of proficient native English speakers and English language learners.

Making Connections

Must Read Versus Want to Read

Directions: List some examples of texts that students must read and texts that they want to read.

MUST READ	WANT TO READ

Five Stages of Reading Appreciation

Carlson (1974) described the following five stages of reading appreciation. While these stages appear as steps in a progression, a reader's reading experiences may include one or more of these stages, depending on the text and the reader's purpose(s), background knowledge, and experience.

Reading for enjoyment

Carlson (1974) describes this stage as the one in which readers completely lose themselves in what they are reading. Readers are not even aware that they are reading. They are totally absorbed by the text, whether captivated by narrative, engrossed in wonder, mesmerized by mystery, fascinated by facts, or tickled with humor. As one student who became a reader said, "[I enjoy reading] because for me reading a book is like being in another world" (Allen, 2003, p. 269).

Reading for vicarious experiences

Human beings are generally a rather curious lot. We want to know what it's like to be someone else, how it feels to be in someone else's shoes. Reading to learn about other people, places, and events provides us with some answers. We may never truly know the experience(s) for ourselves, but we can know through the eyes and stories of others.

Reading to find yourself

A quick review of the best–selling self–help titles on booksellers' Web sites reveals titles such as *How to Win Friends and Influence People* by Dale Carnegie, Dorothy Carnegie, and Arthur R. Prell (1998), *Being Perfect* by Anna Quindlen (2005), and *The 8th Habit: From Effectiveness to Greatness* by Steven R. Covey (2005). Whether teenagers or adults, people strive to find ways to make their lives better, and one of the ways they can accomplish this is through reading about other people's lives and experiences. Great literature, such as Jane Austin's *Pride and Prejudice*, can also serve this purpose as readers accept the characters as models for their own behavior or problem solving.

Reading to understand issues

Our ever–changing world demands that we have an understanding of social, political, economic, and philosophical issues as they occur within and across cultures. The interdependent nature of the world's societies forces the recognition that none is isolated. For young adults, literature, daily newspapers, and news magazines help to open this door as they read about societies and individuals in the past as well as today, and through discussion they come to recognize that, while times change, people's responses to what goes on around them does not.

Reading for aesthetic appreciation

What can be more enchanting and enveloping than having words of a text ring in your ears, dance on your tongue, and sing in your heart? The beauty of the language as crafted by skillful, talented writers evokes wonder and pleasure that the reader enjoys reading and then rereading time and time again.

~

Motivation

"Motivation (in reading) can be defined as the cluster of personal goals, values, and beliefs with regard to the topics, processes, and outcomes of reading that an individual possesses" (Guthrie & Wigfield, 2000, p. 404, cited in Kamil, 2003, p. 7).

A Reading Interest Inventory for Primary Grade Readers

Name: _____ Date: _____ Grade: _____

1. My favorite toys are _____.

2. When I grow up, I want to be a _____.

3. I like to make _____.

4. I have a pet. My pet is a _____. Its name is _____.
   I like to _____ my pet.

5. I don't have a pet. If I could have one, I'd want a _____.
   I'd like to _____ my pet.

6. My favorite person to play with is _____.
   We like to _____.

7. My three wishes are _____.
   _____.
   _____.

8. In school, I like to _____.

9. My favorite TV show is _____.

10. My favorite movie is _____.

11. Check the sentences that tell about you.
    _____ I like funny stories.
    _____ I like true stories.
    _____ I like stories about real people and animals.
    _____ I like stories about make–believe people and animals.
    _____ I like *Once upon a time…* stories.
    _____ I like stories with words that rhyme.
    _____ I like riddles.
    _____ I like pop–up books.

12. My favorite book is _____.

This page may be reproduced for classroom use.

Chapter 2

A Reading Interest Inventory for Intermediate Grade Readers

Name: _____ Date: _____ Grade: _____

1. Which of these activities do you like to do? Check as many as you want.

_____	ride bikes or ATVs	_____	play basketball
_____	play baseball	_____	play football
_____	play soccer	_____	play ice hockey
_____	swim	_____	skate
_____	skateboard	_____	rollerblade
_____	ski	_____	ice skate
_____	play with friends	_____	play computer games
_____	watch TV	_____	play card games

   Other activities? _____

2. What do you like to do when you're not in school?

   _____

3. Do you read the newspaper? _____ Yes _____ No

   If yes, what parts of the newspaper do you read? Check all that apply.

_____	Headlines	_____	Sports
_____	Comics	_____	News
_____	Advertisements	_____	Classifieds
_____	Regional News	_____	Arts & Entertainment
_____	Feature Articles	_____	Travel
_____	Weather	_____	Editorials
_____	Letters to the Editor	_____	Style & Fashion

   Other parts? _____

4. What are your two favorite TV shows?

   _____

   _____

5. What are your two favorite movies?

   _____

   _____

6. Who are your two favorite movie stars?

   _____

   _____

7. Who are your favorite music groups or singers?

_____

_____

8. What collections do you have?

_____

_____

9. If you could go anywhere, where would you like to go and why?

_____

_____

10. If you have a pet, what is it and what is its name?

_____

_____

11. If you could have a pet, what would you have and why would you want it?

_____

_____

12. When you read, what do you like to read? Check all that apply.

_____ adventure		_____ jokes and riddles
_____ animals		_____ letters
_____ autobiography		_____ magazines
_____ biography		_____ maps
_____ books that are movies		_____ movie stars
_____ comic books		_____ mystery
_____ cookbooks		_____ plays
_____ crossword puzzles		_____ poetry
_____ diaries		_____ rock stars
_____ e–mail		_____ romance
_____ fact books		_____ science
_____ fantasy		_____ science fiction
_____ history		_____ supernatural
_____ how–to manuals		_____ teen stories
_____ humor		_____ word search
_____ interviews		

13. What are the titles of your two favorite books? Why are they your favorites?

_____

_____

_____

_____

14. Something else I'd like to say is _____

_____

_____

A Reading Interest Inventory for Middle School Readers

Name: _____ Date: _____ Grade: _____

1. Which of these activities do you like to do? Check as many as you want.

_____ ride bikes or ATVs	_____ play basketball
_____ play baseball	_____ play football
_____ play soccer	_____ play ice hockey
_____ swim	_____ skate
_____ skateboard	_____ rollerblade
_____ ski	_____ ice skate
_____ play with friends	_____ play computer games
_____ watch TV	_____ play card games

   Other activities? _____

2. What do you like to do when you're not in school?

   _____

3. Do you read the newspaper? _____ Yes _____ No

   If yes, what parts of the newspaper do you read? Check all that apply.

_____ Headlines	_____ Sports
_____ Comics	_____ News
_____ Advertisements	_____ Classifieds
_____ Regional News	_____ Arts & Entertainment
_____ Feature Articles	_____ Travel
_____ Weather	_____ Editorials
_____ Letters to the Editor	_____ Style & Fashion

   Other parts? _____

4. What are your two favorite TV shows?

   _____

   _____

5. What are your two favorite movies?

   _____

   _____

6. Who are your two favorite movie stars?

   _____

   _____

This page may be reproduced for classroom use.

7. Who are your favorite music groups or singers?

_____

_____

8. What collections do you have?

_____

_____

9. If you could go anywhere, where would you like to go and why?

_____

_____

10. If you have a pet, what is it and what is its name?

_____

11. If you don't have a pet and could have one, what would you have and why would you want it?

_____

12. When you read, what do you like to read? Check all that apply.

_____	adventure	_____	jokes and riddles
_____	animals	_____	letters
_____	autobiography	_____	magazines
_____	biography	_____	maps
_____	books that are movies	_____	movie stars
_____	comic books	_____	mystery
_____	cookbooks	_____	plays
_____	crossword puzzles	_____	poetry
_____	diaries	_____	rock stars
_____	e-mail	_____	romance
_____	fact books	_____	science
_____	fantasy	_____	science fiction
_____	history	_____	supernatural
_____	how-to manuals	_____	teen stories
_____	humor	_____	word search
_____	interviews		

13. What are the titles of your two favorite books? Why are they your favorites?

_____

_____

_____

_____

14. Read each of the following passages. Circle the word that best describes your interest in reading more about the topic.

Passage 1

Before Fernando Santiago was called "The Boss," he was called Ferdo. To those in his hometown, the prize–winning professional wrestler still is. "That's what we call him to this day," his father, José Santiago, said in an interview on the Jessie Jordan TV Talk Show. "I never call him Fernando."

No interest   A slight interest   Some interest   A lot of interest

Passage 2

There was a large black SUV parked in the driveway behind the beautiful log and stone house. Fifteen years ago it had been a two–room log cabin. That's when the Barkers lived there and the road was a one–lane dirt road. Now, driving past on the smooth asphalt, I wondered if anyone knew what really happened to them.

No interest   A slight interest   Some interest   A lot of interest

Passage 3

McDonald's is one of the most recognized names in the world. Driving along America's roads, you'll see the familiar golden arches welcoming hungry travelers to a comfortable restaurant with familiar menu items. Today, you can find McDonald's in Argentina, Croatia, Egypt, Japan, and 56 other countries around the world. McDonald's is truly the world's community restaurant.

No interest   A slight interest   Some interest   A lot of interest

15. Something else I'd like to say is _____

_____

_____

Advocate Reading!

Public service announcement #1

(30 seconds)

HABITS ARE SOMETHING YOU DO ALL THE TIME. THERE ARE GOOD HABITS AND BAD HABITS. READING FOR THE FUN OF IT IS A GOOD HABIT. IF YOU DON'T YET HAVE THE READING HABIT, HOW ABOUT STARTING ONE? CHOOSE STUFF YOU LIKE TO READ AND READ REGULARLY. BEFORE LONG, YOU WON'T BE ABLE TO GET ALONG WITHOUT READING—BECAUSE IT'S A HABIT. LIKE ALL GOOD HABITS, YOU WILL SEE POSITIVE RESULTS. YOUR READING SPEED WILL INCREASE. YOUR GRADES WILL IMPROVE. YOUR PARENTS WILL BE IMPRESSED, AND YOU WILL STRETCH YOUR IMAGINATION. ISN'T IT NICE TO KNOW YOU CAN BEGIN NOW TO DEVELOP A GOOD HABIT—A READING FOR THE FUN OF IT HABIT? SPONSORED BY [NAME OF LIBRARY OR SCHOOL].

Public service announcement #2

(15 seconds)

DEVELOP A READING HABIT DURING TEEN READ WEEK, OCTOBER 14 TO 20. READ IN SMALL BYTES (sic)—10 MINUTES ON THE WAY TO SCHOOL, 15 MINUTES BEFORE GOING TO SLEEP, 10 MINUTES WAITING FOR FRIENDS. ASK YOUR FRIENDS, FAMILY, AND LIBRARIANS FOR GOOD BOOKS. READING IS LIKE A BRIEF VACATION. TAKE A READING VACATION TODAY.

60

Advocate Reading! *(continued)*

Public service announcement #3
(15 seconds)

3a. A TEEN READ WEEK THOUGHT: "*THE LITTLE PRINCE* IS A BOOK I THINK EVERY HUMAN SHOULD READ AT LEAST ONCE A YEAR. IT HELPS PEOPLE REMEMBER HOW INNOCENT AND BEAUTIFUL LIFE CAN BE!"
—MELISSA JOAN HART, ACTRESS

3b. A TEEN READ WEEK THOUGHT: "ONE OF MY GREATEST SOURCES OF PLEASURE IS READING. I KNEW AT A YOUNG AGE THAT READING FOR ME WAS THE ULTIMATE SOURCE OF FREEDOM. WITH KNOWLEDGE, YOU HAVE THE POTENTIAL TO REACH GREAT HEIGHTS."
—OPRAH WINFREY

3c. A TEEN READ WEEK THOUGHT: "BOOKS ARE UNIQUELY PORTABLE MAGIC. YOU NEVER KNOW WHEN YOU'LL WANT AN ESCAPE HATCH. AT SUCH TIMES I FIND A BOOK VITAL."
—STEPHEN KING

Source: Colorado Department of Education, 2001.

Internet Resources for Books Too Good to Miss

Organization	Types of Information	Internet Link
American Library Association	Best Books for Young Adults Book Lists and Book Awards Teens' Top 10	www.ala.org/ala/yalsa/booklistsawards/booklistsbook.htm
Children's Book Council	Children's Book Week Young People's Poetry Week New Books	www.cbcbooks.org
International Reading Association	IRA's Children's Books Award Lee Bennett Hopkins Promising Poet Award Paul A. Witty Short Story Award	www.reading.org/association/awards/childrens.html
About, Inc.	A part of The New York Times Company, has links to other Web sites	childrensbooks.about.com
National Science Teachers Association	New Books NSTA Book Club Outstanding Science Trade Books for Children—titles of recommended books selected in conjunction with Children's Book Council. Lists are available beginning with 1996 and are updated yearly.	www.nsta.org
Scholastic	Printz Award Winners—outstanding literary books for adolescents All About Reading—books for children from birth to Grade 5, and Grades 6–8 Titles for reluctant readers, advanced readers, and all readers.	www.scholastic.com
Social Studies	Notable Trade Books—titles of books that emphasize human relations and represent a diversity of groups. The lists are compiled in conjunction with the Children's Book Council (www.cbc.com). Current lists are available to members only, but the lists from 2000–2004 are available.	www.socialstudies.org
Carol Hurst's Literature Site	Reviews of good books for student activities to use in the classroom Professional materials	www.carolhurst.com

What's Different About Teaching Reading to Students Learning English?
Study Guide

Internet Resources for Books Too Good to Miss (continued)

Organization	Types of Information	Internet Link

The Children's Literature Web Guide	Internet resources related to books for children and young adults
	  Children's Book Awards
	  The Year's Best Books
	  Children's Best Sellers
	The Doucette Index: Teaching Ideas for Children's Books
		www.ucalgary.ca/~dkbrown

Bookspot	What to Read—for children and adults
	  Bestsellers
	  Book Awards
	  Book Reviews
	  Online Books
	  First Books, etc.
	Genre Corner
	  Children's Books
	  Comics
	  Mystery, etc.
	Behind the Books
	  Authors
		www.bookspot.com

Teen Reads	Books for Teens Coming Soon (new titles) Teenread Chats (discussions with authors) Cool New Books Books into Movies Reviews Manga Reviews (Japanese print comics) Christian Reviews Recent Bookreporter.com Titles Perfect for Teens	www.teenreads.com
The Two Rs: Reading and Riding	Horses, ponies, cowboys, toys, games, and books Books for babies–8 years Books for reluctant readers	www.the2rs.com

Guiding Reading Comprehension

Comprehension

When readers comprehend a text, they actively construct meaning in their minds by drawing from the text itself and from their own knowledge. The goal is to have the two sources of input interweave and make sense.

This is the constructivist theory of comprehension (Kintch & Van Dijk, 1978). In this view of comprehension, readers independently and purposefully make connections between the text and their own body of knowledge and personal experiences that are relevant to what they are reading, which makes reading an interactive process (Grabe & Stoller, 2002). As readers recognize words rapidly, they hold them in their short–term memory as they analyze the structure of sentences to make meaning and monitor their comprehension, all the while drawing background information from their long–term memory (Grabe & Stoller, 2002). In other words, readers actively use what they already know about the language and couple it with their personal background to make sense of what they are reading.

"Great readers are thinking all the time as they read" (Keene & Zimmerman, 1997, p. 85). This means they are continually making connections, asking questions, drawing inferences, visualizing, and so forth. Of these, it is making connections to prior knowledge and experience that deepens their comprehension (Harvey, 1998). Such connections usually take place in these three forms:

• Text–to–self connections
• Text–to–text connections
• Text–to–world connections (Keene & Zimmerman, 1997, p. 55)

Keene and Zimmerman (1997) and Harvey (1998) recommend that teachers help students learn to make these connections by modeling how they, as readers, make these connections when they read. Being able to connect text to self, text, and the world enables readers to more actively engage in drawing on their own experiences, thus improving comprehension (Harvey, 1998).

Harvey (1998, pp. 73–74) suggests that teachers may want to teach students to use the following codes:

* for interesting	I for Important
BK for background knowledge	L for learning something new
? for a question	W for wondering something
C for confused	S for surprising information

Pleasure Reading in a Second Language

Pleasure reading provides valuable input for second language acquisition. Pleasure reading in a second language has two requirements:
- The topic is understandable to the reader, and
- The topic is one the reader would read about in the first language.

Teachers can encourage English language learners to read for pleasure. They can select appropriate reading materials for English language learners, such as universally known stories or tales or longer texts on topics with which readers are familiar (Knutson, 1998; Krashen, 1982).

Making Connections

Why make connections?
- Investigations show that most students forget most of what they have been taught.
- Students who "see the connections" are more likely to understand, remember, and use what they learn (Perkins, 1993, cited in Grognet, Jameson, Franco, & Derrick–Mescua, 2000).

Making connections helps English language learners achieve the following:
- Approach a topic from a variety of perspectives.
- Learn how the use of English is the same and yet different from topic to topic and subject to subject (Grognet, Jameson, Franco, & Derrick–Mescua, 2000, p. 255)

Increase Readers' Comprehension

Use a lesson sequence that proceeds…

- from _____ knowledge to new knowledge;
- from the _____ to the abstract;
- from _____ language to written text; and
- from _____ contextual support to less contextual support.

Use contextual support (_____, _____, non–_____ clues) to communicate the overall message, then correlate the message with the _____.

Source: Jameson, 1998.

Teach the Text Backwards

◆ Read the text.

◆ Answer the questions.

◆ Discuss the material.

◆ Do the applications/expansions.

Source: Jameson, 1998.

A Nation is Born: Study questions

Directions: Read the questions below and write the answers that you know.

1. Who were the founding fathers of the United States?

_____

2. When did the founding fathers meet in Independence Hall?

_____

3. Who wrote the Declaration of Independence?

_____

4. Who were some people who signed the Declaration of Independence?

_____

5. Who took the Declaration of Independence to the printer?

_____

6. Why did John Hancock make his signature so large?

_____

Directions: Use one or more of the texts on pages 66–68 to practice using Teach the Text Backwards.

A NATION IS BORN

Many important colonists helped the United States become a separate nation. They were called the "founding fathers."

America's founding fathers met in Independence Hall in Philadelphia on July 4, 1776. They declared independence from England so that the thirteen colonies could form their own government. The United States of America was born.

Thomas Jefferson was one of the founding fathers. He wrote the Declaration of Independence. It is one of the most important documents in U.S. history.

John Hancock was another founding father. He wrote his signature at the end of the declaration with a quill pen. Hancock wrote his name in big letters so King George III could read it without his glasses.

Benjamin Franklin and John Adams were founding fathers, too. They also signed the Declaration of Independence. Then, they took it to a printer. The printer printed many copies on a printing press so that a lot of people could read it.

Printers also printed political drawings, cartoons, and pamphlets for the people. Benjamin Franklin drew a famous cartoon of a snake cut into pieces. He wrote the words "Unite or Die" under the picture so that people could understand the importance of becoming one nation.

Source: The Oxford Picture Dictionary for the Content Areas: Content Readings. © Oxford University Press 2000. Used by permission.

PREHISTORIC ANIMALS

Millions of years ago many different types of animals lived on the Earth. They are called prehistoric animals. Some of these animals were dinosaurs.

Many dinosaurs were herbivores. They only ate plants. The anatosaurus and the dryosaurus were herbivores. The triceratops was an herbivore, too. It had three horns on its head. The ankylosaurus and the stegosaurus were also herbivores. The ankylosaurus had spikes on its back. The stegosaurus had spikes on its tail.

The apatosaurus and the diplodocus were very long dinosaurs. The apatosaurus was 70 feet long and the diplodocus was 90 feet long. The brachiosaurus was one of the tallest dinosaurs. It was 40 feet tall.

Some dinosaurs were carnivores. They ate meat. Sometimes they ate other dinosaurs. The allosaurus was a carnivore. It had very sharp teeth. The tyrannosaurus was a carnivore, too. It had 60 teeth. People call the tyrannosaurus the king of the dinosaurs. The pteranodon was a carnivore, too. Pteranodons could fly.

Dinosaurs lived more than 65 million years ago. Smilodons lived less than two million years ago. The smilodon was a large cat with two large saber teeth. Some people call these cats saber–toothed tigers.

These prehistoric animals are extinct. They are not alive today. But we can see their fossils in museums. Fossils are bones and other parts of prehistoric animals or plants. Fossils can stay in rocks in the ground for millions of years. Scientists find fossils and study them. We can learn a lot about prehistoric animals from fossils.

Source: The Oxford Picture Dictionary for the Content Areas: Content Readings. © Oxford University Press 2000. Used by permission.

PARTS OF THE BODY

Sam is going surfing today. Surfing is fun, but it is also hard work.

Sam has to use many parts of his body. Sam listens to the ocean with his ears. He feels the wind in his hair. He smells the salty air with his nose. He watches the waves with his eyes.

Sam walks into the ocean with his surfboard. He has to hold his surfboard with two hands, or it will float away. He has to watch the ocean, or else he won't see the best wave.

Finally, Sam sees a big wave. Now, he has to get ready. He puts his chest on the surfboard. He has to keep his head up, or else the wave will go past him. He has to keep this mouth closed, or else he will swallow water.

The wave comes to Sam. He puts one foot on the surfboard. Then, he puts his other foot on the board. He stands up. He can feel the surfboard with his toes.

Sam has to bend his knees, or else he will fall. He has to put his arms out for balance. He doesn't fall! He rides the wave!

Source: The Oxford Picture Dictionary for the Content Areas: Content Readings. © Oxford University Press 2000. Used by permission.

Using Graphics to Generate Oral or Written Text

What can teachers do to help English language learners learn academic content that is written or spoken in English? What can they do to help these students demonstrate what they know using English? What can they do to help these students use English to make connections with what they know and link it to the new knowledge? Graphic organizers are vehicles that can help English language learners learn new academic content, demonstrate what they learned, and make connections between what they know and what they have learned (Rosenshine, 1997; Tang, 1992/1993).

The ways in which this technique can be used might be as simple as using the illustrations or photographs in a text to help students generate language, either oral or written. For example, students can name all the items they know that are in a picture, and the teacher can record these words on the chalkboard or chart. Then, working in pairs or small groups, students organize the words, generate sentences, or produce other language products, such as narratives, descriptions, verses, and so on.

This activity can also be conducted with advance graphic organizers, such as charts, tables, webs, or other formats. Before the lesson, the teacher designs a graphic organizer that matches the way the content is organized in the text. The graphic then forms the basis for the teacher's presentation of how the content is organized and the linguistic devices that are critical for understanding the content. The graphic organizer also functions as a device students can use repeatedly to review the information and language structures because it displays the content schema of the information. Ultimately, students are able to use the graphic organizer to generate their own sentences, either oral or written, and may also create their own graphic organizers to display content information.

A Nation is Born: Knowledge structures

Concepts	Definitions	Details
founding fathers	• the men who helped the United States become a separate nation	• Thomas Jefferson • John Hancock • Benjamin Franklin • John Adams
independence	• freedom from the control of another person or country	• the 13 colonies formed their own government
Declaration of Independence	• a written statement saying the United States was no longer under the control of the King of England	• one of the most important documents in U.S. history • printed in many copies so a lot of people could read it
King George	• the King, or ruler, of England and the 13 colonies	• after the Declaration of Independence was signed, he no longer had control of the 13 colonies
political drawings, cartoons, and pamphlets	• pictures and written words that tell readers what a person thinks or feels about how public matters are handled	• Unite or Die—a famous cartoon drawn by Benjamin Franklin • people understood the importance of becoming a new nation

Directions: How do these sentences emerge from the information in the chart?

The founding fathers were the men who helped the United States become a separate nation.

Some of the founding fathers were Thomas Jefferson, John Hancock, Benjamin Franklin, and John Adams.

Use the information in the chart to generate another sentence.

_____

_____

Chapter 2

A Nation is Born: Linguistic devices

Signal Words	Subject	Predicate
one	Thomas Jefferson	– wrote the Declaration of Independence – signed the Declaration of Independence
another	John Hancock	– signed the Declaration of Independence in very large letters
too	Benjamin Franklin	– signed the Declaration of Independence – took the Declaration of Independence to a printer – drew a famous political cartoon
	John Adams	– signed the Declaration of Independence – took the Declaration of Independence to a printer

*Thomas Jefferson was **one** of the founding fathers.*

***One** of the founding fathers was Thomas Jefferson.*

*John Hancock was **another** founding father.*

Directions: Use the word *too* and the information in the chart to write a sentence about Benjamin Franklin and John Adams.

_____

_____

_____

Six Strategies to Improve Comprehension

◆ Self–Monitoring of Comprehension

◆ Graphic Organizers

◆ Semantic Organizers

◆ Story/Text Structure

◆ Questions and Answers

◆ Summarization

Source: National Reading Panel, 2000.

Graphic Organizers and Language Needed

Kind of Graphic Organizer	Kind of Language Needed
Chronology What is the sequence of events? _____ _____ _____	first last next soon after while later finally at last in the end eventually in the meantime since in 2004
Compare and Contrast How are they similar? _____ _____ How are they different? _____ _____	**Comparison** **Contrast** and however too yet also but similarly although both even though in the same way on the other hand as...as in contrast like rather alike

Graphic Organizers and Language Needed (continued)

Kind of Graphic Organizer	Kind of Language Needed
Simple Listing What are the attributes of this object/person? _____ _____ _____	such as include others for example some a few a, an the
Cause and Effect What are the cause and effect of this event? _____ _____ _____	**Cause** **Effect** because lead to due to result in since because given that effect of cause as a result

Sources: Levine, 1995; Mikulecky, 1985.

Directions: Use the following text to practice Using Graphics to Generate Oral or Written Text.

THE UNIVERSE

Our world is a very small place. The Earth is just one planet. There are eight other planets in our solar system. The Sun is the center of our solar system. All the planets go around Sun once every year.

Mercury is the closest planet to the Sun. Venus is next. The Earth is the third planet from the Sun. Mars is the fourth planet. Jupiter is fifth. It's the largest planet. Saturn is sixth. It has big rings around it. Uranus is seventh. Neptune is eighth. Pluto is ninth. Pluto is the farthest planet from the Sun.

The Moon isn't a planet. It doesn't go around the Sun. It goes around the Earth. The Moon is very close to the Earth. You can see it at night. The Moon is the biggest and brightest light in the night sky.

Comets and meteors are in our solar system, too. Comets are bodies of dust, rocks, and gas. Meteors are small rocks in space. Meteors enter the Earth's atmosphere and make bright streaks of light in the sky.

Stars aren't planets. Stars are very large bodies of gas. The Sun is a star. A constellation is a group of stars with a name. Ursa Major is a constellation. It looks like a big spoon, or big dipper. People call it the "Big Dipper." You can see Ursa Major at night.

Galaxies have thousands and thousands of stars. Our solar system is part of a galaxy. Out galaxy is the Milky Way. There are many other galaxies in the universe. They are very far from our solar system.

Source: The Oxford Picture Dictionary for the Content Areas: Content Readings. © Oxford University Press 2000. Used by permission.

Directed Reading–Thinking Activity (DRTA)

The Directed Reading–Thinking Activity (DRTA) as developed by Russel G. Stauffer (1969) is an instructional strategy that guides readers through the process of reading text to access meaning. Throughout the DRTA, the teacher serves as a guide, and the steps in the strategy serve as a blueprint for the instruction (Maney, n.d.[a]). The DRTA includes the following five steps: Preview, Predict, Read, Check, and Summarize.

Preview	
Teacher Actions	**Student Actions**

Prepares for the lesson:
    reads the text
    notes new vocabulary
    notes new language structures
    notes text cues
    notes unfamiliar content
    divides text into sections	

Uses *Teach the Text Backwards*	Makes connections with the content
Guides students to make connections with prior knowledge, personal experiences, and previous learning	Makes connections with the content
Introduces new vocabulary and language structures	Learns new vocabulary and focuses on new language structures
Guides students to develop an overview of the text	Begins to see the big picture

Predict

Teacher Actions	Student Actions
Guides students to make predictions about the content and to answer these questions: *What is it about?* *What does it mean?* *What do I expect to learn?* *What does it mean to me?*	Reads the title, headings, and bold print and looks at illustrations and graphics to get the big picture Makes predictions about the content Turns headings into questions Examines the questions at the end of the text
Guides students to set purposes for reading	Identifies personal questions

Read

Sets purposes for reading Guides students to read the text in sections or reads the text aloud as students follow along Assists students in checking predictions Guides students to make connections with the text Guides students to ask additional questions	Reads the text silently, orally with a partner, or orally with a group, or listens as someone reads the text aloud Notes places in the text where predictions are verified or refuted Notes places in the text where additional questions or uncertainties arise

Check

Guides students to check predictions	Reports findings about predictions Indicates text locations relating to the predictions

Summarize

Guides students to summarize the content	Locates and reads aloud main points in the text States or writes the main points in own words Draws conclusions about the content and identifies what was learned Predicts what will follow

Reading Lesson Plan and Reflections on Instruction

Student(s) Information

Grade Level(s) _____

Native Language(s) _____

Level(s) of English Proficiency

___ Beginning   ___ Early Intermediate   ___ Intermediate   ___ Transitioning

Reading Level(s) in English

___ Beginning   ___ Primer   ___ First Grade   ___ Second Grade

___ Third Grade   ___ Fourth Grade   ___ Fifth Grade   ___ Sixth Grade

___ Seventh Grade ___ Eighth Grade   ___ Ninth Grade   ___ Tenth Grade

Lesson Plan

Title _____

New Vocabulary

Language Structure(s) or Grammar

   Stages

      Before Reading

      During Reading

      After Reading

Reflections on Instruction

What worked well in the lesson?

What did not work well? Why do you think this happened?

What, if anything, did you change in the lesson? Why?

If you were to do the lesson again, what would you change and why?

Directions: Use the following text to create a DRTA lesson using the Reading Lesson Plan and Reflections on Instruction.

OUR ENVIRONMENT

People, plants, and animals all live in the same environment. That environment is the Earth. People and animals need food, water, and air. Plants need food, water, air, and soil.

This town had serious environmental problems several years ago. Water pollution was one problem. There were oil slicks on the lake.

Air pollution was another problem. People drove their cars everywhere and they ignored the exhaust. Hundreds of smokestacks polluted the air with smoke. The smoke mixed with fog and then the town had smog.

Soil pollution was a problem, too. People threw litter and garbage on the sides of the roads. Cans and bottles filled big, ugly landfills.

But things have been changing recently. The town has been solving its environmental problems. People have been reducing their litter. They have been reusing plastic and glass bottles. They have been recycling metal cans and newspapers. Some people have been making compost from their uneaten food, banana peels, and other garbage.

People have been riding together in carpools. Some people have been walking or biking to work. They haven't been polluting the air with their cars.

Now, the sky and lake are blue, and the trees and grass are green. Plants are growing and people are breathing clean air.

Source: The Oxford Picture Dictionary for the Content Areas: Content Readings. © Oxford University Press 2000. Used by permission.

What's Different About Teaching Reading to Students Learning English?
Study Guide

Why Reading Is Hard: Reading Texts

Why Reading Is Hard: Reading Text Passages

Directions: Use pages 80–85 as you view the video clip.

Icebergs and Glaciers
by Seymour Simon
©1993, Creative Education

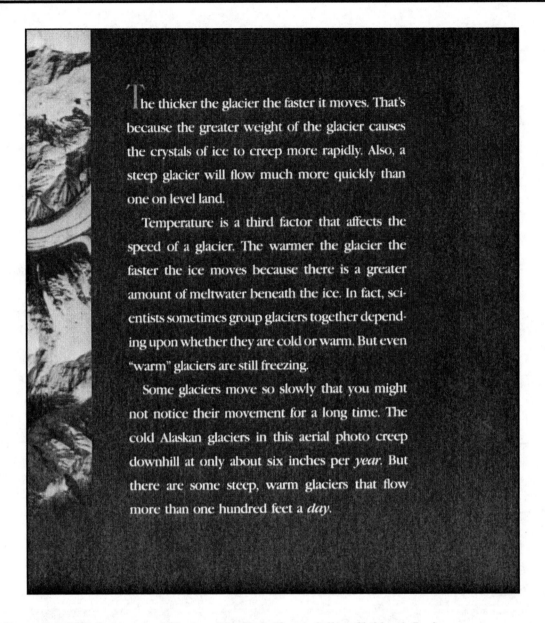

The thicker the glacier the faster it moves. That's because the greater weight of the glacier causes the crystals of ice to creep more rapidly. Also, a steep glacier will flow much more quickly than one on level land.

Temperature is a third factor that affects the speed of a glacier. The warmer the glacier the faster the ice moves because there is a greater amount of meltwater beneath the ice. In fact, scientists sometimes group glaciers together depending upon whether they are cold or warm. But even "warm" glaciers are still freezing.

Some glaciers move so slowly that you might not notice their movement for a long time. The cold Alaskan glaciers in this aerial photo creep downhill at only about six inches per *year*. But there are some steep, warm glaciers that flow more than one hundred feet a *day*.

Source: Simon, S. (1993). *Icebergs and Glaciers.* New York: HarperCollins Children's Books. Reprinted with permission.

What I think will be difficult for readers is...	What readers found was difficult was...

82

Collecting Rocks and Crystals:
Hold the Treasures of the Earth in the Palm of Your Hand
by John Farndon
©1999, Quartz, Inc.

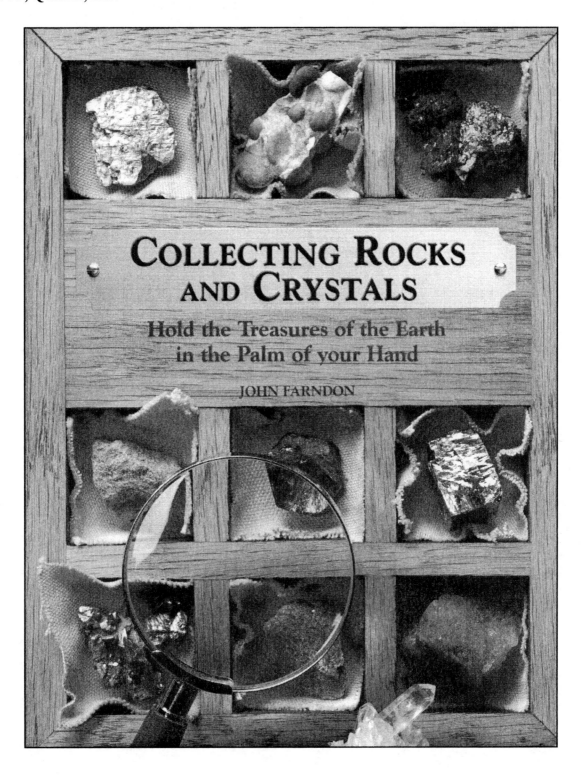

Introducing Rocks and Crystals

ROCKS AND CRYSTALS are the raw materials of the Earth's surface—the material beneath every hill and valley, mountain and plain. Some are just a few million years old. Others are almost as old as the Earth.

What are rocks?

ROCKS ARE NEVER far beneath the ground. They are only exposed on the surface in a few places—such as bare rock outcrops, cliff faces and quarries. But dig down almost anywhere on the Earth's surface and you will come to solid rock before long.

Like the other smaller planets in the solar system, our world is made almost entirely from rock. The Earth is a bit like a perfectly boiled egg—with a semi-liquid yolk or "core," surrounded by a thick, soft layer called the mantle, and covered by a thin hard shell called the crust. The core in the very center is metal but the crust and mantel are made entirely from rock.

ROCKS AND MANKIND

No wonder, then, that rocks have played such an important part in mankind's history. Rocks were used by humans for their very first cutting tools, millions of years ago. At least three million years ago, early hominids (manlike creatures) were chipping the edge off hand-sized round pebbles, perhaps to use as weapons. Two million years ago, hominids began using flints to make two-sided hand-axes, which is why the first age of man is known as the Stone Age.

Later, clay was used to make pottery, and since then mankind has found an increasing variety of ways to use rocks. They can be broken up and reshaped to provide building materials for everything from cottages to cathedrals, harbor walls to roads. Certain minerals—the natural chemicals they are made from—can be extracted or processed to make a huge range of materials. All metals, such as iron, copper, and tin, come from minerals contained in rock. So do most

ROCK SOURCE *(below)*
One of the best places to see living rock is in quarries, where it is blasted and dug from the ground to provide building stone and other materials.

•6•

Source: Farndon, J. (1999). *Collecting Rocks and Crystals.* London: Quarto. Reprinted with permission.

What I think will be difficult for readers is...	What readers found was difficult was...

Caterpillars, Bugs and Butterflies
by Mel Boring
©1996, T & N Children's Publishing

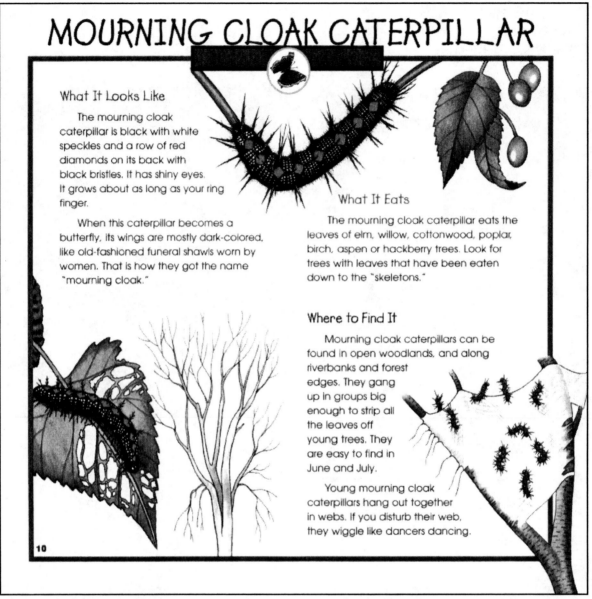

MOURNING CLOAK CATERPILLAR

What It Looks Like

The mourning cloak caterpillar is black with white speckles and a row of red diamonds on its back with black bristles. It has shiny eyes. It grows about as long as your ring finger.

When this caterpillar becomes a butterfly, its wings are mostly dark-colored, like old-fashioned funeral shawls worn by women. That is how they got the name "mourning cloak."

What It Eats

The mourning cloak caterpillar eats the leaves of elm, willow, cottonwood, poplar, birch, aspen or hackberry trees. Look for trees with leaves that have been eaten down to the "skeletons."

Where to Find It

Mourning cloak caterpillars can be found in open woodlands, and along riverbanks and forest edges. They gang up in groups big enough to strip all the leaves off young trees. They are easy to find in June and July.

Young mourning cloak caterpillars hang out together in webs. If you disturb their web, they wiggle like dancers dancing.

10

Source: Boring, M. (1996). *Caterpillars, Bugs and Butterflies.* Minnetonka, MN: T & N Children's Publishing. Reprinted with permission.

What I think will be difficult for readers is...	What readers found was difficult was...

Teaching Comprehension

What Teachers Can Do to Teach Comprehension

1. Read aloud to students.

2. Select motivating and culturally appropriate reading materials that make sense to the students.

3. Use prereading activities to have students think about the topic, make their own connections with it, and establish a purpose for reading.

4. Draw attention to how the text is written.

5. Explicitly teach reading strategies and refer to them by name.

6. Model how to do the reading strategies.

7. Teach students when and why to use each strategy.

8. Provide many opportunities for students to practice the strategies.

9. Build in frequent opportunities for students to review their understanding of what they are reading.

10. Develop students' metacognitive skills.

Recommended Prereading Activities

Preview the text to identify the words and language features that are critical to understanding and reading the text; then do the following:

- Build background to help students identify and use what they already know about the topic.

- Use field trips, videos or films, simulations, and experiments to give students direct experiences to learn new words.

- Use pictures, realia, diagrams, actions, or demonstrations to teach the new words.

- Involve students in using and expanding the meanings of words through activities such as brainstorming, clustering, or webbing.

- Use songs, chants, or pattern practice to have students practice the language structure(s) used in the text.

- Strengthen sight word recognition with word cards, games, or computer–based activities.

- Teach the meanings of the words in the text that have multiple meanings.

- Teach the more complex language structures such as idioms and figurative language, as needed.

- Construct preview guides or anticipation guides to help students to identify purposes for reading.

Sources: Cloud, Genessee, & Hamayan, 2000; Peregoy & Boyle, 2001.

What's Different About Teaching Reading to Students Learning English?
Study Guide

Questions to Ask When Reading

Teach students to ask the following:

◆ What do the title, special kinds of print, and illustrations tell me?

◆ What are the most important words?

◆ For whom did the author write the text?

◆ What does the author want me to understand, learn, or do?

◆ What words did the author use to connect the ideas?

◆ Why am I reading this? What do I want to accomplish?

◆ Do I understand what I am reading?

◆ What reading strategies am I using, and how well am I using them?

◆ What else can I do?

From One Teacher's Perspective

Coast–to–Coast: A Directed Reading–Thinking Activity

This lesson was created and taught by Rebecca Zieminski, literacy coach, in collaboration with Danielle Rivet, ELL teacher, Marlborough Intermediate School, Marlborough, Massachusetts, and is used with permission.

Content objective

Students will be able to name and describe the landforms and bodies of water of the United States.

Key vocabulary

coast	volcano	river	canyon
ocean	desert	lake	mountain

Materials

Freeman, M. S. (1999). *Coast to Coast*. Skokie, IL: Rand McNally.

clay	cookie sheet or heavy cardboard
toothpicks	small pieces of paper (for labels)
sticky notes	

Before Reading

Activating Prior Knowledge

- Supply students with sample sentences about places visited in the United States using photos and pictures.
- Ask students to name and describe places in the United States where they have traveled for vacations or places they have visited.

Teaching the Text Backwards

- Provide clay and a cookie sheet or heavy cardboard for the students to create some of the places they have seen or been to, such as a lake, a river, the ocean, or mountains.
- As students work cooperatively on this building task, encourage and monitor their use of the new vocabulary words and sentence formations.
- After the structures are built, have the students label their structure with signs made of toothpicks and paper.
- Conduct a picture walk of the book, pointing out places that might be familiar to the students.
- Review the vocabulary, making connections to cognates.

Vocabulary Words in English	Cognates in Spanish
coast	costa
ocean	océano
volcano	volcán
desert	desierto
river	río
lake	lago
canyon	cañón
mountains	montañas

- Discuss the genre of the text: a nonfiction text. Specifically point out the bold print words, the captions under the pictures, the table of contents, and the picture index.
- Answer questions that the students have.
- Set the purposes for reading: The "What are we going to learn?" questions.
- Read the text.

During Reading

- Students are expected to "text code" the text.
- Students are shown how to "code" their text to get the meaning and take notes about what they read. Students then make text–to–self, text–to–text, and text–to–world connections, writing the connections on sticky notes and later organizing them in their writing journals. Students also note any questions that arise when they are reading and write a brief summary of what they read.
- Following the reading, students do a paired reading of the text and discuss the questions and points of interest that they found when reading.
- After the paired reading activity, students discuss any questions that linger and reread the text to locate the information that answers the questions.

After Reading

- Students draw an illustration of a created country or island that includes at least five landforms or bodies of water that were mentioned in the reading.
- Students create drawings and label them with the correct vocabulary words.
- The teacher introduces the atlas, demonstrates how maps are made, and explains the Map Key.
- Small groups of students display and talk about their island/country drawings with a partner and point out their five landforms/bodies of water.
- Pictures are posted in the classroom for the students to refer to throughout this unit of study and to reinforce the vocabulary.

Reflections on Instruction

The Coast–to–Coast lesson was one part of an assignment for teachers attending a reading workshop. The second part of the assignment was to reflect on how the instruction had gone by answering three questions (A, B, and C below). The following comments were those made by the teacher who planned and taught the Coast–to–Coast lesson.

A. What parts of the lesson worked well?

Teaching the Text Backwards was a tremendously successful strategy to employ! After discussing this project with the teacher of English language learners with whom I would be working, we were unsure whether or not the students would buy into the hands–on activity with the clay. I was also afraid that it would be too time–consuming because our days are so busy and jam–packed with work. She thought her students would love it, so we decided to try it out.

What I found out was that, yes, the hands–on activity took some time to implement and complete; however, the students became actively involved in their learning. The backward approach, starting with the application/expansion, proved to be a wonderful way for the students to really focus on and practice the new vocabulary. The time invested on this prereading activity provided an opportunity for the students to chat socially while they constructed rivers, lakes, mountains, and valleys. They used the vocabulary while talking to each other. This was a natural time to discuss the cognates and how the words in English sounded similar to the words in Spanish.

As the students worked, I could see that not all of the necessary landforms and bodies of water were being created, so I assigned a different one to each student to create. I also gave them a time limit. After seeing how detailed some students were, I could see this part of the lesson taking up to 45 minutes, so I cut it short after 15 minutes and asked them to put their completed forms on the tray I had provided. The students created labels with the toothpicks and paper and stuck their labels into their landforms when they were finished.

At the conclusion of the construction, all of the pieces were put together to create a unique island that had many different landforms in close proximity. This gave us an opportunity to discuss where the different landforms really exist. Next, we took a picture walk through the book and discussed where the geographic locations were. That prompted us to take out an atlas with a map of the United States to show us where the various places in the book were in relation to Massachusetts.

We set purposes for reading the text and discussed what we thought we were going to learn. I distributed sticky notes to the class and instructed them to text code the material as they read. Text coding is a strategy they have already been taught. They mark the text if they have a question, a connection, or a thought/comment. They have a reference sheet they can refer to if they need to.

As the students completed this first reading, the teacher of English language learners and I moved around the group and listened to individual students read, and encouraged good reading strategies. Because this was such a short book, we decided to have the children reread it with a partner and do a shared reading, sharing what they marked with their sticky notes the first time they read it. Then as a whole group, we reread the book again, answering any questions that they still had and wished to discuss.

We assigned the "after reading" assignment for homework because we were out of time for the lesson. We have not collected the pictures of the children's imaginary island or country. I am eager to see how they incorporate the vocabulary they learned into this open–ended project.

B. How was what you did different from the way you usually teach reading?

This was a new approach for me to try with my fourth graders. Starting with the project/ application/expansion first was very much the way I would have taught my former class of first graders. I always started with something concrete with them and then moved toward more abstract concepts. I never thought to do something like this with my intermediate grade students and not with English language learners either.

I enjoyed listening to the children talk as they created the clay forms. This casual, yet focused, discussion of their work really impressed me. They talked about beaches they had visited, mountains they had seen, and lakes they had been to.

By the time the students actually started reading, they were very comfortable having heard and pronounced the words before the reading. There were other bold print words in the book, and we discussed them in our picture walk.

Having two teachers with a small group of six English language learners was a treat. I enjoyed working with Danielle, the teacher of English language learners, and even though I intended to just observe, I found myself in the middle of the lesson with her as we supported each other as co–teachers.

C. What does this experience tell you about teaching reading to students who are learning English?

What this experience tells me about teaching reading to students who are learning English is that students experience greater success when they have concrete examples and strategies to utilize (that have been modeled effectively). Also, the opportunity to reread the text several times helps students increase their fluency and comprehension. Although I know this to be true, I don't always provide the structure and time for my students to practice and participate in multiple readings. This experience reminds me that this is a valuable use of the students' reading block.

Chapter Summary and Beyond the Workshop

Chapter 2: Comprehension
What's Different About Teaching Reading to Students Learning English?

Some native English speakers may

- share much of the same knowledge and experiences because they have grown up in the United States (Hirsch, Jr., 2006); and
- share many of the same values, beliefs, and attitudes about school and learning because they have attended U.S. schools (Hirsch, Jr., 2006).

Some English language learners may

- enjoy pleasure reading in English if the topic is one that they would read about in their native language (Krashen, 1982);
- need to learn about a new culture and the ways language is used in social and academic contexts (TESOL, 1997);
- not have the prior knowledge needed to understand written texts because of socioeconomic status, educational background, cultural knowledge, or a combination of these factors (Kamil, 2003; Peregoy & Boyle, 2001); and
- benefit from using their native language to discuss a topic before and after reading about it in English (Snow, Burns, & Griffin, 1998; Tankersley, 2005).

Beyond the Workshop

1. Outside reading

Have participants read *A Focus on Comprehension*, a review of what research tells us about factors that affect reading comprehension. It also describes the content and direction for instruction that will help students better comprehend what they read. Have participants respond to the reading by describing those suggestions and strategies that are appropriate for English language learners and explaining the reasons for their choices.

The report is available at www.prel.org/products/re_/re_focuscomp.pdf.

2. Reading interest inventory

Administer a Reading Interest Inventory to one or more students. Briefly discuss the responses together. Select some materials and introduce them. When the students finish with the reading, talk about how satisfied they feel with the reading experience.

3. Teach a lesson

Plan and teach a reading lesson. Use Teach the Text Backwards or the Directed Reading–Thinking Activity. Complete the Reading Lesson Plan and Reflections on Instruction (see page 79). Share the lesson plan and reflections at the next session. Be prepared to share your thoughts on how this lesson sequence helped all readers, and English language learners in particular, become familiar with the language needed to read the text with comprehension.

4. Reading with a student

Ask a student to read a text (a book, a part of a book or a section of text). Use Teach the Text Backwards or the Directed Reading–Thinking Activity. Record your observations and then answer the following questions:

- What did you observe the student doing?
- What did you do to support the student's reading?
- What is the student ready to learn next?
- What do you plan to do in preparation for the next session with the student?

Share your lesson plan and notes on the experience in the next session.

CHAPTER 3
Vocabulary Development

Goal and Objectives

Goal
Participants will achieve the following:

- Understand the role of word roots and affixes and of vocabulary development in learning to read.

- Understand the characteristics of effective instructional strategies to teach vocabulary.

Objectives
Participants will be able to do the following:

- Define word affixes and roots and describe their contributions to the reading process.

- Define and describe the roles of sight vocabulary, cognates, and idioms in teaching reading to native English speakers and English language learners.

- Identify the characteristics of effective instructional techniques to teach vocabulary to both native English speakers and English language learners.

- Select effective vocabulary learning techniques to use in the classroom.

Words, Words, Words

A Word...

◆ Is a basic unit of all languages.

◆ Can be either spoken or written.

◆ Can be one sound or a group of sounds that have meaning.

◆ Can be one letter or symbol or a group of letters or symbols that have meaning.

◆ Can be composed of one or more syllables.

Young Readers' Concepts of Oral and Written Words

Many experts agree that most children, whether English speakers or speakers of other languages, go through five stages of literacy development:

- Awareness and exploration
- Experimenting with reading and writing
- Early reading and writing
- Transitional reading and writing
- Conventional reading and writing (International Reading Association and the National Association for the Education of Young Children, 1998)

As they grow and develop into conventional readers, young readers will perform with different degrees of success at a variety of phases along this reading and writing continuum (McGee & Richgels, 2003).

During the awareness and exploration stage, children become aware that everyday spoken language is different from print. Through many experiences with oral language, they have learned that human speech has meaning. They have learned the meanings of many words and can say them and use them to communicate messages. (Researchers have reported that typical English–speaking students come to school with somewhere between 2,500 and 26,000 words [Beck & McKeown, 1991].) They have also learned how to take turns in conversations and to use culturally expected nonverbal behaviors, such as making appropriate eye contact with the speaker (McGee & Richgels, 2003). They are able to make sense of the "streams of sounds that is the whole sentence" (McGee & Richgels, 2003, p. 16) and the words' meaning as they figure out the meaning of the speaker's message.

During this same stage, children become aware of the environmental print (e.g., print on restaurant signs, traffic signs, and products) that is present in most contemporary cultures (McGee & Richgels, 2003). This awareness is heightened as they engage in activities that draw their attention to environmental print and its messages. Through activities such as noticing and pointing to the *M* that appears with the world–recognized golden arches, the unconscious awareness moves into conscious exploration, and children come to know that print carries meaning.

Children's early writing attempts may start as scribbles, but as they develop, the writings begin to show evidences of linearity, directionality, and intentionality. Children's early writing of a story heard read aloud or of a letter to daddy is an indication that they are consciously aware that print conveys meaning. This development then allows them to develop concepts about print and the stability of a message that appears in print: The message remains the same each time it is seen (McGee & Richgels, 2003).

As young children move into the experimenting with reading and writing stage, they develop an understanding of two more concepts—the concept of written words and the alphabetic principle (McGee & Richgels, 2003). It is in this stage that children begin to use finger–reading to point to one written word to match a spoken word, noticing that English words are separated by white space (McGee & Richgels, 2003).

By the stage of early reading and writing, young children have developed three concepts that are critical for literacy development: 1) that oral and written language is used to communicate messages, 2) that written language is displayed via print, and 3) that written language utilizes a consistent set of sound–symbol relationships (McGee & Richgels, 2003).

Students who are speakers of other languages and who come to school needing to learn English, learn a lot of English through conversations (McGee & Richgels, 2003). They try to communicate through the use of English as their teachers use gestures, pantomime, drama, or repetition to confirm and extend their meaning. Initial communication relies on the intended message and not on correctness of form (McGee & Richgels, 2003).

Research suggests that early literacy experiences support later literacy development, "regardless of language" (Reese, 2000, cited in Genesee, Lindholm–Leary, Saunders, & Christian, 2006). Many English language learners who have early emergent literacy experiences and skills in their native language are able to draw on these native language competencies to develop second language literacy and to make sense of second language reading. This means they may translate or think of words and ideas in their native language when the second language reading task is difficult (Cohen, 2006; Genesee, Lindholm–Leary, Saunders, & Christian, 2006).

According to the International Reading Association (1998), children begin to read more and more fluently in the transitional reading and writing stage. They also begin to use some reading strategies such as rereading and asking questions when their understanding of text breaks down. As writers, children at this stage are able to use a variety of genres and may include both simple and complex sentences. During the conventional reading and writing stage, children continue to grow and develop their reading and writing skills to accomplish a wide range of tasks for many different purposes and with different audiences.

Roots and Affixes

Directions: Use the prefixes, roots, and suffixes below to create words. They are not aligned across the page. Write the new words on the lines provided.

Prefix	Root	Suffix	Word
pre	break	ed	_____
mal	care	ful	_____
un	heat	ing	_____
over	pay	ance	_____
in	perspire	able	_____
non	access	ible	_____
re	comply	ant	_____
anti	adjust	ment	_____

Directions: Review the lists of roots and the affixes and the new words. What generalizations about prefixes and suffixes can you make?

_____

_____

_____

_____

Directions: Review the information below. What generalization(s) can you draw?

Most Frequently Occurring English Affixes

Prefixes	Suffixes
un– (not) uncooked re– (again) revisit in–, im–, il–, ir– (not) invisible dis– (do the opposite of) disengage en–, em– (put into or onto) encase non– (not) nonacid over– (so as to exceed) overreach mis– (badly) mistake	–s (plural) boys –es (plural) wishes –ed (past tense) washed –ing (participle) eating –ly (like) motherly –er (comparative) faster

Inflectional Suffixes

Suffixes	Designations	Examples
–s/–es –'s –s	plural possessive third person singular	birds/dishes bird's, children's sings
–ed	past tense	walked
–ed/–en	past participle	(has/had) climbed
–ing	participle	(is/was/were) eating
–er	comparative form	taller
–est	superlative form	tallest

Word Mapping: Latin and Greek Roots

Directions: Select one Latin or Greek root. Write it in the center of the word map. In two minutes, write as many Latin or Greek words as you can.

Latin Roots	Meanings	Greek Roots	Meanings
–aud–	to hear	chrom–	color
–dict–	to tell, to speak	–cycle–	circle
–duc–, –duct–	to lead	–gen–	race
–form–	to form	–helio–	sun
–ject–	to throw	–hyper–	above, beyond
–port–	to carry	–phil–	having a love for
–scribe–	to write	–phon–	sound
–tract–	to drag	therm–	heat
–vert–	to turn		

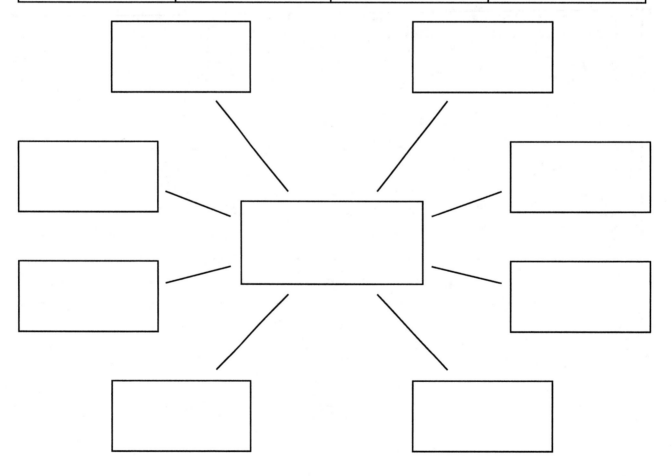

Sight Vocabulary

Kinds of Vocabularies

Directions: Write the missing words.

Receptive vocabulary

_____ vocabulary

_____ vocabulary

Productive vocabulary

_____ vocabulary

_____ vocabulary

Four Ingredients for Learning a Language

◆ Exposure to the language

◆ Opportunities for imitation

◆ Practice in a nonthreatening environment

◆ Reinforcement

Stages of Second Language Acquisition

Silent Period/Preproduction

The student—	The student is able to—	
is verbally unresponsive may often feel uncertain and confused may respond nonverbally develops listening skills begins to associate sound and meaning	listen point move mime match	draw choose dramatize circle underline

Early Production

The student—	The student is able to—	
makes connections between sounds and the environment is able to understand more understands main ideas learns keywords and sight words can use context clues can answer orally using one–, two–, or three–word responses	name label group respond use a dictionary	list categorize tell or say answer

Speech Emergence

The student—	The student is able to—	

can produce words that have been heard and understood
    many times
may mispronounce words
may omit words in speaking or writing
can produce words that are heard, such as nouns, verbs,
    and adjectives
	recall
	retell
	compare
	use phonics
		describe
		role play
		contrast
		restate

Intermediate/Advanced Fluency

The student—	The student is able to—	
makes more errors as speech becomes more complex has not mastered grammar because focusing on grammar is not productive at this stage displays extensive vocabulary development	analyze create defend debate complete define explain	evaluate justify support examine describe summarize use word analysis

Sources: Colorado Department of Education, 1997; Maine Department of Education, 1991.

Sight Vocabulary Word Identification

Directions: Below is a list of words. Cross out the words you think <u>do not</u> appear in all of the well–known lists of sight words.

a	look	there
all	my	they
an	name	this
and	not	to
ball	oil	up
can	on	was
come	over	water
did	please	went
do	said	what
friend	see	will
go	she	wish
had	some	with
his	sure	word
horse	that	you
in	the	your
like	then	

The Role of Sight Vocabulary

Native English speakers

◆ Native English speakers start to read and write as they become aware of onset and rime patterns.

◆ At first, they use visual cues to word recognition.

◆ Later, they use initial letter–sound cues.

◆ Still later, they draw on spelling pattern recognition to read new words.

English language learners

◆ Preproduction readers begin to develop a small sight vocabulary.

◆ Early Production readers recognize a larger variety of words and can use a dictionary.

◆ Speech Emergence readers use phonics and context clues for word recognition.

◆ Intermediate/Advanced Fluency readers use word analysis or word clues to decode new words.

Dolch Basic Sight Word List

List 1	List 2	List 3	List 4
1. _____ the	1. _____ at	1. _____ do	1. _____ big
2. _____ to	2. _____ him	2. _____ can	2. _____ went
3. _____ and	3. _____ with	3. _____ could	3. _____ are
4. _____ he	4. _____ up	4. _____ when	4. _____ come
5. _____ a	5. _____ all	5. _____ did	5. _____ if
6. _____ I	6. _____ look	6. _____ what	6. _____ now
7. _____ you	7. _____ is	7. _____ so	7. _____ long
8. _____ it	8. _____ her	8. _____ see	8. _____ no
9. _____ of	9. _____ there	9. _____ not	9. _____ came
10. _____ in	10. _____ some	10. _____ were	10. _____ ask
11. _____ was	11. _____ out	11. _____ get	11. _____ very
12. _____ said	12. _____ as	12. _____ them	12. _____ an
13. _____ his	13. _____ be	13. _____ like	13. _____ over
14. _____ that	14. _____ have	14. _____ one	14. _____ your
15. _____ she	15. _____ go	15. _____ this	15. _____ its
16. _____ for	16. _____ we	16. _____ my	16. _____ ride
17. _____ on	17. _____ am	17. _____ would	17. _____ into
18. _____ they	18. _____ then	18. _____ me	18. _____ just
19. _____ but	19. _____ little	19. _____ will	19. _____ blue
20. _____ had	20. _____ down	20. _____ yes	20. _____ red
/20	/20	/20	/20

Source: Shanker, J., & Ekwall, E. (1998). *Locating and Correcting Reading Difficulties* (pp. 261, 263). Columbus, OH: Merrill. Reprinted with permission.

Dolch Basic Sight Word List (continued)

List 5	List 6	List 7	List 8
1. _____ from	1. _____ away	1. _____ walk	1. _____ tell
2. _____ good	2. _____ old	2. _____ to	2. _____ much
3. _____ any	3. _____ by	3. _____ or	3. _____ keep
4. _____ about	4. _____ their	4. _____ before	4. _____ give
5. _____ around	5. _____ here	5. _____ eat	5. _____ work
6. _____ want	6. _____ saw	6. _____ again	6. _____ first
7. _____ don't	7. _____ call	7. _____ play	7. _____ try
8. _____ how	8. _____ after	8. _____ who	8. _____ new
9. _____ know	9. _____ well	9. _____ been	9. _____ must
10. _____ right	10. _____ think	10. _____ may	10. _____ start
11. _____ put	11. _____ ran	11. _____ stop	11. _____ black
12. _____ too	12. _____ let	12. _____ off	12. _____ white
13. _____ got	13. _____ help	13. _____ never	13. _____ ten
14. _____ take	14. _____ make	14. _____ seven	14. _____ does
15. _____ where	15. _____ going	15. _____ eight	15. _____ bring
16. _____ every	16. _____ sleep	16. _____ cold	16. _____ goes
17. _____ pretty	17. _____ brown	17. _____ today	17. _____ write
18. _____ jump	18. _____ yellow	18. _____ fly	18. _____ always
19. _____ green	19. _____ five	19. _____ myself	19. _____ drink
20. _____ four	20. _____ six	20. _____ around	20. _____ once
/20	/20	/20	/20

Dolch Basic Sight Word List (continued)

List 9	List 10	List 11
1. _____ soon	1. _____ use	1. _____ wash
2. _____ made	2. _____ fast	2. _____ show
3. _____ run	3. _____ say	3. _____ hot
4. _____ gave	4. _____ light	4. _____ because
5. _____ open	5. _____ pick	5. _____ far
6. _____ has	6. _____ hurt	6. _____ live
7. _____ find	7. _____ pull	7. _____ draw
8. _____ only	8. _____ cut	8. _____ clean
9. _____ us	9. _____ kind	9. _____ grow
10. _____ three	10. _____ both	10. _____ best
11. _____ out	11. _____ sit	11. _____ upon
12. _____ better	12. _____ which	12. _____ these
13. _____ hold	13. _____ fall	13. _____ sing
14. _____ buy	14. _____ carry	14. _____ together
15. _____ funny	15. _____ small	15. _____ please
16. _____ warm	16. _____ under	16. _____ thank
17. _____ ate	17. _____ read	17. _____ wish
18. _____ fall	18. _____ why	18. _____ many
19. _____ those	19. _____ own	19. _____ shall
20. _____ done	20. _____ found	20. _____ laugh
/20	/20	/20

Chapter 3

Word Lists Available on the Internet

The Academic Word List (Coxhead, 2000) is a list that shows the most frequent words in each family in italics. There are 570 headwords and about 3,000 words altogether. For more information, see www.uefap.com/vocab/vocfram.htm.

The General Service List of English Words (West, 1953) is a list of the 2,000 most useful word families in English. Coxhead's (2000) review of the list suggested that its contents cover approximately 80% of the words in academic texts. See www.uefap.com/vocab/vocfram.htm.

Combined, these two lists cover the words that appear in about 90% of academic texts.

Three Tiers of Vocabulary

Tiers	Definitions	Examples	
Tier 1	basic, common high–frequency words that native English speakers usually know when they come to school	hand dog clock	happy house baby
Tier 2	words that are characteristic of mature English users and are used frequently but that need to be taught so that students are exposed to them and have knowledge of their range of meaning and specific uses	fortunate maintain remote absurd merchant delinquent travesty coincidence	
Tier 3	low–frequency words that rarely appear in general reading texts, but are used in specific content areas	irksome pallet retinue geography biology radius concentric	

Source: Beck, McKeown, & Kucan, 2002.

Three Tiers of Vocabulary for Spanish Speakers

Directions: Compare the words in the three tiers below with those on page 110. How are the lists similar and different?

Tier	Definitions	Examples
Tier 1	basic words that students will know in Spanish and may need to learn in English	dog find cat hate song tooth
	words of idioms, metaphors, and everyday expressions	Let's play bridge. Make up your mind.
	Spanish cognates for which students know the concept	family/familia color/color
	false cognates that need to be pointed out with a correct translation	rope/ropa embarrassed/embarazada
Tier 2	high–frequency words in students' reading and listening comprehension texts academic words needed to understand the texts (Many of Beck's Tier 2 words are Spanish–English cognates, common Tier 1 Spanish words.)	coincidence/coincidencia absurd/absurdo concentrate/concentrar fortunate/afortunado
	words that have multiple meanings so students can use them in many contexts	trunk ring tree deep
Tier 3	words that are used infrequently and are limited to specific academic disciplines and content areas	sum biology multiplication

Source: Calderón, 2004.

_____

_____

_____

_____

Cognates

◆ Cognates are words in different languages that have the same original source.

◆ Cognates are found only in languages that belong to the same family. The Indo–European family is the largest family, with such language branches as Germanic, Romance, and Slavic.

◆ For reading in English, cognates are especially helpful for speakers of Romance languages.

◆ Romance languages are a group of languages that developed from Latin. They are the languages that are spoken in places that were once part of the Roman Empire. They include French, Italian, Portuguese, Romanian, and Spanish.

The Cognate Connection

Directions: Arrange the letters in the envelope to make a set of cognates for the languages below. Write them in the chart.

ENGLISH	SPANISH	FRENCH	ITALIAN	PORTUGUESE
territory	territorio	territoire	territorio	territorio

Learning a Foreign Language: One Student's Use of Cognates and Strategies

While learning Spanish as a foreign language, one high school student's use of cognates changed as she continued to develop literacy in the new language. The excerpts below describe the student's cognate usage at three different proficiency levels (Barnhardt, 1997). These examples begin to shed some light on how English language learners may also use cognates when they read English.

Level 1 high school Spanish student

"This looks like a dentist because there's a DDS and my uncle is a dentist and he has that. It says limpiar dentales and I know what limpiar means so I guess that means 'to clean your dentures' and something about root canals. I guess canales. Then it says tratamiento which I guess means 'treatment.'"

Level 2 high school Spanish student

"It's a dialogue. There's a conversation between A and B in a dialogue form. I'm looking at the title to know what they're talking about. Some of the words I won't know but if you know what they're talking about, you might get it. It's saying the lady is much older than her husband."

Level 3 high school Spanish student

"It's about the chocolate industry and how popular it is now and the importance of it in the past in history. Is that right? That's what I thought. It's saying that this Quetzalcoatl, this ruler, he obviously said that chocolate was important in his empire and there is another thing in here that it has some religious connotation. Where is it? Origen divino like a divine origin and so that implies religion and polytheism. So it's saying that chocolate is popular now possibly because it was very important then."

In the above examples, we can see that the student starts out using word–based strategies, such as recognizing cognates, as well as relying on her world experience to verify meaning. As she progresses through her study of the language, she builds on these strategies. She continues to use cognates and background knowledge, but she expands her strategies repertoire by using text structure and academic knowledge to construct meaning. In level 2, she is translating full sentences and, by level 3, she is summarizing the gist of the text and self–questioning to see whether her summaries make sense. She also increasingly relies on inferencing meanings in the text. Her strategy use has grown with her language knowledge and adapted to the level of text complexity (Barnhardt, 1997).

Source: Barnhardt, S., 1997.

Idioms and Other Stumbling Blocks

What's the BIG Idea?

Directions: List as many idioms as you can in 1 minute.

_____

_____

_____

_____

_____

_____

_____

_____

_____

_____

_____

_____

_____

_____

_____

_____

_____

_____

Some English Stumbling Blocks

Denotations: Many words may seem to mean the same thing, but they are not always used in the same way.

small and *puny*

small —dictionary definition: not large or great, little in size

puny —dictionary definition: small and weak

One can say a present is *small*, but one would not want to say a present is *puny*.

Connotations: Many words seem to be synonyms at first, but they imply a meaning that goes beyond their literal meanings.

Chubby, plump, stout, and *obese* have meanings related to "fleshy."

A chubby face suggests roundness and youthfulness.

A stout man implies dignity.

An obese person suggests unsightly fat.

Collocations: Many words are commonly used together, and speakers know which words to expect within a given context.

For a story about going camping, would you expect to read about a *happy camper* or a *joyful camper*?

Effective Strategies for Vocabulary Development

How Native English Speakers and English Language Learners Learn Vocabulary

Young children learn most of their vocabulary indirectly through the following:

◆ having conversations with other people, but mainly with adults;

◆ listening to others read to them and talking about the text that was read aloud; and

◆ reading extensively on their own (Adler, 2001; Center for the Improvement of Early Reading Achievement (CIERA), 2001).

Challenges With Learning Vocabulary for English Language Learners

◆ Children may not have any adults who speak English in their environment.

◆ Parents or adults may not read to them in English or their first language.

◆ Parents or adults may not have time to speak with and read to them.

◆ They may not have books in either their first language or their second language.

◆ As a result, they do not know the 5,000–7,000 words that their English–speaking peers know before they begin formal reading instruction in school, and they do not have the intuitive sense of English grammar that their peers have (Singer, 1981, as cited in Grabe, 1991).

Successful Classroom Vocabulary Teaching Activities

Directions: Work with a partner. List some successful activities that you have used to teach vocabulary to first and second language learners.

First Language	Second Language

118

The Role of Vocabulary in Reading Instruction

Directions: What do these statements suggest for reading instruction in your classroom?

1. There is a need for direct instruction of vocabulary items required for a specific text.

2. Repetition and multiple exposure to vocabulary items are important. Students should be given items that will be likely to appear in many contexts.

3. Learning in rich contexts is valuable for vocabulary learning. Vocabulary words should be those that the learner will find useful in many contexts. When vocabulary items are derived from content learning materials, the learner will be better equipped to deal with specific reading matter in content areas.

4. Vocabulary tasks should be restructured as necessary. It is important to be certain that students fully understand what is asked of them in the context of reading, rather than focusing only on the words to be learned. Restructuring seems to be most effective for low–achieving students.

5. Vocabulary learning is effective when it entails active engagement in learning tasks.

6. Computer technology can be used effectively to help teach vocabulary.

7. Vocabulary can be acquired through incidental learning. Much of a student's vocabulary will have to be learned in the course of doing things other than explicit vocabulary learning. Repetition, richness of context, and motivation may also add to the efficacy of incidental learning of vocabulary.

8. "Dependence on a single vocabulary instruction method will not result in optimal learning. Various methods were used effectively with an emphasis on multimedia aspects of learning, richness of context in which words are to be learned, and the number of exposures to words that learners receive" (National Reading Panel, 2000, p. 4).

What Research Says: How Well Children Will Learn New Words

- A good predictor of how well children will learn a new word is the number of times they encounter it.
- The best predictor of how well children will learn a new word is the richness and diversity of meaningful contexts in which they encounter it.

(McKeown, Beck, Omanson, & Pople, 1985, pp. 522–535)

Activities for Vocabulary Development

Charades: Students mime or act out the meanings of words, and their peers guess the meanings.

Cloze Sentences: Teachers prepare sentences omitting selected vocabulary words or phrases. Students read each sentence aloud and brainstorm possible answers. The teacher or a student then gives the correct response.

Debates: Students prepare and present a talk about reasons for or against something.

Games: Teachers use entertaining and challenging contests that involve one side against another.

Interviews: Students ask questions of others and record their responses.

Language Experience Approach: Students discuss shared experiences and then dictate phrases or sentences that the teacher records on poster paper or the chalkboard. The dictated work then serves as reading material.

Personal Dictionaries: Students construct their own dictionaries by selecting the words of their choice. These dictionaries serve as meaning and spelling resources. Pairs or small groups may work together as they create their individual dictionaries.

Read Aloud: A teacher or a student reads the material aloud, and a discussion of important vocabulary follows.

Role Play/Dramatization: Role play: Students draw on their personal experiences to select and express the roles of characters in given situations. Dramatization: Students act out what happened in a story or other event.

Semantic and Concept Maps: Teachers use some visual form to organize vocabulary or concepts, such as a Venn diagram, T–chart, or other graphic organizer.

Sources: Echevarria, Vogt, & Short, 2004; McLaughlin et al., 2000.

Sample Activities for Vocabulary Development

Concept Map

concept/vocabulary word
_____

What is it?   *What is it like?*

_____   _____

_____   _____

What are some examples?

_____

_____

_____

Completed Concept Map

weather
_____

What is it?   *What is it like?*

the condition of the air   *the air can be hot or cold*

that surrounds the earth   *the air can be clear or foggy*

What are some examples?

rain

snow

sunshine

Word Square

concept/vocabulary word	definition
examples	what it is not

Sample Activities for Vocabulary Development (continued)

Completed Word Square	
triangle	a plane figure consisting of three sides and three angles
isosceles—at least two equal sides equilateral—three equal sides scalene—three unequal sides	not a square

Thematic Instruction: Category Classification Matrix

	Topic				
Examples	Descriptors				

Thematic Instruction: Completed Category Classification Matrix

	Animals					
Members	Features					
	Land	Water	Feet	Wings	Hair	Carnivore
catfish		✔				✔
ladybug	✔		✔	✔		✔
horse	✔		✔		✔	

Completed Word Sort: The Misfits

Cross out the words that do not belong with the others.

hummingbird	bison	parrot
beak	nest	wing
feather	robin	horse

Sample Activities for Vocabulary Development *(continued)*

Word Sort: Semantic Scale

Measurement: Arrange these time measurements from largest to smallest.

largest

second

decade

week

day

year

eon

month

_____

_____

_____

_____

_____

_____

_____

smallest

Completed Word Splash: Teacher Generated

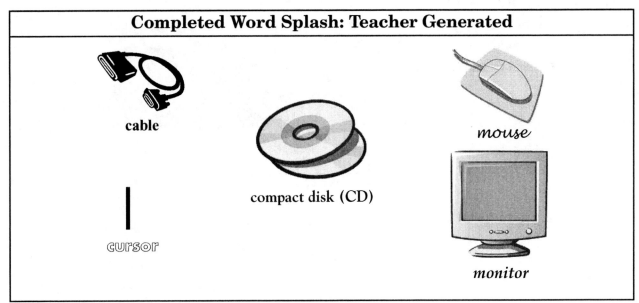

cable

compact disk (CD)

cursor

mouse

monitor

Write a title or sentence.

Sample Activities for Vocabulary Development (continued)

Songs and Chants

Traveling West

I've been walking.
We've been floating and boating.
They've been pulling so strong.
We've been riding.
We've been bouncing.
We've been traveling along.

I'd been walking.
We'd been floating and boating.
They'd been pulling so long.
We'd been riding.
We'd been bouncing.
We'd been traveling so long.

I stopped walking.
We stopped floating and boating.
They stopped pulling so strong.
We stopped riding.
We stopped bouncing.
We stopped traveling along.

Written by Dorothy Kauffman

From One Teacher's Perspective

The Rodeo

This lesson was created and taught by Lois Mason, Mill Pond Intermediate School, Westborough, Massachusetts, and is used with permission.

Student information
- A class of fifth–grade students with two English language learners who are native speakers of Portuguese
- English proficiency level—transitioning
- Reading level—second grade

Language objectives

Key Vocabulary

rodeo	buckle	barrel	racing
hush puppies	bronco	steer wrestling	succotash

Language Structures

adjectives
question words
similes
comparisons

Objective

The purpose of the lesson is to introduce and practice the strategy of visualization. Research shows that this strategy not only deepens the reader's enjoyment of what is read, but helps the reader accomplish four tasks: 1) fill in missing information; 2) merge prior experiences with the text to create visual images; 3) gain a better understanding of the dimensions of size, space, and time; and 4) use all of the senses to comprehend text (Harvey & Goudvis, 2000).

Before reading

The lesson started by asking the class to assess their background knowledge about rodeos. Some native English speakers were able to jump in with prior experiences at county fairs. As they shared their experiences, we began to create a word splash[1] on the board. I broke the class into small groups and had them continue to work on the word splash.

---

[1]Word Splash—The teacher provides students with a list of words from the text. Students use the words to predict the content and then write sentences with them. Students then read the text and confirm or refute their predictions and make additional predictions. An alternate way to do it is to give students the topic and have them brainstorm the words they expect to find in the text. Students may categorize the words and use them to write sentences about the topic. For more information see www.turningpts.org/pdf/Word_splash2.doc.

With the two Brazilian students, I took them to a class computer and brought up Google images to help them see the setting, clothing, and actions found at rodeos. We then rejoined the class and together completed the word splash on the board.

Next, I read aloud a short description of a rodeo from *National Geographic* as the students followed along. As they listened, I asked them to highlight the words that caused them to see pictures in their minds, that is, the words that helped them to make a movie in their minds. After the read–aloud, I drew a three–column graphic organizer on the board and explained it to them. The graphic organizer contained the following headings.

Words That Help Me Visualize	What I See in My Mind	Questions and Responses

During reading

As the class reread the text to complete the graphic organizer, I worked with one of the Brazilian students who had no prior knowledge about rodeos. To complete the graphic organizer, we again referred to the Internet images as we reread the text. In the first column, he expressed his interest in several bits of information—the cowboy's buckle, the size of the bull, the cowgirl, and the barrel racing. In the second column, he followed up with drawings to match the information in the first column. This worked better than expressing his thoughts in words. He made some connections in the third column that involved questions and responses. He wondered how heavy the buckle was, how big (how tall and how long) the bull was, and finally, he filled in a missing piece of information about the barrel racing by asking if the racers kicked the barrel during the race. At the conclusion of this part of the lesson, it became clear that the student who had some knowledge about horses now had a whole new body of information that he could draw on about horses, bulls, and calves.

After reading

New vocabulary was abundant in this selection, so I chose to simplify things by keeping the number of words to only the most essential ones. I am a firm believer that it is better to reduce the vocabulary load and master a smaller number of words than to overwhelm and lose the students' interest in the text.

I wrote five new words on the white board for the two Brazilian students and asked them to go back to the text to find them and underline them, if they hadn't already done so. We then talked about these words and how they were used in context to see whether we could guess their meanings. One student was able to infer that hush puppies had to be some kind of bread because it was used to mop up gravy. We also discussed other foods that people use to mop up other liquid food.

When it came to decoding the word *succotash*, we drew on our skill of clapping–out syllables. We have been working on the fact that every syllable has a talking vowel, and one of the students was able to decode this three–syllable word. The definition followed the appearance of the word in the text, and he was able to use this combination of strategies to understand the meaning of the term.

Checking comprehension is an ongoing and usually informal process, particularly with the two Brazilian students. Their use of the graphic organizer enabled me to see that these students were able to transfer the instruction of how to use it along with my modeling of visualization into their inner conversations and images.

Reflections on Instruction

The Rodeo lesson was one part of an assignment for teachers attending a reading workshop. The second part of the assignment was to reflect on how the instruction had gone. The following comments (parts A and B below) were those made by the teacher who planned and taught The Rodeo lesson.

A. What strategies did you use?

The multiple strategies used in this lesson were—
- Explicitly stating the objective for the class (visualization).
- Thinking about what you already know about the topic.
- Underlining or circling words that help create a picture/movie in the mind.
- Using a graphic organizer to organize information and ask questions.
- Rereading the text to clarify the meaning of vocabulary words.

B. Describe the interventions that you are currently using to teach reading.

I am daily using the following three strategies.

- Working at a slower pace and providing extra wait time when presenting information and waiting for an answer. (This extra wait time also occurred in test situations.)

- Using visuals to reinforce information. In the areas of phonemic awareness and phonics, I am using both Project Read Phonology and Telian–Cas Learning Concepts (TLC) Cards to provide a multisensory approach. I am starting to meet with some success with this approach.

- Color coding short vowels, long vowels, and blends on index cards. Students are starting to make breakthroughs in spelling tests by practicing with these color–modified lists. Sometimes it helps to put a dot under the initial consonant and tell them, "Get your mouth ready for the first sound" or a dot under the ending consonant or consonant blend and remind them to "take a look at the ending sound(s)." This has greatly reduced the random word calling in oral reading practice.

I feel the following quotes directly relate to the critical need for me to go back and fill in missing pieces of instruction for students if they are to move forward and achieve functional literacy within the next few years. Consider this statement: "In terms of reading instruction, this means that the English words and letters students are learning need to be familiar to them. Using familiar letters and words, teachers can begin to teach phonemic awareness, vocabulary words and their meanings, and pronunciation simultaneously" (Hiebert et al., 1998, cited in Antunez, 2002). In other words, meet students at the point they are and rigorously move forward from there. Also of note, "Although readers may not be consciously aware of it, phonological awareness is crucial for alphabetic reading with comprehension. Readers are able to successfully attend to matters of comprehension when they can easily, accurately, and rapidly recognize the words of the text" (Birch, 2002).

Clearly, students learning English as a second language usually require extra effort and methods to acquire the automaticity that allows text to be understood rather than merely decoded (word calling).The second strategy of employing visuals has clearly been a strong teaching method for this student. All in all, they have strongly favored the visual TLC cards as a way to remind themselves of the different lip positions and production of each letter to differentiate between the subtle similarities of short –a /æ/ and short –e /e/, p and b, and so on. I will be watching carefully to see whether these skills spill over into their writing. With effort and great strategies, I feel confident that I can make a positive difference in the students' literacy journey at Mill Pond.

Chapter Summary and Beyond the Workshop

Chapter 3: Vocabulary Development
What's Different About Teaching Reading to Students Learning English?

Some native English speakers may

- know and use many more words than their peers who are learning English (Colorado Department of Education, 1997; Snow, Burns, & Griffin, 1998);
- already know basic, common, high–frequency words (Tier 1) but need to be taught low–frequency words that are used in written texts and specific topic domains (Tiers 2 and 3) (Beck, McKeown, & Kucan, 2002); and
- understand and use many English idioms from growing up in the U.S. culture (Hirsch, Jr., 2006).

Some English language learners may

- need many opportunities to listen to English but not be required to produce the language immediately (Burt, Peyton, & Adams, 2003; Krashen, 1982);
- use both English and their native language to accomplish a variety of communicative and literacy tasks (Escamilla, 2000);
- find their bilingualism is a strength (Escamilla, 2000; Valdés, 2003);
- benefit from having similarities between their native language and English pointed out to them (Durgunoglu, Nagy, & Hancin–Bhatt, 1993);
- not find their native language helpful when learning to read English (Bernhardt, 2003; Birch, 2002; Snow, Burns, & Griffin, 1998);
- not know the academic concepts in their native languages that they are learning in English;
- need to learn Tier 1 as well as Tier 2 and 3 words (Calderón, 2004);
- find understanding idioms difficult because they cannot rely on the usual meanings of the words;
- rely on their vocabulary knowledge more than their English–speaking peers do when they read (McLaughlin et al., 2000); and
- be able to benefit from recognizing cognates between their native language and English, but may be confused by false cognates.

Beyond the Workshop

1. Outside reading

Read *Meeting the Literacy Needs of English Language Learners*, a description of who English language learners are and a discussion of the literacy challenges they face and their developmental patterns. After reading the article, consider the suggestions in light of the contents of the information presented in Chapters 1, 2, and 3. What are the implications for teaching reading to your students? The article is available at http://knowledgeloom.org/elemlit/ells_meetnds.jsp.

2. Web resources

Explore the numerous resources available at www.manythings.org. This site contains many interactive activities that encourage students to explore language through a variety of formats such as phone calls, onscreen magnetic boards, and songs. There is also a link to questions for students and teachers.

3. Multimedia/technology exploration

Visit and explore activities that promote pronunciation, rereading, and reading fluency at the award–winning online library available at www.repeatafterus.com. The site contains a wide range of free texts and audio clips such as poetry, drama, nonfiction, nursery rhymes, and stories from around the world. In what ways could you use this site with your students?

4. In the classroom

Select one or more of the suggestions for teaching vocabulary mentioned in this chapter or in any of the outside readings. Plan and teach a lesson using the activity and reflect on what worked well, what didn't work, and what you changed or would change if you repeated the lesson. Be prepared to share the results in the next session.

CHAPTER 4
Beginning Reading

Goal and Objectives

Goal
Participants will achieve the following:

- Develop an understanding of the basic components of learning to read in English for native English speakers and English language learners.

Objectives
Participants will be able to do the following:

- Describe the role that oral English proficiency plays in beginning reading instruction.

- Define the three most important predictors of beginning reading success for all elementary school students: phonemic awareness, concepts of print, and understanding phonics.

- Explain the differences between phonemic awareness and phonics.

- Describe activities to teach phonemic awareness, concepts of print, and phonics.

Factors to Keep in Mind When Teaching Second Language Speakers to Read in English

1. Not all languages have alphabetic writing systems; neither do they share the same syntactic characteristics (August & Shanahan, 2006).

2. Reading models include the same set of three processing dimensions:
   - visual
   - phonological
   - syntactic

3. What is not considered in reading models is the second language reader's prior knowledge of the sound–letter correspondences in the native language, which may not match the correspondences of the English text.

4. English language learners come from around the globe and bring different sets of language experiences with them.

5. Teachers need to understand the similarities and differences between students' languages and writing systems and English in order to be able to teach English language learners.

Phonemic Awareness

Eechee Nee Sahn

Eechee Nee Sahn

Ee - chee, Nee, Sa - hn, Ee - chee, Nee, Sa - hn,

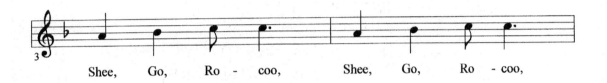

Shee, Go, Ro - coo, Shee, Go, Ro - coo,

Shee - chee, Hah - chee, Coo, Joo, Shee - chee, Hah - chee, Coo, Joo,

Hah - chee, Coo, Joo, Hah - chee, Coo, Joo.

Japanese Numbers, Characters, and Their Phonetic Spellings

Pronunciation Guide			
[ee] as in *feed*	[o] as in *go*	[oo] as in *food*	[ah] as in *Say "Ah"*

Number	Character	Preferred reading	On reading	Kun reading
0	零 / ○	zero	rei / れい	(none)
1	一	ichi	ichi / いち (ee–chee)	hito(tsu) / ひと(つ)
2	二	ni	ni, ji / に、じ (nee)	futa(tsu) / ふた(つ)
3	三	san	san / さん (sahn)	mi(ttsu) / み(っつ)
4	四	yon	shi / し (she)	yo(ttsu) / よ(っつ)
5	五	go	go / ご (go)	itsu(tsu) / いつ(つ)
6	六	roku	roku / ろく (ro–ku)	mu(ttsu) / む(っつ)
7	七	nana	shichi / しち (shee–chee)	nana(tsu) / なな(つ)
8	八	hachi	hachi / はち (hah–chee)	ya(ttsu) / や(っつ)
9	九	kyū	kyū, ku / きゅう、く (coo)	kokono(tsu) / ここの(つ)
10	十	jū	jū / じゅう (joo)	tō / とお

Sources: Allen, C. (1992). *Japanese Numerals From Japan: Traditions and Trends*. Torrance, CA: Good Apple; and Wikipedia, the free encyclopedia. This chart is licensed under the GNU Free Documentation License. It uses material from the Wikipedia article, "Japanese Numerals." Permission is granted to copy, distribute, and/or modify this chart under the terms of the GNU Free Documentation License, Version 1.2 (http://en.wikipedia.org/wiki/GNU_Free_Documentation_License), or any later version published by the Free Software Foundation.

Directions: Use the Japanese characters to write the answers to the items below.

1. Write the number of toes you have using Japanese numerals.

   _____

2. Write the answer to the math problem 4 + 4 using Japanese numerals.

   _____

3. Write the number of days in a week using Japanese numerals.

   _____

4. Write your phone number using Japanese numerals.

   _____

What Is Phonemic Awareness?

"Knowing the sounds of a language is a prerequisite to being able to start to match it with print" (Ramirez, 2000, p. 15).

"Phonemic awareness is the ability to notice, think, and work with the individual sounds in spoken words" (Adler, 2001, p. 4). This means that individuals are aware of how the individual sounds in words work. They can break words into their component sounds, identify onsets and rhymes, and make new words by deleting or replacing sounds.

Words are made of speech sounds called phonemes. Phonemes are the small, discrete spoken sounds of a language that help to distinguish one word from another.

For example, change the first phoneme in the word *bat* to /h/. Changing the /b/ to /h/ changes the word from *bat* to *hat* and also changes the meaning of the word.

Some Ways Children Develop Phonemic Awareness

Word Play	
What is left if I take away the *m* in mice?	*ice*
What is left if I take away the *s* in eyes?	*eye*
What is left is I take away the *p* in bump?	*bum*
Rhyming Games	
One, two, buckle your shoe. Three, four, shut the door. One, two, stir the stew. Three, four, lie on the floor.	
Nursery Rhymes	
Three little kittens lost their mittens	

Some Ways Children Develop Phonemic Awareness (continued)

Picture Books With Rhymes

It's Theresa

Mirror, mirror in my claw

Who's the prettiest

    dinosaur of all?

Her horns are purple, and her lips are red.

There's a scalloped frill behind her head.

Theresa Triceratops it must be.

No dinosaur in the world is

    prettier

        than she.

Written by Dorothy Kauffman

Source: Kauffman, D. (1994). Getting to Know Theresa. In W. A. Bennett et al. (Eds.), *Tapir* (p. 76). Benque Viejo, Belize: Cubola Productions. Adapted with permission. Illustration by Greg Dayman, 2004. Used with permission.

37 Essential Phonograms

–ack	–ain	–ake	–ale	–all	–ame	–an
–ank	–ap	–ash	–at	–ate	–aw	–ay
–eat	–ell	–est	–ice	–ick	–ide	–ight
–ill	–in	–ine	–ing	–ink	–ir	–ock
–oke	–op	–or	–ore	–uck	–ug	–ump
–unk						

Source: Wylie & Durrell, 1970.

English Consonants and Vowels

Initial Consonants

b bat	c cat	d dog	f fat	g got	h hat	j jet
k kit	l log	m met	n net	p pat	q quit	r rat
s sat	t tin	v van	w wet	x xylem	y yet	z zip

Initial Consonant Digraphs

ch– chin	ph– phone	sh– she	th– this th– thin	wh– white

Initial Consonant Blends

bl– blot	br– brat	cl– clap	cr– crab	dr– drag
fl– flat	fr– frog	gl– glad	gr– grin	pl– plot
pr– prod	sc– scat	scr– scrap	sk– skit	sl– slot
sm– smug	sn– snap	sp– spot	spl– splat	spr– sprig
st– stop	str– strap	sw– swim	thr– three	tr– trip

Final Consonants

–b Bob	–d bud	–f if	–g rug	–k/ck rock	–l/ll tall
–m hum	–n man	–p hop	–r car	–s/ss yes	–s/z is	–t cat

Final Consonant Blends

–ct act	–ft left	–lf self	–lk silk	–lt melt	–mp stamp	–nd bend
–nk ink	–rd board	–sk dusk	–sp wasp	–st best	–st waist	–xt next

Final Consonant Digraphs

–ch bench	–ck back	–dge– edge	–ff off	–gh laugh	–ng sing
–nk ink	–ph graph	–sh fish	–tch itch	–th bath	–th tenth

Short Vowels

a cat	e wet	i bit	o cot	u cut

Long Vowels

a	e	i	o	u
say break	meet niece	ice aisle	soap bow	rule Ruth
lake grey	beat fee	sigh guide	sold hoe	blue juice
sail sleigh	be baby	eye my	home corn	fruit flew
	people			

Vowel Digraphs—two adjacent vowels that spell one sound, such as *ai* in *sail, oa* in *soap, ee* in *seed, au* in *taught, aw* in *paw*, and *ay* in *say*.

Vowel Diphthongs—two adjacent vowels that spell two sounds, such as *ou* in *mouse, oi* in *oil, oy* in *boy*, and *ow* in *cow*.

Phonemic Awareness Skills

Directions: Add one additional example to each part of the assigned section. Be prepared to share your examples.

1. **Onset and Rime:** Children recognize the correspondence of the ending sounds of words and their different beginning sounds (also, sometimes referred to as rhyming words or phonograms).

    Example: Listen to these words: *Hickory, dickory, dock, the mouse ran up the clock.* Say the words that rhyme. (hickory, dickory and dock, clock)

2. **Phoneme Identity:** Children recognize the same sounds in different words.

    a. alliteration
    Example: Listen to these words: *Six seagulls soared silently.* What sound do you hear that is the same? /s/

    b. assonance
    Example: Listen to these words: *We see three green trees.* What sound do you hear that is the same? /ee/

3. **Phoneme Categorization:** Children recognize the word in a series of words that sounds different.

    a. rhyming words
    Example: Which word does not rhyme: *cat. rat, sun, hat*? (sun)

    b. beginning consonants
    Example: Which words begin with the same sound: *dish, bag, dog, door*? (dish, dog, door)

    c. ending consonants
    Example: Which words end with the same sound: *salt, melt, sing*? (salt, melt)

    d. medial sounds (long vowels)
    Example: Which words have the same middle sound: *bean, kite, bite*? (kite, bite)

    e. medial sounds (short vowels)
    Example: Which words have the same middle sound: *sun, can, bun*? (sun, bun)

    f. medial sounds (consonants)
    Example: Which two words have the same middle sound: *summer, cotton, getting*? (cotton, getting)

4. **Phoneme Isolation:** Children recognize individual sounds in words.

   a. initial consonants

     Example: Listen to this word: *can*. What sound do you hear at the beginning? (/k/)

   b. final consonants

     Example: Listen to this word: *box*. What sound do you hear at the end? (/x/)

   c. medial consonants

     Example: Listen to this word: *bottle*. What sound do you hear in the middle? (/t/)

   d. initial consonant blends

     Example: Listen to this word: *shrimp*. What sounds do you hear at the beginning?
       (/sh/.../r/)

   e. final consonant blends

     Example: Listen to this word: *held*. What sounds do you hear at the end? (/l/…/d/)

   f. short vowels

     Example: Listen to this word: *cut*. What sound do you hear in the middle? (/æ/)

   g. long vowels

     Example: Listen to this word: *rake*. What sound do you hear in the middle? (/a/)

5. **Phoneme Blending:** Children listen to a sequence of separately spoken phonemes, combine them, and pronounce the word.

   a. syllables

     Example: Listen to these word parts then say the word: *bas...ket*. What's the word?
       (basket)

   b. phoneme by phoneme

     Example: Listen to these word parts then say the word: /s/.../u/../n/. What's the word?
       (sun)

6. **Word Segmentation:** Children listen to words and break them into their separate sounds, identify the number of sounds in them, and say and count the syllables in them.

   a. phoneme by phoneme

     Example: Listen to this word and say it sound by sound: *robe*. (/r/.../o/.../b/)

     Example: Listen to this word and count the number of sounds in it: *bathtub*. How many
       sounds do you hear? (6)

   b. syllables

     Example: Listen to this word and say it syllable by syllable: *trapezoid*. (trap – e – zoid)

7. Phoneme Deletion: Children recognize the word that remains following the removal of a phoneme from the word.

    a. initial consonants
      Example: Listen to this word: *pin.* Say the word without the /p/. (in)

    b. final consonants
      Example: Listen to this word: *rocks.* Say the word without the /s/. (rock)

    c. initial consonant blends
      Example: Listen to this word: *blink.* Say the word without the /bl/. (ink)

    d. final consonant blends
      Example: Listen to this word: *mind.* Say the word without the /nd/. (mi)

    e. initial consonant digraphs
      Example: Listen to this word: *chair.* Say the word without the /ch/. (air)

    f. final consonant digraphs
      Example: Listen to this word: *tenth.* Say the word without the /th/. (ten)

8. Phoneme Addition: Children make a new word by adding a phoneme to a word.

    a. initial consonants
      Example: Listen to this word: *in.* What word do you get if you add /p/ to the beginning? (pin)

    b. final consonants
      Example: Listen to this word: *me.* What word do you get if you add /t/ at the end? (meet)

9. Phoneme Substitution: Children replace one phoneme with another to make a new word.

    a. initial consonant substitution
      Example: Replace the first sound in *book* with /t/. (took)

    b. final consonant substitution
      Example: Replace the last sound in *beg* with /d/. (bed)

    c. medial vowel substitution
      Example: Replace the middle sound in *mit* with /e/. (met)

Sources: Beck, 2006; Maney, n.d. [b]; Shanahan, 2006.

Chapter 4

Activities for Developing Phonemic Awareness

> **Directions:** Work with a partner. Select one activity from the list below. How would you use or modify this activity with English language learners? How could you modify it for use with older English language learners?

1. **Singing and Chanting Aloud**—Sing and chant songs, nursery rhymes, and chants. Add motions or movement as appropriate.

2. **Let's Go on a Rhyme Hunt**—Go on a rhyme hunt around the classroom or school. Have students find objects in the environment that rhyme with a given word, for example, look – book, hair – chair, floor – door, or tag – flag.

3. **A Rhyme–Time Band**—Distribute wood blocks, drumsticks, or other percussion instruments. Say three words, two of which rhyme. Have students play the instruments whenever they hear the second word of a rhyming pair.

4. **Seek and Say**—Create a set of picture cards that contains two or more pictures of objects that begin with the same sounds or contain the same vowel sounds, using drawings or magazine pictures. Mix the cards and have students turn over the cards one by one. Have students say the sound that begins the word or the sound of the vowel. Students then continue to search for other cards that contain pictures with the same beginning or vowel sound.

5. **Odd Man Out**—Display sets of picture cards that begin with the same initial, final, or medial sound and include at least one that does not belong. Have students select the card that doesn't belong.

6. **Match–Mates**—Distribute picture cards to all students. Have them walk around to find the person who has a picture that has the same sound, ends with the same sound, or rhymes with the word that they have.

7. **Riddle Me, Riddle Me**—What am I? Create rhyming riddles. Say the riddle and have students supply the final rhyming word.

   Example: I rhyme with sled,   I rhyme with dozen.
                 You sleep in me.   I am related to you.
                 I am a _____. (bed)   I am your _____. (cousin)

---

8. **Follow the Bouncing Ball**—Use a small soft ball. Say a word that begins with a sound. Toss the ball to a student who says another word that begins with the same sound. Play continues with this sound until no one can think of another example. Play the game using ending sounds, medial sounds, etc.

9. **Rhyming Words Walk–About**—Arrange students in a circle. Have them listen to the words that you say. Each time they hear a rhyming word, they take one step forward. When a word doesn't rhyme with the others, students stand still.

   Example: look, book, hook, toy, shook, brook, took.

Alphabet Recognition

Teaching Alphabet Recognition

1. Teach letter names first. (Begin by using the children's names.)
2. Teach the shapes of the letters.
3. Direct attention to similarities and differences among the shapes of the letters.
4. Incorporate visual discrimination activities for students who have difficulties identifying letters. Begin with visual discrimination tasks that are grossly different and gradually increase the level of difficulty. Begin with letter forms and follow them with word forms (Maney, n.d.[b]).

   Circle the letters that are the same.

t w o	y e h	y e h	t w o	y e h
A G I	A G I	F J Q	F J Q	F J Q

   Use tasks that require visual discrimination of letters in the initial position.

l I f t	s I f t	l I f t	s I f t	s I f t
f l a s h	s p l a s h	s p l a s h	f l a s h	s p l a s h

   Use tasks that require visual discrimination of letters in the final position.

s t a r t	s t a r k	s t a r k	s t a r k	s t a r t
t r a I n	t r a I l	t r a I n	t r a I l	t r a I l

   Use tasks that require visual discrimination of omitted letters.

w r e a t h	w r a t h	w r a t h	w r a t h	w r e a t h
p a l a c e	p l a c e	p l a c e	p a l a c e	p l a c e

   Use tasks that require visual discrimination of medial letters.

b a t h	b a t h	b o t h	b o t h	b o t h
m o u t h	m o n t h	m o u t h	m o n t h	m o n t h

   Use tasks that require visual discrimination of reversed letters.

p e a r s	p a r e s	p a r e s	p a r e s	p e a r s
f r I e d	f I r e d	f I r e d	f I r e d	f r I e d

5. Provide opportunities for letter–writing practice, including tracing, copying, and independent writing.

Activities for Developing Alphabet Recognition

Directions: Work with a partner. Select one activity from the list below. How would you modify this activity with English language learners? How could you modify it for use with older English language learners?

1. **Alphabet Area**—Set up an area of the room for alphabet exploration and practice. Stock it with a variety of alphabet books and types of letters, such as stencils, alphabet puzzles, magnetic letters, etc.; different kinds paper; writing tools, such as crayons, markers, and pencils; and any other materials of your choice, such as play–dough, shaving cream, finger paint, etc. Schedule students into the alphabet area as part of other area features of exploration, such as a reading area or listening area.

2. **Alphabet Concentration**—Make a set of letter cards (lower case and upper case for each letter). Mix the cards and place them face–down on a table. Have students turn over the cards one by one, say the names of the letters, and try to collect as many cards that match as they can.

3. **Now You See It. Now You Don't**—Fill clear plastic bags with a paste made of food coloring, cornstarch, and water. Use the bags to have students write letters. You may direct the writing or have a student give the directions. After writing a letter, students erase it by smoothing out the bag.

4. **Alphabet Stick–Up**—Distribute a set of letter cards, one to each student. Take students for a walk around the classroom or school. Have students identify words that begin with the letters that are on the letter cards. Then have students use masking tape to tape their matching card on the letter.

5. **Alphabet Sorts**—Place a pile of alphabet cereal on a napkin for each students. Have them sort the letters and count the number of times they found each one. Create a class graph.

6. **Alphabet Song**—Teach students the Alphabet Song. Give each student a letter card. Begin singing the alphabet song. As students hear their letter sung, they hold it up or stand up.

7. **Alphabet Twister**—Challenge pairs or small groups of students to use their bodies to make the letters of the alphabet and have their classmates identify them.

8. **All Aboard!**—Construct a train using 26 small boxes of the same size. Write the letters of the alphabet on the train and connect the train cars with yarn. Mix a set of letter cards and distribute them to students. Have the student with the A card go to the car with the A and pick it up. The student then starts to walk around the room with the train. Additional students join the train as it passes them until all students are aboard.

Concepts of Print

Concepts of Print Checklist

◆ Holds a book correctly (beginning with the cover)

◆ Points to text using left–to–right and top–to–bottom page sequence

◆ Points to and reads words aloud with one–to–one matching

◆ Points to illustrations, pictures, or graphics when asked

◆ Responds to punctuation marks correctly, when reading aloud

◆ When asked, points to
- a dictated word
- a dictated uppercase letter
- a dictated lowercase letter
- a letter that represents a dictated initial sound
- a letter that represents a dictated final sound
- a space between words
- . ? ! " "

Activities for Teaching Concepts of Print

Directions: Work with a partner. Select one activity from the list below. How would you use or modify this activity with English language learners? How could you modify it for use with older English language learners?

1. **Teacher Read–Aloud**—When reading aloud to students, point to the words and talk about left–to–right and top–to–bottom direction, the function of punctuation marks, the way words are separated by spaces, and the letters of the alphabet, noting the function of capital and lower case letters.

2. **Tactile Punctuation**—Copy sentences from stories and poems onto paper strips. Do not include the punctuation. Have students use glue and the following items to replace the punctuation:
   - Elbow macaroni for commas or apostrophes
   - Orzo for periods
   - Plastic paper clips as quotation marks
   - Pieces of spaghetti for exclamation marks

3. **Choral Reading**—Have students use pointers, pencils with erasers, rulers, etc. to point to words on a chart or in a book during choral reading activities.

4. **Word Puzzles**—Cut the words in titles or sentences apart and have students put them back together. Allow them to check their work with the printed text.

Phonics

What Is Phonics?

Phonics is a way of teaching

- graphophonemic relationships

- letter–sound associations

- letter–sound correspondences

- sound–symbol correspondences

- sound–spellings.

Source: The Partnership for Reading. (2001). *Put Reading First: The Research Building Blocks for Teaching Children to Read* (p. 8). Washington, DC: Author.

Phonics is....

...the predictable relationship between the sounds (phonemes) of spoken language and the letters and spellings (graphemes) that represent those sounds in written language (Antunez, 2002).

Phonics instruction is...

...a way of teaching reading. It focuses on teaching children to understand the relationships between the sounds of the spoken words they hear and the letters of written words they see in print so they can use these relationships to read and write words (Adler, 2001; Heilman, 1968).

Chapter 4

Activities for Developing Phonics Skills

Directions: Work with a partner. Select one activity from the list below. How would you use or modify this activity with English language learners? How could you modify it for use with older English language learners?

1. **Singing and Chanting Aloud**—Copy the words of familiar songs, nursery rhymes, and chants onto chart paper. Use your hand or a pointer to track the print from left to right and top to bottom as you and the students say and read the text together. Ask students to come to the chart and point to the rhyming words. As appropriate, write additional verses for the rhymes, songs, and chants.

2. **Odd Man Out**—Display a set of picture cards with the words written on them. In each set, include at least one picture and word card that does not belong because the initial, final, or medial sound is not the same. Ask students to identify the picture and word card that does not belong.

3. **Bag–It**—Write letters and letter combinations on the outside of small paper bags. Give students picture cards. Have them say the name of the picture and place it in the bag with the matching letters.

4. **Hang–Ups**—You will need a set of picture and letter cards, clothes hangers, and clothespins. Hang a picture card on the left side of a hanger. Have a student say the name of the picture and then find the matching letter among the letter cards. Have the student use a clothespin to hang up the letter beside the picture card on the hanger.

5. **Rhyming Clues**—Write sentences and insert a blank line where a target word is needed. Write a rhyming word under the blank line. Ask students to read the sentence aloud and use the rhyming clue to identify the missing word.

   Example: Mr. Brown lives on a _____. (farm)
                                        arm

   Example: Sara added spices to _____ the soup. (season)
                                         reason

Evaluating Phonics Instruction Programs: A Checklist

Directions: Work with a partner. Select one activity from the list below. How would you use or modify this activity with English language learners? How could you modify it for use with older English language learners?

	Yes	No
1. Does the program teach students the following skills systematically and explicitly? How to relate letters and sounds		
How to break spoken words into sounds		
How to blend sounds to make words		
2. Does it help students understand why they are learning phonics?		
3. Does it help students apply their phonics knowledge as they read… words?		
sentences?		
connected text?		
4. Does it help students apply their phonics knowledge to their own writing?		
5. Can it be adapted to meet the needs of individual students, based on assessment?		
6. Does the program include each of the following areas? Alphabetic knowledge		
Phonemic awareness		
Explicit and systematic phonics instruction		
Vocabulary development		
Reading of text		

Source: Adler, 2001.

~

The Requirements for Skilled Reading

Skilled reading clearly requires skill in both decoding and comprehension … A child who cannot decode cannot read; a child who cannot comprehend cannot read either. Literacy—reading ability—can be found only in the presence of both decoding and comprehension. Both skills are necessary; neither alone is sufficient (Gough, Hoover, & Peterson, 1996, p. 3, as cited in Grabe & Stoller, 2002).

From One Teacher's Perspective

I Went Walking: A Shared Reading/Shared Writing Lesson Plan

This lesson was created and taught by Harriet R. Griffin, Title I reading specialist, and Diane Fuimara, sheltered English immersion teacher, Medford Public Schools, Medford, Massachusetts, and is used with permission.

Materials

Williams, S. (1990). *I Went Walking*. New York: Harcourt, Brace, & Javanovich.

Students

Students	Student #1	Student #2	Student #3
Native Language	Somali	Arabic	Portuguese
Level of English Proficiency	Beginning	Early Intermediate	Beginning
English Reading Level	Beginning	First Grade	First Grade

The three girls are at different stages of second language acquisition because of a number of factors. Student #1, a second grader, arrived in the United States almost a year ago. Little is known of her educational background in Somalia. She is able to name some objects in the environment, has learned some keywords, and can answer simple questions. Student #2 is a well–educated second grader who received English instruction in her native Kuwait. She is the most verbal of the girls and is making connections between words. She is able to make lists and demonstrate her understanding by using keywords, stating main ideas, and answering orally in phrases. Student #3, a second grader, arrived from Brazil only a few weeks before this lesson. She is in the silent/preproduction stage of language acquisition and is very shy and verbally unresponsive. She appears to be listening intently and can point to some words. She also seems to be beginning to associate some words with their meanings. Her parents do speak some English that they learned on earlier visits to the United States.

Key Vocabulary

Animal Words	cat, horse, cow, duck, pig, dog
Color Words	black, brown, red, green, pink, yellow
Ordinals	first, second, third, etc.
Sequence	first, next, last
Language Structures	irregular tenses—see/saw
	participles—walking, looking, following
Articles	a
Conjunctions	and
Question and Answer Patterns	what

Purpose

The lesson was designed to address the following benchmarks described in the *Massachusetts English Language Proficiency and Benchmarks Outcomes* (ELPBO).

- To connect reading and writing through shared reading and shared writing

- To understand a story by using prior knowledge and visual cues

- To read previously learned words presented in print and classified by topics

- To demonstrate phonemic awareness

- To recognize letters and letter–sound correspondences in familiar words

- To recognize features of written English, such as capitalization and punctuation, that convey meaning

- To identify items in chronological order

- To retell a story

- To ask and answer questions about a familiar topic

- To identify audience and purpose for writing

Before reading

Before the initial reading, much attention was given to key vocabulary. Color words were introduced in several ways: crayons were used with color names written on each; pictures of crayons colored by students and labeled were put into individual notebooks and reviewed at home; a color chart was posted; color flash cards were practiced; color poems, including "I Like Stars" by Pamela Johnson, were read and reread by both the teacher and students; and colors in the environment were named. Animal words were introduced similarly with pictures and labeled cards, and through numerous read–alouds.

The meaning of *following* was demonstrated through activities that involved students lining up and following a leader. Ordinals were used continuously throughout the playing of follow the leader.

The article *a* was used orally to name objects, for example, a pencil, a desk.

Verbs ending in *–ing* were used orally by the teacher and in short written sentences.

The use of *and* was emphasized orally when it occurred in poems and short texts by framing the word and talking about how it was used. Additionally, shared writing activities included the word *and* as an important word, and it was also included in the class Word Wall.

Questions words, such as *what*, and providing answers to questions were practiced throughout the day.

Predicting and previewing, important prereading activities, were included by having students look at the book cover to predict what would happen in the story and to debate whether the child on the cover is a boy or a girl. The picture walk through *I Went Walking* enabled the students to make further predictions. The arrangement of animal body parts on specific pages, for example, a duck's tail and rump, a dog's tail and feet, helped the children make good predictions and allowed them to quickly confirm their predictions.

During reading

The teacher read the story using a Big Book and emphasizing pronunciation, intonation, and use of punctuation as cues to meaning. This first reading was for the girls to get the gist of the story. Subsequent readings focused on other elements of reading and writing and included the following:

• Questioning preceding a reading to recall ideas: What animal was red? Green? Pink?

• Matching color words from the text with the color words in a list.

• Reading and matching phrase cards of each animal and color: a pink pig.

• Focusing on the first sound in a color word and locating another example:

"What's this?" (a feather). "Find the picture of a feather in the Letter and Sound Basket."

- Direct teaching of the question word *what*, the sound of an interrogative sentence, and the question mark as a feature of such a sentence.

- Finding high–frequency sight words in the text.

- Using cloze techniques for repetition of vocabulary.

- Encouraging students to ask clarifying questions: Student #2, "Is this the dog?"

- Asking students to recall the order of the animals and recognizing and using the word *following*.

- Discussing present and past tense verbs in terms of *today* and *yesterday*.

After reading

Shared writing gave the girls an opportunity to bolster their oral language and to connect the reading and writing. The girls reviewed the story orally before writing about it together. The results of their oral discussion and retelling were recorded on chart paper.

> A girl went walking.
>
> She saw animals. She
>
> Saw a cat, a horse, a cow,
>
> a duck, a pig, and
>
> a dog.

Although the teacher recorded most of the story, the girls were given several chances to use the marker and write the word *and*, the first letters of *girl* and *dog*, and *cat*. During the shared writing, rereading to edit was modeled and many elements of writing were discussed during the writing of this short text. These included the following:

- Capitalizing the beginning letter of sentences
- Matching letters with beginning sounds of words
- Finding correct spellings of frequently used words in the text
- Placing periods at the ends of sentences
- Finding the correct spelling of words on the Word Wall
- Using commas in a series
- Using carets when we forget to write a word (the article *a* was forgotten several times)
- Segmenting words into individual sounds.

The girls shared their shared writing piece by choosing animals to draw and color for the story. Each girl already had a copy of the book in her book basket, and they were reminded that they could take the story home to share with their parents. This provided the girls with another purpose for reading, another opportunity to use their new vocabulary, and an audience for their efforts.

Reflections on Instruction

The *I Went Walking* reading lesson was one part of an assignment for teachers attending a reading workshop. The second part of the assignment was to reflect on how the instruction had gone by answering three questions. The following comments were those made by the teacher who taught the Coast–to–Coast directed reading activity.

Scaffolding to teach reading and writing strategies to our English language learners expands the dimensions of and increases the time and flexibility necessary for good instruction. Modeling requires teachers to be even more thoughtful of their goals and more detailed in their lessons. Our work before reading becomes increasingly important. Shifting responsibility to our students will call for more support and opportunities to work at various levels in shared activities.

No longer can the classroom teacher or Title I teacher depend on children coming to school with similar experiences and common vocabulary. Short prereading explanations of vocabulary formerly considered general knowledge for most kindergartners and first graders are insufficient for English language learners. Climate, terrain, homes, clothes, and animals of our country may be far different from those of the native countries of our immigrant children. Vocabulary development must be accomplished in a much more deliberate and thorough way. Vocabulary must be built ever more slowly and carefully with much repeated attention to picture clues and opportunities for oral language usage. Students must be encouraged to clarify meaning by asking questions.

When matching children and texts, teachers need to ensure accessibility to both the vocabulary and the language structures. Syntactic and structural cueing systems with questions normally including "Does it sound right?" may yield little help for the second language readers. Graphophonic/visual cues may be different from those in the student's native language and take more time to learn. Meaning and making connections must be explored through language experience activities that reflect the particular students and their stage of second language acquisition.

Awareness and appreciation of our newest students must precede any successful teaching. Cultural sensitivity and understandings are required in our communities, schools, and classrooms. As the population continues to change and to become more diverse, we all face the additional challenges of teaching reading to more and more children who are English language learners. Our success as teachers depends on our knowledge of best practices in reading instruction and our increasing understandings of teaching reading to English language learners. Our patience, persistence, and hard work will be measured through the achievements of our newest citizens.

Chapter Summary and Beyond the Workshop

Chapter 4: Beginning Reading
What's Different About Teaching Reading to Students Learning English?

Some native English speakers may
- outperform their peers in tasks involving reading and spelling in early elementary grades if they have received systematic phonics instruction in kindergarten and first grade (Adler, 2001).

Some English language learners may
- speak languages that do not have the visual, phonological, or syntactic matches of spoken and written English (Bernhardt, 2003);
- be literate in their native language but know very little oral English (Bernhardt, 2003);
- not be literate in their native language, so English is the language in which they develop literacy (Bernhardt, 2003);
- need to develop a phonological concept for English words (Bernhardt, 2003);
- develop early reading skills in many of the same ways as native English speakers (Ramírez, 2000);
- be able to use what they know about the phonological features of their native language to develop phonemic awareness in English (Durgunoglu, Nagy, & Hancin–Bhatt, 1991),
- need to learn the alphabetic writing system of English because the writing system of their native language is different from that of English (Walqui, 2000); and
- benefit from instruction in phonemic awareness and phonics that teaches English speech sounds alone and letter–sound associations (Adams, Foorman, Lundberg, & Beeler, 1998; Oudeans, 2004, as cited in August & Shanahan, 2006).

Chapter 4

Beyond the Workshop

1. Outside reading

Read *Implementing Reading First with English Language Learners*. Following a brief history of Reading First, the article summarizes research and offers instructional suggestions for use with English language learners, looking at each of the five components identified by the National Reading Panel. Examine the suggestions that are made regarding phonemic awareness and phonics and comment on how they could be used with the students in your classroom. If appropriate, try out one or more activities and report on the success of the practice. The article is available at:http://ncela.gwu.edu/pub/directions/15.pdf.

2. Explore words and sounds

Locate and share one or more children's books that contain easy language patterns or rhythmic and rhyming text, such as *Fish Faces* by Norbert Wu, a brief rhythmic, alliterative text that is accompanied by colorful photographs of deep sea creatures. After sharing the book, examine the language patterns together, noting the letter combinations and their corresponding sounds. Have students re–read the text to practice reading the words and then challenge them to supply additional words or phrases that contain the same patterns and sounds. Share the results of the experience in the next workshop.

3. Alphabet books

Locate and share one or more alphabet books that address classroom topics or focus on language, such as *Jambo Means Hello: Swahili Alphabet Book* by Muriel Feelings (1992), a Penguin Young Readers Book, an introduction to the 24 letters and sounds of the Swahili language as well as glimpses of African life and culture. After sharing the book, focus on the information that describes the Swahili language and compare it with students' native languages and with English and create a new alphabet or language book. How are the languages alike and in what ways do they differ? Share the results of this experience in the next workshop.

4. Lyrics to songs

For older students who need experiences with phonemic awareness or phonics, draw on the availability of current lyrics in songs that the students know and enjoy. Clarify the meanings of the songs before exploring what makes the words appealing and how the lyrics fit with the music. Students may then want to write additional lyrics for the songs or even create their own melodies and lyrics. Share the results of this experience in the next workshop.

CHAPTER 5
Reading Fluency

Goal and Objectives

Goal
Participants will achieve the following:

- Understand the role that reading fluency plays in reading comprehension.

Objectives
Participants will be able to do the following:

- Define fluency and identify effective techniques to develop reading fluency for native English speakers and English language learners.

- Describe ways to help native English speakers and English language learners build on their knowledge of how English works so they can read texts effectively, efficiently, and fluently.

What's Your WCPM?

Reading Sample

Poland	1
Summer 1929	3
DEAR EVA,	5
I LIKE YOU VERY MUCH.	10
I WILL SEE YOU IN THE AFTERNOON.	17
JOE	18

I checked my letter carefully for spelling, and I folded it two times. I slid   33
from the chair, and I carried the letter to Veronka. I was six years old, and in   50
September I was scheduled to enter first grade of the Rozwadow Elementary School.   62
For quite some time, I had been reading children's books with my   75
mother's help, and later newspaper headlines and advertisements. Then I copied   86
capital letters from newspapers, and I started to write. My first printed letters were   99
written to Eve, or as I called her in Polish "Eva." Eva was a beautiful smart girl,   116
and she was my first love.   123

As it turned out, this love was rather enduring. For the past several years   137
she and her younger sister Mimi visited from Vienna and spent part of every   151
summer vacation with Dr. and Mrs. Schwartz, their uncle and aunt. Eva was about my   164
age, and both girls were great company. The Schwartzes lived almost across the street   177
from us. They had no children. Mrs. Schwartz loved children, and   190
whenever Eva, Mimi and their parents were not there in the summer, Mrs. Schwartz   204
invited two other nephews Adam and Felek. I played with all of them, but Eva was   218
very special.   223

I went into our kitchen and afterward gave the letter to Veronka, our maid.   236
I told her to please carry the letter to Eva. Veronka was a slim woman, about twenty   252
years old. She had blue eyes and long blond hair, which was disarranged most of the   266
time. She was very busy cleaning and cooking and taking care of me....   279
    283

Word count 283

Page 2

"You will see Eva in just a few hours, after dinner, this afternoon,"   13
Veronka protested mildly. "We'll eat at two in the afternoon, and at three you will   27
be on your way just like every day," she continued. "Besides, things are boiling on   41
the stove."

She stood barefoot, as usual, near the wood and coal–fire stove. She was   58
busy cooking. I was not tall enough to see what was cooking on the stove.   73
Veronka was tossing her hair back and wiping off the perspiration from her   86
forehead. Her flower–printed cotton dress clung to her body. She gave me a rather   99
perturbed look, reflecting her reaction to my asking her to deliver my note.   113

"Just move the stuff a little bit off the stove for a minute," I persisted. "It is   129
only across the road; nothing will burn or boil over. I'll get up on the chair and   147
watch it."   149

"Don't you dare," she said. She pushed a couple of pots away to the side.   164
She took the letter from my hand and then ran down the steps. When she left, I   181
went quickly onto the balcony overlooking the street and I saw Veronka running   194
across the road. She opened the gate to the Schwartzes' house, passed Dr.   207
Schwartz's office window, which in summertime always had a net over it. Then   220
she knocked on the door. Mrs. Schwartz appeared and took the letter. I could   234
actually see her smile. Mrs. Schwartz nodded. No words were exchanged.   245

Veronka ran back to the house.... She went back to her chores in the   259
kitchen....   260

"Thank you," I said, and went back to the living room.   271

Word count 271

Source: Taler, J. (1995). *In Search of Heroes* (pp. 3–4).Baltimore: Gateway. Reprinted with permission.

Hasbrouck and Tindal 2005 Oral Reading Fluency Data

Grade	Percentile	Fall WCPM	Winter WCPM	Spring WCPM
1	90		81	111
	75		47	82
	50		23	53
	25		12	28
	10		6	15
2	90	106	125	142
	75	79	100	117
	50	51	72	89
	25	25	42	61
	10	11	18	31
3	90	128	146	162
	75	99	120	137
	50	71	92	107
	25	44	62	78
	10	21	36	48
4	90	145	166	180
	75	119	139	152
	50	94	112	123
	25	68	87	98
	10	45	61	72
5	90	166	182	194
	75	138	156	168
	50	110	127	139
	25	85	99	109
	10	61	74	83
6	90	177	195	204
	75	153	167	177
	50	127	140	150
	25	98	111	122
	10	68	82	93
7	90	180	192	202
	75	156	165	177
	50	128	136	150
	25	102	109	123
	10	79	88	98
8	90	185	199	199
	75	161	173	177
	50	133	146	151
	25	106	115	124
	10	77	84	97

Source: Hasbrouck, J., & Tindal, G. (2005). *Oral Reading Fluency: 90 Years of Measurement.* Eugene: University of Oregon, Behavioral Research and Teaching. (241 Education, 5262 University of Oregon, Eugene, OR 97403–5262, http://brt.uoregon.edu)

Automaticity and Fluency

Automaticity is fast, effortless, and accurate word recognition.

Fluency is the ability to recognize words and comprehend meaning simultaneously. Fluent readers can

◆ Recognize words automatically,

◆ Group words into meaningful chunks,

◆ Read aloud effortlessly, and

◆ Read aloud with expression in order to make connections between what they know and the meaning of the words to understand what they are reading (Adler, 2001).

Venn Diagram

Directions: Complete the Venn diagram below using the terms *Automaticity* and *Fluency*. Write *Automaticity* in the the top circle and *Fluency* in the bottom circle.

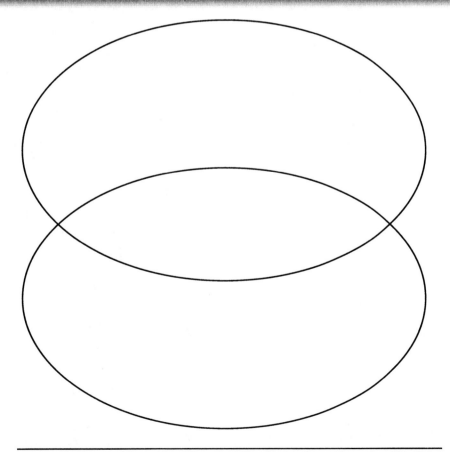

Automaticity and Fluency Diagram

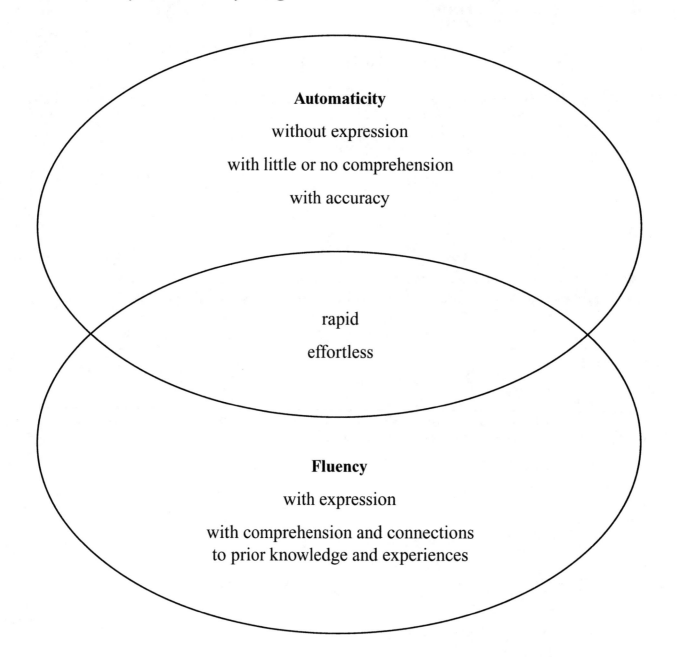

Automaticity

without expression

with little or no comprehension

with accuracy

rapid

effortless

Fluency

with expression

with comprehension and connections
to prior knowledge and experiences

Fluent Readers

Native English speakers

◆ See individual letters of the words they read.

◆ Seek familiar letter sequences and patterns.

◆ Decode words rapidly, effortlessly, and accurately.

◆ Group words into meaningful chunks.

◆ Use punctuation and meanings as cues for reading connected text with expression and comprehension.

◆ Make predictions from context.

◆ Draw on their background knowledge and experiences.

◆ Decode words rapidly and accurately.

English language learners

◆ Decode words quickly, effortlessly, and accurately.

◆ Transfer knowledge about the alphabetic principle and vocabulary from their first language to their second language.*

◆ Make predictions from context.

◆ Draw on their background knowledge and experiences.

◆ Decode words rapidly and accurately.

* This is what sets English language learners apart from their native–English–speaking counterparts. English language learners who know how the alphabetic principle works in their first language can transfer this knowledge to their learning to read in English. Those who recognize and know how to use cognates of words in their first language can transfer this knowledge of the meanings of words to their reading in English (Birch, 2002).

Sources: Adams, 1990; Adler, 2001; Birch, 2002; Moats, 1999.

Chapter 5

Activities Involving Repeated Oral Reading

> **Directions:** Work with a partner. Share your experiences using each of the following activities.

Adult–student reading
- An adult reads the passage first, demonstrating fluent reading.
- The student reads the text as the adult provides guidance.
- The student continues reading (perhaps as many as five times) until the reading is fluent.

Choral reading
- A fluent reader models the reading, and then students read aloud with the reader.
- Repeat the procedure (perhaps four or five times), so students are likely to be able to read the text independently.

Tape–assisted reading
- A student reads aloud with a taped reading.
- At first, the student listens to the reader and follows along in the text.
- On subsequent readings, the student reads aloud with the tape until the oral reading can be performed independently without the tape.

Partner reading
- Pairs of students take turns reading aloud to each other.
- The better reader reads first; the weaker reader reads second.
- The better reader offers encouragement and assists with word recognition.
- The weaker reader reads the text until the oral reading can be done independently.

Readers' theatre
- Students select a script and rehearse reading it orally.
- Students perform an oral reading of the script for an audience of peers or others.

Source: Adler, 2001.

How to Develop Fluent Reading

Directions: List one or more reasons why English language learners can benefit from each activity.

Hear texts read orally with expression.	
See and talk about the texts and the cues the reader used to read fluently.	
Practice reading the same texts they have heard read.	
Repeatedly read texts with guidance and feedback.	
Read texts that are enjoyable.	
Read texts that are easy.	

Kindergarten Through Grade 3 Developmental Continuum Oral Reading Rubric for Fluency, Rate, Expression, and Self–Monitoring

Directions: Compare the information on the rubric on pages 166–169 with that on your Continuum for Emerging Readers, Developing Readers, and Advanced Readers.

Fluency

Fluency is the flow of a reader's delivery in an oral reading.

5   The advanced reader in fluency reads aloud with appropriate pauses, stops, starts, and signals for transitions.
   • The reader reads whole passages for meaning as opposed to single words or phrases.
   • Line breaks or hyphenated words are smooth and unnoticeable.
   • Substitutions or corrections are unobtrusively made, and meaning is always maintained.

3   The developing reader in fluency reads aloud with some appropriate pauses, stops, starts, and signals for transitions.
   • The reader reads in chunks, applying meaning to phrases of single sentences instead of whole passages.
   • Line breaks or hyphenated words are often noticeable.
   • Substitutions are sometimes inappropriate in maintaining the context, and meaning is sometimes distorted.

1   The emerging reader in fluency reads aloud with awkward pauses, stops, and starts. There are usually few signals for transitions.
   • The reader reads each word as a single entity, limiting the flow of the passage. Meaning is usually obscured by this flow.
   • Line breaks and/or hyphenated words are confusing and usually halt the progress of the oral reading.
   • Substitutions are typically guesses at words with little attempt to maintain meaning or context.

Rate

Rate is the speed and pattern a reader follows in an oral reading.

5 The advanced reader selects and maintains an appropriate rate and speed for an oral reading.
- The rate corresponds to the meaning of the passage, and the reader uses the ability to speed up or slow down different sections of the text to create an appropriate emphasis on the meaning of the text.
- The rate and speed are well coordinated and enable the oral reading to sound natural.

3 The developing reader sometimes selects an appropriate rate and speed for an oral reading.
- The rate does not always correspond to the meaning of the passage and attempts to add emphasis through rate sometimes produce a bumpy oral reading.
- The rate and speed do not always correspond to the meaning of the text, and it can sound forced.

1 The emerging reader is not yet able to select an appropriate rate and speed for an oral reading.
- The rate does not correspond to the meaning of the passage, and sometimes a monotone or excessively hurried speed is the result.
- Meaning and context are actually obscured by the difficult rate and speed employed by the reader.

Chapter 5

Expression

Expression is the use of time, inflection, speed, and fluency in an oral reading.

5 The advanced reader reads with appropriate expression in his or her voice during oral reading.
  • The reader accurately adjusts tone, inflection, rate, speed, and fluency to match the intended meaning of the passage.
  • The reader is confident in his or her choice of expressive intent and uses it well to incorporate an oral interpretation of the text that is evident in the reading.

3 The developing reader incorporates some expressiveness in his or her voice during an oral reading.
  • The reader sometimes adjusts tone, inflection, rate, speed, or fluency to attempt an expressive interpretation of the text.
  • The reader is ambivalent about expressive choice, often overdoing it or underdoing it through hesitation.
  • An oral interpretation is not always evident.

1 The emerging reader does not yet incorporate expressiveness in his or her voice during an oral reading.
  • The reader does not yet recognize the use of tone, inflection, rate, speed, or fluency to attempt an expressive interpretation of the text.
  • The reader is unsure about expressiveness, and an oral interpretation is not evident.

Self–Monitoring

Self–Monitoring is the management of strategies for accuracy and appropriateness that a reader uses in an oral reading.

5 The advanced reader employs a variety of self–monitoring skills to check his or her oral reading for accuracy and appropriateness.
- The reader thoughtfully and purposefully uses rereading, sounding out, substitutions, skipping over, searching for help, and asking questions to monitor comprehension and fluency during oral reading.
- The reader rarely needs assistance when reading age–appropriate materials.

3 The developing reader employs some self–monitoring skills to check his or her oral reading for accuracy and appropriateness.
- The reader uses some skills including rereading, sounding out, substitutions, skipping over, searching for help, or asking questions to aid his or her ability to self–monitor.
- The reader relies on other readers, listeners, or coaches to help when he or she gets stuck.
- The reader sometimes needs assistance when reading age–appropriate materials.

1 The emerging reader does not employ very many self–monitoring skills to check his or her oral reading for accuracy or appropriateness.
- The reader is still developing the skills of rereading, sounding out, substitutions, skipping over, searching for help, or asking questions to aid his or her ability to self–monitor.
- The reader relies heavily on other readers, listeners, or coaches to orally read a passage.
- The reader needs great assistance when reading age–appropriate materials.

Source: Northwest Regional Educational Laboratory. (n.d.). *K–3 Developmental Continuum Oral Reading Rubric for Fluency, Rate, Expression, and Self–Monitoring.* Portland, OR: Author. Reprinted with permission.

Assessing Students' Oral Reading Fluency

Resources for Assessing Students' Oral Reading

AIMSweb Standard Reading Assessment Passages (RAPs)

A Curriculum–Based Measurement (CBM) set of passages for quick oral reading assessment, the field–tested, validated results can assist teachers in making instructional decisions and monitoring students' progress. The system includes a Web–based software management program for data collection and reporting. Available at www.aimsweb.com/measures/reading.

Dynamic Indicators of Basic Early Literacy Skills (DIBELS)

Designed for students in first through third grades, the DIBELS (Good & Kaminski, 2003) contains a subtest of Oral Reading Fluency and Retell Fluency. The standardized oral reading passage requires students to real aloud for 1 minute. The number of words read per minute provides the oral fluency reading rate, and the retell fluency measures comprehension. Available at http://dibels.uoregon.edu/.

Gray Oral Reading Test Fourth Edition (GORT–4)

This is a norm–referenced measure that assesses students' rate, accuracy, fluency (rate and accuracy combined), comprehension, and overall reading ability (rate, accuracy, and comprehension combined). Available at www.agsnet.com/group.asp?nGroupInfoID=a11445.

National Assessment of Educational Progress (NAEP) Fluency Scale

The students' naturalness of reading is assessed through a four–point scale involving phrasing of words, syntax, and expressiveness (Pinnell, et al, 1995, cited in Hudson, Lane, & Pullen, 2005). The number of words read correctly per minute provides the data for rate and accuracy. Available at http://nces.ed.gov/pubs95/web/95762.asp.

Reading Fluency Benchmark Assessor by Read Naturally

Grade–level passages are available for Grades 1 through 8. Fall, winter, and spring evaluations are suggested, and there is a software program for recording and reporting data. Available at www.readnaturally.com/products/rfmInfo.htm.

Sample Oral Reading Passages for Grades 1–8

Grade 1. The Hare and the Tortoise

	Running Words
One morning, Tortoise	3
woke up early. He was cold. He	10
said to himself, "I think I'll go	17
sit in the sun." So off he went.	25
That same morning, Hare	29
woke up early. He was cold. He	36
said to himself, "I think I'll go	43
for a run around the meadow.	49
That will warm me up." So off	56
he went.	58
Tortoise walked and	61
walked. At last, he came to a	68
big rock in the sun. He crawled	75
onto the top of the rock. "Ah,"	82
he said to himself, "this feels	88
so nice and warm. I feel better	95
already. I think I will stay here	102
for a while."	105

Source: Critical Thinking with Literature. © The
Continental Press, Inc. 1999, 1997, 1992.
Used by permission.

This page may be reproduced for classroom use.

Grade 2. The Clever Maggie

	Running Words
One day Maggie Mouse was	5
very hungry. There was no corn in	12
her cupboard. "I'll get some corn	18
from the barn," she said to herself.	25
Maggie came to the barnyard	30
gate. Oops! There was Casey Cat	36
hiding in the grass. "If Casey sees	43
me," thought Maggie," he'll have	48
me for lunch. I'll cross the	54
barnyard on the other side."	59
Maggie crossed the other side	64
of the barnyard. She went into the	71
barn and filled a basket with corn.	78
Maggie started back across the	83
barnyard. Oops! There was Harry	88
Hawk sitting on the fence. "If Harry	95
sees me, he'll have me for lunch,"	102
Maggie thought. "I'll wait until he	108
flies away."	110

Source: Critical Thinking with Literature. © The
Continental Press, Inc. 1999, 1997, 1992.
Used by permission.

Grade 3. Who's Superstitious?

	Running Words
My brother Billy always carries a lucky	7
rabbit's foot. Last night I guess it didn't	15
work. Billy spilled the salt at dinner. Do	23
you know what he did next? He tossed a	32
little salt over his left shoulder! Billy is so	41
superstitious!	42
Superstitious people have strange	46
reasons for eating some foods. They say,	53
"Eat an apple a day to keep the doctor	62
away." They also say, "Eat the crusts of	70
bread to have rosy cheeks." Or they say,	78
"Eat fish because it's brain food."	84
Maybe you have heard someone say,	90
"Things come in threes." Have you ever	97
been told, "Toads cause warts"? How	103
about, "When bulls see red, they get	110
angry." Of course, everyone knows,	115
"Thirteen is an unlucky number." But did	122
you know, "Thirteen is a lucky number"?	129

Source: Critical Thinking with Literature. © The
Continental Press, Inc. 1999, 1997, 1992.
Used by permission.

Grade 4. Mirages: Nature's Tricks

	Running Words
Of all your senses, sight may be one of the	10
most important. Your eyes probably tell you	17
more about the world than any of your other	26
senses.	27
You use your eyes to do lots of everyday	36
things. When you get dressed, your eyes help	44
you find the right color clothes to wear	52
together. When you borrow a marker from a	60
friend, your eyes tell you how far away the	69
marker is and where you have to reach for it.	79
Most of the time, you believe what your	87
eyes tell you. But you have probably noticed	95
that sometimes your eyes can fool you.	102
Picture this. It is summertime. It's a hot	110
day. The sun is beating down on the trees, the	120
bushes, the car in which you are riding, and the	130
road ahead. The temperature in the car is rising	139
higher and higher. You are thirsty. You can	147
only think of getting water. Thoughts of	154
"Water! Where can I get some water?" run	162
through your mind.	165
Then suddenly, just up ahead….on the	172
road…is…water! A pool of cool, rippling	180
water lies just "up there."	185

Source: Critical Thinking with Literature. © The
Continental Press, Inc. 1999, 1997, 1992.
Used by permission.

Grade 5. From Slow to Fast

	Running Words
For thousands and thousands of years,	6
the speed at which people traveled did not	14
change. People used foot–power to get from	21
place to place. Carrying even a light load, a	30
person could travel only 15 to 20 miles a	37
day.	38
Then somehow, someone learned that	43
waterways could be used as roads. On the	51
very simple early boats, passengers and	57
loads of goods had to be balanced just so.	66
A mistake could prove costly, if not wet.	74
Still, sailing was faster than walking.	80
At about the same time, traders were	87
learning the fastest way to travel long	94
distances over desert lands. They used	100
camels. These animals traveled at about	106
two and a half miles an hour. Sudden	114
sandstorms or a lame animal might slow	121
them down. But a camel caravan could	128
often get goods to market in half the time it	138
would take for someone to carry them on	146
foot.	147
The first wheel was the next big step.	155
Neither the exact time nor the inventor is	163
known. But we do know that by 3500 BC	170
or so, a solid, round wheel was being used	179
in the lands between the Tigris and	185
Euphrates rivers in the Middle East. It	189
would be another 1,500 years until the	195
spoked wheel was invented. This let cart	202
makers build much lighter wagons that	208
could be pulled by horses. The top speed	217
a person could travel now rose to 15 to 20	224
miles an hour!	227

Source: Critical Thinking with Literature. © The
Continental Press, Inc. 1999, 1997, 1992.
Used by permission.

This page may be reproduced for classroom use.

Grade 6. Where Did You Get Those Jeans?

	Running Words
Did you know your jeans are really over 500 years	10
old? Long before Columbus discovered America, cloth	16
makers in Nîmes, France, were making a strong cotton cloth.	25
This cloth was called *serge de Nîmes*, or "cloth from Nîmes."	32
Because the word Nîmes is pronounced *Neem*, the cloth	40
eventually became known as *denim*. Then, when Columbus set	50
sail across the ocean in 1492, he naturally needed good, strong	60
sails. His ships' sails may have been made of denim.	65
We do know that around this same time, Italian sailors used	75
denim sails on their voyages to India. Now, the Indian word for	85
denim is *dungri*. So it's easy to see where the word *dungaree*	97
came from. But the Indians didn't use dungri, or denim, just to	108
make sails. They used it to make pants, too.	116
The Italian sailors liked their dungri pants so much	124
they took some home to Genoa (JEN–oh–uh). English sailors in	130
Genoa saw the pants. The sailors thought the pants were great	142
because they could be worn and worn without wearing out. So,	154
of course, the pants went home to England with the sailors. And	163
Genoa pants were soon called *jeans*.	167

Source: Critical Thinking with Literature. © The Continental Press, Inc.
1999, 1997, 1992. Used by permission.

Grade 7. Who Designed the First United States Flag?

	Running Words
At the beginning of the American Revolution, the	8
colonists fought under a number of different flags.	16
Between 1775 and 1777, many of the soldiers fought	25
under a flag known as the Grand Union Flag or the	36
Continental Colors. This flag, with a small British flag	45
placed in the upper left corner, suggested that the	55
colonies felt some loyalty to England. But with the	66
signing of the Declaration of Independence in 1776,	75
the symbol of the British flag was no longer fitting.	85
The new country needed to have a new flag.	90
Almost a year later, in June of 1777, the	99
Continental Congress declared that the flag should	107
have 13 alternating stripes of red and white. It also	117
suggested that the Union be shown as 13 white stars	130
in a blue field.	138
One of the members of the Continental	146
Congress was Francis Hopkinson. Mr. Hopkinson	157
was the delegate from New Jersey. He was one of	166
the signers of the Declaration of Independence. He	174
was also an artist, writer, lawyer, and judge.	182
Historical records suggest that Mr. Hopkinson	186
designed the first flag. Most scholars believe this to	192
be true.	202
Some people, however, believe Betsy Ross	209
designed and made the first United States Flag. Born	219
in Philadelphia, Betsy married John Ross, an	230
upholsterer. Not long after their marriage, John was	239
killed and Betsy had to take over the business. She	241
soon became known as an excellent seamstress.	251
She also made flags for the Pennsylvania Navy.	258
The story goes that in June 1776 a committee	269
from the Continental Congress visited Betsy Ross.	277
George Ross, one of Betsy's husband's uncles and a	286
signer of the Declaration of Independence, was a	292
member of this committee. The men showed Betsy a	301
rough design and asked her to make the flag.	310

Source: Isaacs, S. (2000). *JEI Self–Learning English.*
    Seoul, Korea: Jaeneung Educational Institute.
    Reprinted with permission.

This page may be reproduced for classroom use.

Grade 8. What a Funny Girl!

	Running Words
"Did you ever wonder where pasteurized milk gets	8
its name? Maybe it is because cows are kept in a	20
pasture, so cow's milk is naturally pasteurized."	25
Years and years ago, a joke similar to this was often	35
told by a famous comedian. Acting as a smarty–pants	45
7–year–old named Baby Snooks, Fannie Brice could	54
make audiences forget themselves and laugh.	59
Born in 1891 as Fannie Borach, she decided very	68
early that she wanted to be a performer. Although	78
she always wanted to be a serious actress, it was	90
her gift for comedy that brought her stardom.	95
Fannie grew up in New York City. She left school	105
after eighth grade and got a job as a chorus girl. At	119
the age of 14, she changed her name to Brice and a	131
year later appeared on Broadway. Fannie sang and	140
danced in the show, a musical comedy called *The*	149
College Girls. Her performance was so funny it	158
brought the house down. This was but the beginning	168
of her road to stardom.	173
In 1910, Fannie got a job in vaudeville, a kind of	179
entertainment that features many different kinds of	187
acts. For example, a typical performance would	195
include as many as 8 or 10 acts. These acts might	206
include such performers as jugglers, animal acts,	215
singers, and, of course, comedians. There, Fannie's	222
reputation began to grow.	226

Source: Isaacs, S. (2000). *JEI Self–Learning English*.
Seoul, Korea: Jaeneung Educational Institute.
Reprinted with permission.

From One Teacher's Perspective

Reading Fluency

This commentary was written by Carolyn W. Patton, Coordinating Literacy Teacher, Wake County Public Schools, Raleigh, North Carolina.

As a reading specialist who consults with general education, English as a second language (ESL), and special education teachers, I find questions regarding students' reading fluency have increased in the past year because of the impact and increased awareness of reading research. Fluency, the critical bridge that links word recognition and vocabulary to comprehension, is most easily gained when a student achieves automaticity in the aforementioned aspects of reading. As a result of this awareness, the following instructional question frequently arises: "How do I expect my English language learners to become fluent when they are still developing English?"

Fluency instruction with connected text does not begin in regular kindergarten classes because these learners are developing automaticity with the sound–symbol system, with high–frequency words, and with the phrasing of those high–frequency words. Preparing the novice English language learner for the successful acquisition of reading fluency begins in a similar manner, by providing exposures that allow them to attain automaticity at the foundational levels of English. With developed proficiency, novice English language learners will greatly reduce the cognitive load they encounter when trying to read text, thus allowing for greater processing in the comprehension realm.

A wonderful tool for providing quick, efficient, daily practice is *Great Leaps* (available at www.greatleaps.com), a program that utilizes the research–proven practices of repeated readings and monitored oral feedback to build mastery of letter–sound relationships, common rimes, proficiency with high–frequency word phrases, and the reading of connected text. Students enjoy charting their progress and measuring their growth. This tool is easily implemented by paraprofessionals and volunteers.

Students at the intermediate through advanced levels will continue to benefit from any emphasis placed on vocabulary instruction. Simultaneously pairing vocabulary instruction with English phrasing helps readers develop the breaks, not always signaled by punctuation, that enhance intonation and reflection of mood, leading to increased comprehension.

All students whether novice, intermediate, or advanced, benefit from choral reading activities. Choral readings provide modeling of English as well as participation and practice in a sheltered learning environment. Choral readings afford the teacher the opportunity to blend elements of instruction. For example, Shel Silverstein's "The Twistable, Turnable Man," presents students with vocabulary exposure while teaching the suffix *–able* and modeling the rhythm of English. Awareness of the sounds of *–ed* can be practiced through the reading of, *When the Fly Flew In* by Lisa Westberg Peters while being paired with vocabulary development and sequence instruction.

No matter the language level of the student, text given to the student for oral reading practice must be provided at the independent level. After determining the student's reading level, a personal reading list for the student can often be generated through the databases used by media specialists to order media resources. Such a personal list allows for selection not only by reading level but also by area of interest and age (e.g., Titlewave available at www.titlewave.com/login/?side=C).

Another question that arises all too frequently is "What do I do with the student I have been teaching for 2 years who is not showing the expected growth?" If a review of the instruction provided shows evidence of appropriateness, yet the student is still not reading independently, the texts offered to the student may need further scaffolding. Many teachers are unaware of the different types of text: patterned, decodable[1], transitional, easy reader, and authentic. Furthermore, the student may benefit from instruction at one of the more discrete foundational levels previously mentioned, if that instruction has not already been provided. Finally, the intensity of the program should be reviewed. The student may require more repetitions per day to demonstrate acquisition of the material.

Another consideration in the development of reading fluency is that of stamina. English language learners develop their ability to listen and comprehend; they must also develop a stamina for reading. So, in addition to scaffolding text, the length of the text must also increase to ensure that students are reading for longer and longer durations. Just as an athlete trains to run a marathon, a reader must train to read lengthy texts.

How should fluency be measured? Most fluency is measured by the number of words the student reads correctly within one minute (WCPM). The norms by Hasbrouck and Tindal (2005) are used to gauge student performance. Many districts are also using Curriculum–Based Measurements (CBMs) such as *Dynamic Indicators of Basic Early Literacy Skills* (DIBELS) to measure student growth.

Fluency is more than rate and accuracy; it also incorporates a student's prosody. Students who read quickly and accurately, but without expression, may very well impact their ability to visualize and comprehend what has been read. Students who do not learn to reread familiar text will rarely learn to develop their stride when reading. No stride, no stamina. It is our job not only to condition these students to run the race, but also to keep them in the race, and ultimately to watch them cross the finish line.

---

[1]Decodable texts have been difficult to find in the past several years. These are some source to consider: Books to Remember (FlyLeaf Publishing), Travels with Ted (Wilson Reading System), J &J Readers (Sopris West), www.readinga-z.com/newfiles/levels_descriptions/levelaabooks.html

Chapter Summary and Beyond the Workshop

Chapter 5: Reading Fluency
What's Different About Teaching Reading to Students Learning English?

Some native English speakers may

- be able to read connected text accurately, effortlessly, and with appropriate speed and prosody (Hudson, Lane, & Pullen, 2005).

Some English language learners may

- not benefit from reading fluency instruction until they have strong English word–recognition skills (Snow, Burns, & Griffin, 1998; Spangenberg–Urbschat & Pritchard, 1994);
- be able to meet reading fluency goals of oral reading assessments that are used with native English speakers;
- recognize that what they know about their native language can help them with reading English (Birch, 2002);
- benefit from reading texts related to their native culture (Fitzgerald & Graves, 2004);
- demonstrate fluency in reading connected text orally when they understand its meaning and have discussed it orally before reading; and
- benefit from teachers' and other students' modeling fluent reading of brief text passages.

Chapter 5

Beyond the Workshop

1. Outside reading (1)

Read "Promoting Language Proficiency and Academic Achievement Through Cooperation," a description of the features of a bilingual cooperative learning model combined with a classroom management model for instruction. The article highlights the findings from a study conducted in Texas and outlines the features and strategies of this Bilingual Cooperative Integrated Reading and Composition (BCIRC) project. Respond to the reading by describing the practices you might include in your classroom and explain the reasons for your choices. The article is available at www.cal.org/resources/digest/cooperation.html.

2. Outside reading (2)

Read the article "Reading Fluency Instruction and Assessment: What, Why, and How?" Select one or more of the instructional suggestions for assessing accuracy, prosody, and rate and try them with your students. Describe the activities you selected and explain the reasons for your choice(s). Also describe how well the activities worked. The article is available at www.fcrr.org/publications/publicationspdffiles/hudson_lane_pullen_readingfluency_2005.pdf.

3. Reading with a student

Ask a student to read a passage aloud. (Use the Kindergarten Through Grade 3 Developmental Continuum Oral Reading Rubric with one of the oral reading passages in the study guide, one of the passages from the resources on the Internet, or another text of your choice.) Then answer the following questions:
- What aspects of fluent reading did the student perform well?
- What aspects of fluent reading did the student have difficulty performing?
- What did you do to support the student's reading?
- What does the student need to improve?
- What do you plan to do in preparation for the next session with the student?

Share your notes on the experience in the next session.

4. In the classroom

Assist students in investigating how composers use music to communicate ideas to listeners, and then explore how oral reading can communicate ideas to listeners. Begin by playing recordings of Villa–Lobos' *The Little Train of Caipira*, Rimsky–Korsakoff's *Flight of the Bumblebee*, or Copeland's *Appalachian Spring*. After listening to the music, ask the following questions:
- What places or animals did the music make you think about or see in your mind?
- What actions did the music make you think of?
- How did the music make you feel?
- What are some words that describe how the music moved?

Next, investigate how the human voice can cause listeners to think of different places, actions, and feelings. Display the poem "Echo" (page 184) on an overhead transparency. Begin by reading it in a straight–forward manner, then read it again and produce the echo effect by diminishing the loudness of the repeated words in each line. You may also want to read it a third time as students standing in different places read the repeated words, again producing the echo effect.

If times allows, display the poem "Sand Crab Catch" (page 186) on an overhead transparency. Reveal and read each stanza one by one. Pause after each stanza to have students describe the images they see in their mind's eye. Ask them to describe any sounds or smells that the poem makes them think about.

Again, ask students to describe what they saw in their mind's eye and how the poem made them feel with each of the different oral readings.

Echo

From the top of a mountain, mountain, mountain.
Or the top of a cliff, cliff, cliff.
Call Hello! Hello! Hello!
To someone down below, below, below.

Just listen, listen, listen
To the echo, echo, echo
In the air, air, air.

Sound bounces, bounces, bounces
From here to there, there, there.
That's why you hear an echo, echo, echo,
In the air, air, air.

Written by Dorothy Kauffman

Sand Crab Catch

Come down to the shoreline,
with a shovel and a cup.
Get some sand on the shovel.
Just scoop it right up.

Put the sand in the cup.
Pat it down nice and tight.
Set the cup on the sand
Then squeeze left and right.

When you lift up the cup,
There's a cone of sand.
Oh, please look! Look! Look!
There's a sand crab in my hand!

Written by Dorothy Kauffman

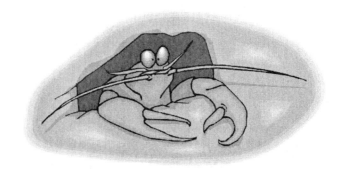

CHAPTER 6
Content Area Reading and Study Skills

Goal and Objectives

Goal

Participants will achieve the following:

- Understand that reading to learn is a complex process that involves a reader's knowledge of how English works, how content is represented in print, and how to select and employ appropriate reading strategies and study skills to meet specific purposes.

Objectives

Participants will be able to do the following:

- Describe ways to help native English speakers and English language learners build on their knowledge of how English works so they can read texts effectively and efficiently.

- Describe reading behaviors used by proficient native English speakers and English language learners.

- Select effective strategies to teach content area reading and study skills to native English speakers and English language learners.

Characteristics of Social and Academic Language

Directions: Read the two passages in the chart below and list some characteristics of social and academic language.

A. Well, other than herb tea, what is anyone's favorite tea? B. Earl Grey. I love Earl Grey. C. Well, actually, I like raspberry–flavored tea. D. Uh? E. It's quite good. It's regular tea, and a tea that…, but I haven't lately. I'm not a big fan of tea. F. My dad always put milk in his tea, and I thought that was barbarous until I went to England. I found out that's what they do. G. Ha.	In 1767 the British Parliament put a tax on some items imported into America. Many colonists became angry and decided not to pay the taxes. In 1770 the British repealed all of the taxes except the one on tea. Later, in 1773, the British passed the Tea Act to help the East India Tea Company survive its financial problems. The act allowed the company to sell tea in America at a very low price, but the colonists still had to pay taxes on the tea. Some colonists thought the low price for tea would cause them to go out of business. Others thought paying the tea tax would make the British put taxes on more goods.

Characteristics of Social Language	Characteristics of Academic Language

Anticipation Guide: Comprehension of Content Texts

Directions: Read each statement. Based on your knowledge and experience, decide whether you Agree or Disagree with the statement. Place an A (Agree) or D (Disagree) in the blank. Finally, discuss the items you feel least certain about with the person beside you.

_____ 1. Readers comprehend more when they have a purpose for reading and engage in interactions with the text.

_____ 2. The strategy of making connections occurs primarily before reading.

_____ 3. Texts are authoritative repositories of information.

_____ 4. Texts are defined as print tools that readers use to construct knowledge.

_____ 5. Texts that reflect adolescents' interests, social realities, and range of reading levels offer support for their motivation to learn.

_____ 6. English language learners need to interact with text and with their peers to learn more about the content.

_____ 7. A teacher's use of lecture and discussion is sufficient for enhancing English language learners' content learning and academic literacy development.

Seven Principles for Promoting Reading Motivation

◆ Conceptual themes

◆ Real–world interactions

◆ Student self–direction

◆ A variety of texts at different reading levels

◆ Supports for using cognitive strategies

◆ Social collaboration

◆ Opportunities for self–expression

Source: Guthries & Knowles, 2001, as cited in Meltzer & Hamann, 2004.

Building on and Expanding Students' Knowledge
of How English Works

Questions, Questions, Questions

Asking questions enables teachers and students to recall what they know; find out what others know and think; explain a point of view; share interpretations, feelings, and opinions; formulate new ways of thinking about ideas; make evaluations; solve problems; and achieve a sense of acceptance and belonging in a group or classroom (Walker, n.d.).

In 1956, Benjamin Bloom headed a group of educational psychologists who investigated how to write educational objectives. They described and classified six levels of intellectual behavior in the cognitive domain and five levels in the affective domain. These two sets of objectives, known as Bloom's Taxonomy, inform educators about the varieties of thinking in which people engage.

The following chart identifies the range of questions in both domains, provides brief definitions, lists some suggested action verbs, and includes sample questions for each level of questioning.

Bloom's Taxonomy of Educational Objectives: Definitions, Sample Action Verbs, and Examples

Cognitive Domain	Affective Domain
Knowledge—remembers or recalls information define, describe, name *Example:* In your own words, define citizen.	**Receiving**—attends and shows responsiveness to and awareness of ongoing events listens, replies, identifies *Example:* Follows directions given by the teacher.
Comprehension—demonstrates an understanding of the meaning explain, give an example, interpret *Example:* Tell why the Bill of Rights is an important part of the U.S. Constitution.	**Responding**—participates in and reacts to ongoing activities answers, helps, reads *Example:* Works with others to complete a group project, such as a mural or play.

190

Bloom's Taxonomy (continued)

Cognitive Domain	Affective Domain

Application—uses what is known to solve a problem
 	
demonstrate, choose, show
 	
Example:
    Describe a situation when your rights that are guaranteed by the Bill of Rights may have been violated.
	Valuing—demonstrates or places a value on events or concern for others
	
	joins, explains, initiates
	
	Example:
	    Shares materials with others and offers suggestions to the group when uncertainties arise.

Analysis—breaks down the information into parts and recognizes relationships between the parts
 	
diagram, rearrange, tell
 	
Example:
    Represent the relationships among the branches of the United States government.
	Organizing—brings together differing values and sets aside conflicts; begins to construct a consistent value system
	
	adheres, identifies, integrates
	
	Example:
	    Recognizes different roles and considers their value in the way a group of the class functions

Synthesis—produces a solution using original and creative thinking
 	
compose, design, imagine
 	
Example:
    If you were stranded on a desert island with a group of people, what two rights would you feel would be most needed to survive the situation?
	Characterization—demonstrates consistent, predictable behavior based on values
	
	acts, performs, qualifies
	
	Example:
	    Is punctual and self–disciplined.

Evaluation—judges ideas and information based on identified criteria
 	
defend, select, recommend
 	
Example:
    Give some examples that support this statement: "Democracy is based upon the conviction that there are extraordinary possibilities in ordinary people."
    —H. E. Fostick	

Sources: Allen, n.d.; Bloom, 1956; Clark, 1999; Krathwohl, Bloom, & Bertram, 1973; Maryland Department of Education, n.d. [b]; Walker, n.d.

Questioning Strategies

Strategy	Definition	Examples
QtA Questioning the Author (Beck, McKeown, & Kucan, 2002)	This strategy enables readers to ponder the author's intent, meaning, and word choices.	To begin: *What's the author trying to say?* *What's the author's message?* *What's that all about?* *What does the author want us to know from this?* To follow up: *That's what the author says, but what does the author mean?* *X said…. Did anyone else pick that up?* *What did the author say to make X think of that?*
See: http://score.rims.k12.ca.us/score_lessons/content_area_literacy/pages/questioning_the_author.html		
CSI Collaborative Strategy Instruction (Anderson & Roit, 1993)	A combination of thinking aloud and collaborative discussions. By having students think aloud, teachers can identify the strategies students are using, and by asking general questions, students and teachers can have conversations about the text.	*What is it about?* *What do you already know about it?* Other general kinds of questions people might ask when talking about books.
See: http://fcis.oise.utoronto.ca/~ayasnitsky/Reading/collaborative.html		

Strategy	Definition	Examples

CSR
 	
Collaborative Strategic Reading
 	
(Klinger & Vaughn, 1996)
	Preview
	
	<u>Click and Clunk</u>
	Students notice unfamiliar words and use one of four fix-up strategies:
	  –reread
	  –use context clues
	  –look at prefixes and suffixes
	  –break words into syllables
	
	<u>Get the Gist</u>
	Look for the big ideas
	
	<u>Wrap Up</u>
	Identify key ideas and ask teacher–type questions
		What is this about?
		
		What is the most important person, thing, or idea in this paragraph?
		
		How are _____ and _____ the same?
		What do you think would happen if....?
		What do you think caused....?

See: www.ncset.org/teleconferences/transcripts/2002_09.asp		
QAR Question Answer Relationship (Raphael, 1982, 1984)	Students look in the text to find answers to questions, knowing that some answers are— <u>Right There</u> the answers are in the text and the words in the sentences provide the answers <u>Think and Search</u> the answers are implicit within the text but they are more difficult to find than the "right there" answers because the answers lie in different portions of the text <u>On Your Own</u> the answers are in your head and draw from your personal knowledge and experience	 *What color is the _____?* *When did it happen?* *Who is _____?* *Where is the _____?* *How did the _____ get into the _____?* *How do you know....?* *Which is the better choice?* *Why do you think....?* *What would have happened if....?*
See: http://students.lisp.wayne.edu		

Reading to Learn

Ten Strategies to Conduct Text–Based Discussions

1. Ask questions to establish purposes for reading.
2. Use two–column note–taking.
   Interesting Details/Learning Summary
   Double–Entry Diaries
3. Use coding.
4. Conduct follow–up discussions.
5. Allow longer wait time.
6. Conduct think–pair–share activities.
7. Use reciprocal teaching.
8. Conduct small–group and large–group responses to questions and prompts.
9. Compare and contrast text with visuals or another topic to complete graphic organizers.
10. Conduct quick–writes.

Sources: Adger & Peyton, 1999, as cited in Meltzer & Hamann; Anstrom, 1997; Tovani, 2000.

Two–Column Note–Taking: Interesting Details/Learning Summary

Interesting Details	Summary

Source: Adapted from *I Read It, but I Don't Get It* by Chris Tovani, copyright © 2000, with permission of Stenhouse Publishers.

This page may be reproduced for classroom use.

Two–Column Note–Taking: Double–Entry Coding Diaries

Quotation & Page Number	This makes me think of….
Quotation & Page Number	**This makes me wonder….**
Quotation & Page Number	**This makes me see….**
Quotation & Page Number	**This confuses me because….**

Source: Adapted from *I Read It, but I Don't Get It* by Chris Tovani, copyright © 2000, with permission
of Stenhouse Publishers.

This page may be reproduced for classroom use.

Teacher Works Magic With CREDE's Five Standards and Harry Potter

Barbara McKenna
Center for Research on Education, Diversity & Excellence (CREDE)[1]

Most people might write off the magic in the Harry Potter books as the stuff of fiction, but the books did work real magic last year in a Corning, California, elementary classroom. The class of third, fourth, and fifth graders was introduced to the second book in the Harry Potter series by teacher Maria Sudduth, who combined CREDE pedagogy and the Harry Potter craze to help her English language learners successfully read at well above their expected level.

Sudduth, a veteran teacher, conducted the 12–week literature unit as part of her work for a master's program at California State University, Chico. It took place when you couldn't buy children's clothing or fast food without reference to the hapless wizard and his friends. "They so wanted to be a part of the Harry Potter thing," Sudduth remembers. "But it was so far above their reading level. My job was to figure out how to help them be successful."

Right off the bat, Sudduth enacted a CREDE standard—providing challenging curriculum—by recognizing her students' motivation and encouraging it. "So many of our English language learners are being tracked out or tracked down, and I think a lot of that is because people's expectations of what they can achieve are not high enough. If they're well supported, there's no reason you can't teach English language learners rich literature. You just need to provide lots of charting, lots of visuals, and lots of instructional conversation."

All of the CREDE standards played a part in her approach, Sudduth says. "When I discovered the Five Standards, I said, 'Oh, that's completely what I think of when I work with my kids.' These standards are exactly what I try to make happen in the classroom."

Sudduth feels that the instructional conversation (IC) was one of the most important foundations of her approach. The IC is content–focused dialogue between teachers and students in which students do most of the speaking, and the teacher listens, guides the conversation, paraphrases, and introduces content–related vocabulary into the conversation.

"During that unit, we spent about 25 minutes every day in the library with the Harry Potter book. I would read to them, and they would read along in their own books. And then we would discuss what we had read. They were so into the story that they were making predictions and then looking ahead to see if their predictions were right or looking back to verify their understanding.

Because of the IC, we didn't just have the confident kids speaking out and everyone else agreeing with them. They had to develop strategies to back up their thinking and justify their ideas, which gave them enormous confidence in what they were saying."

---

[1] CREDE is a federally funded research and development program focused on improving the education of students whose ability to reach their potential is challenged by language or cultural barriers, race, geographic location, or poverty. For more information, visit www–gse.berkeley.edu/research/crede/index.html.

Sudduth gathered some tangible proof of success as well. "The target of the project was comprehension; my goal was to raise their transferable comprehension strategies," Sudduth says. And it worked. Using the Scholastic Reading Inventory test, the school district's reading specialist tested students before and after Sudduth taught the Harry Potter unit. Students' scores in the pretest ranged from 415 to 780; posttest results were 485 to 935—a significant rise.

"But what really went up," Sudduth notes, "were their battery of language, their spelling, and their skill with syntax and structure. *Harry Potter and the Chamber of Secrets* (Rowling, 1999) was a perfect book to use because the way that [author J. K. Rowling] uses metaphors, similes, and foreshadowing helps them to naturally develop their comprehension."

With her master's work completed, Sudduth returns to the classroom this fall as a full–time teacher. Inspired by last year's success, she plans to implement a similar literacy unit this fall. Besides using ICs, Sudduth recommends the following additional strategies:

- Along with the challenging literature, include reading materials that are at the instructional level of the students.

- Use "wondering questions." A strategy drawn from the Reader Leader program, wondering questions occur after a student "Reader Leader" reads a passage from a book and asks pairs of students to generate questions about the passage.

- Engage students in joint productive activity. Sudduth engaged her students with this strategy in numerous ways, including a regular activity in which she charted the story and students' ideas. "From the beginning of the story on through, I charted the story line and the children's thoughts on butcher paper. When I wrote down their comments, I would put their name alongside them. Then, down the line, when the issue came up again or the question was answered, I would go back to that student and ask, 'What do you think now?'"

- Have students work in pairs. Sudduth paired a stronger English speaker with a less–skilled speaker, creating a symbiotic arrangement that enabled both students to improve their skills—one by receiving some one–on–one tutoring and the other by having to articulate his or her understanding of the language. Sudduth says this arrangement was especially useful for children who were shy about speaking during group discussions. "The one who was less confident about speaking in front of the whole group could tell his or her thoughts to the partner, who would then share with the group."

- Create other activities in which students can apply their learning. Sudduth enlisted Jesus Cortez, one of her professors from CSU Chico, to help engage her students. Taking an idea from the Harry Potter book, Sudduth had her students send Cortez "owl mail" (in this case, e–mail took the place of live owls). "As the book evolved, they started asking him a lot of in–depth, critical thinking questions about the book," she says. "When I read those, I noticed that a lot of the students who were normally the quieter ones during class discussions, especially some of the girls, were stepping up and asking questions."

Source: McKenna, 2002.

Five Standards for Effective Pedagogy

◆ Teachers and Students Producing Together

Facilitate learning through joint productive activity among teachers and students.

◆ Developing Language and Literacy Across the Curriculum

Develop competence in the language and literacy of instruction across the curriculum.

◆ Making Meaning

Contextualize teaching and curriculum in the experiences and skills of students' homes and communities.

◆ Teaching Complex Thinking

Challenge students toward cognitive complexity.

◆ Teaching Through Conversation

Engage students through dialogue, especially Instructional Conversation.

Source: Center for Research on Education, Diversity & Excellence, 2002.

Proficient Reader Behaviors

What Proficient Readers Know

◆ They know what and when they are comprehending.

◆ They know their purposes for reading.

◆ They recognize the style of the text and know how to approach reading it.

◆ They know when and why they are not comprehending.

◆ They know and use a variety of strategies to solve their comprehension problems.

Source: Paric, Cross, & Lipson, 1984, as cited in Keene & Zimmerman, 1997.

Behaviors Exhibited by Students Struggling to Learn English

◆ Students strive to complete the assignment and believe that reading is decoding and pronouncing the words correctly.

◆ They view their two languages as separate and unrelated.

◆ They may consider their first language as detrimental and lack a biliterate perspective.

◆ They fail to integrate their prior knowledge and experiences with the topic.

◆ They do not ask questions to guide their reading and thinking.

Source: Jimenez, 1997.

200

What Proficient Readers Do

◆ They use prior knowledge to—
  • make connections with the topic;
  • evaluate how well they understand what they are reading;
  • make predictions, inferences, and generalizations;
  • draw conclusions; and
  • store new information to create their own interpretations.

◆ They identify the most important themes and ideas in the text and use them to focus their reading and thinking.

◆ They ask questions as they read.

◆ They create mental pictures of what they read.

◆ They use a variety of fix–up strategies to repair comprehension when it falters.

◆ They synthesize what they have read.

Source: Keene & Zimmerman, 1997.

Successful English Language Learners' Reading Behaviors

◆ They hold positive self–images of themselves as readers.

◆ They read in broad phrases and skip unimportant words.

◆ They understand the relationships between their two language systems.

◆ They search for cognates.

◆ They transfer information across their two languages.

◆ They reflect on the meaning of the text in either the first or second language.

Sources: Jimenez, 1997; Singhal, 2001.

Chapter 6

Two Kinds of Reading Strategies for English Language Learners

Unsuccessful strategies

1. Thinking about something else while you are reading.
2. Skipping parts you do not understand and not coming back to make sense of them later.
3. Reading as rapidly as possible.
4. Concentrating on figuring out what the words are.
5. Making a list of every word you do not know.
6. Looking up all of the words that you do not know in a dictionary.
7. Repeating the main idea over and over.

Successful strategies

1. Setting purposes for your reading.
2. Thinking about what you already know about the topic.
3. Thinking about what you do not know about the topic.
4. Concentrating on getting the meaning.
5. Underlining important parts.
6. Asking questions as you read.
7. Asking questions about the parts you do not understand.
8. Using other information to figure out what you do not understand.
9. Taking notes.
10. Picturing information in your head.
11. Checking back through the text to see whether you remember it.

Sources: Vacca, Vacca, & Gove, 1987; Waxman & Padrón, 1987, as cited in Padrón, 1992.

My Strategy Log

Name: _____ Date: _____

Strategy	How I Used It				
	Monday	**Tuesday**	**Wednesday**	**Thursday**	**Friday**

This page may be reproduced for classroom use.

Why Reading Is Hard: The Language of Texts

Why Reading Is Hard

Directions: Use this page as you view the video clip.

Volcanoes
by Michael George
1993 Creative Education

Volcanoes that erupt regularly are known as *Active Volcanoes*. There are about six hundred active volcanoes on the Earth's sur–face. However, only fifty to sixty active vol–canoes erupt in any given year.

~

Whether sitting in silence or erupting with violence, volcanoes have intrigued people for thousands of years. In an attempt to ex–plain the immense power and unpredictable behavior of volcanoes, our ancient ancestors created myths about evil gods that lived within volcanoes. When angered, the gods would display their fury with eruptions.

~

Today, scientists explain volcanoes without relying on angry gods. However, the true causes for *Volcanic Eruptions* are as fasci–nating as the ancient myths.

Questions to ask to unpack the meaning of the passage.

1. _____

2. _____

3. _____

4. _____

Unpacking content with text language

Volcanoes by Michael George

Who or what is doing the acting?	What is the action?
Volcanoes	are known as
600	are on the earth's surface
50–60	erupt in a year
volcanoes	have intrigued people
ancestors	attempt to explain the power and behavior of volcanoes
ancestors	created myths
gods	would display fury
scientists	explain volcanoes
true causes	are fascinating

Source: Schleppegrell & Achugar, 2003.

Directions: Work with a partner. Read the passage and complete the chart below.

Volcanic Structure

A volcano's structure or edifice is cone–shaped. It is more or less symmetric and is built by an accumulation of lava around the volcano's central vent, an exposed opening on the earth's surface. When the volcano erupts, volcanic material is released through the central vent.

Who or what is doing the acting?	What is the action?

Content Area Reading

Academic Language Functions

Academic language functions are specific uses of language to accomplish academic tasks. Knowledge of language functions enables students to communicate both inside and outside the content classroom (Fathman, Quinn, & Kessler, 1992).

Why teach academic language?

◆ Academic language is the key to success in the grade–level classroom.

◆ Academic language is not usually learned outside the classroom.

◆ Most English language learners do not have fluency in academic language.

◆ Academic language provides students with practice in using English.

◆ Learning strategies can be taught through academic language instruction (Clair, 2001; Jameson, 1998).

A List of Academic Language Functions

accepting	inferring
advising	informing
agreeing	interpreting data
analyzing	justifying
cautioning	persuading
classifying	posing alternative solutions
comparing	praising
defining	predicting
describing	questioning
directing	refusing
disagreeing	requesting
encouraging	seeking information
evaluating	sharing findings
explaining	solving problems
expressing opinions	suggesting
generalizing	synthesizing
hypothesizing	understanding time relations

Sources: Chamot & O'Malley, 1986; Fathman, Quinn, & Kessler, 1992; Short, 1994; Valdez–Pierce & O'Malley, 1992.

Major Types of School Text

	Relate or Recount	Narratives & Stories	Science & Social Studies Reports	Explanations	Science & Math Procedures	Discussions & Arguments
Text Type	What happened on the way to school? How I did on my science project	*The City Mouse and the Country Mouse*	*The American Flag* The American flag is red, white, and blue. It has 13 stripes. Seven are red, and six are white. It has 50 white stars on a blue field.	*Physical Changes* Physical changes are changes of matter from one form to another. Thus, there are no changes in taste, odor, solubility, or the ability to react chemically. Melting ice is an example of a physical change.	*How to see the water cycle in a plastic bag* *How to find the area of a rectangle*	*The benefits of space travel* *Why the government should increase spending for space travel*
Purpose	To relate or retell what happened in one or more events To reconstruct a chronological set of events	To entertain or to teach To address problematic events and their resolutions To relate daily newsworthy events	To share information and findings To share a personal or critical response to a cultural work	To explain information following a sequence To interpret a cultural work's meaning	To tell how to do an experiment, make something, or solve a problem	To take a stand and persuade others to take action To take a position for or against an issue and justify that position To argue a case for or against one or more perspectives on a given issue

Organization Style	Tells who, what, where, and when Relates a series of events Involves personal responses or comments Ends with a conclusion	Tells who, what, where, and when Relates a series of events Presents a problem or conflict Ends with a resolution or an open ending	Relates characteristics or descriptions May use headings and subheadings May use a taxonomy	Explains related information about a topic giving one or more definitions and providing examples, comparisons, causes, or one or more theories behind it	Presents the steps in a process or sequence Proposes a hypothesis or makes predictions Includes materials needed May include charts or diagrams	Tells one or more persons' opinions Includes details and reasons that support the position Ends with a suggested or preferred action or conclusion
Cohesive Devices	Addresses time: *first,* *then,* *next,* *then,* *at the same time,* *after*	Addresses time: *Once upon a time...* *Later that same day...* *Finally,*	May indicate connections: *Therefore,* *However,* *On the other hand,* *Consequently,* *For that reason,* *As a result,*	May address relationships: *when...* *so...* *then...* *near...*	Reports a sequence: *First, ...* *Second, ...* *Third, ...* Proposes a hypothesis or makes predictions: *If..., then...* *Given..., then...*	Addresses degrees of importance, notes similarities, or marks relationships: *should...* *the most compelling reason...* *therefore, ...* *because of this, ...*
Additional Language Features	Past tense Adjectives Action verbs Adverbs Dialogues	Past tense Action verbs Adjectives Dialogues	Verbs *to be* and *to have* Specialized vocabulary Clauses Passive Voice	Present tense Adverbs	Imperatives: *pour...* *stir...* *bake...* *cut...* Passive voice	May include persuasive language: *It is obvious that...* *...makes it perfectly clear that...* *...must...* *...should...* May include reasons for or against an argument

Sources: Gibbons, 2002; Unsworth, 2001.

Teach Students How School Texts Are Organized

Directions: Work with a partner. Describe how you might implement one or more of these suggestions with English language learners.

◆ Read and share a sample text with students, perhaps a narrative. Work with students to identify the purpose of the text—to entertain. Then share another variety of text with them and have them identify its purpose and how it differs from the narrative.

◆ Underline or highlight how the text is organized or shaped. For example, science reports often begin with a statement that is followed by a term that is followed by examples.

◆ Point out the specific vocabulary and grammatical features of the text, noting the kind of verbs that are used and why.

◆ Involve students in text reconstruction. That is, have them reassemble text that has been cut into bits or arranged in jumbled paragraphs or sentences. Or, create cloze passages that focus on the grammatical features or specialized vocabulary that are key to understanding the passage (Gibbons, 2002).

_____

_____

_____

_____

_____

_____

_____

_____

_____

_____

_____

_____

210

Preparing English Language Learners to Read Academic Content

◆ Integrate language and content instruction.

◆ Select content objectives—key vocabulary and concepts.

◆ Select language objectives—key language structures.

◆ Explicitly teach new vocabulary. Use visual aids, realia, demonstrations, hands–on activities, graphic organizers, and other concrete experiences to teach concrete vocabulary.

◆ Make connections with students' background knowledge and experiences or current events to teach the vocabulary of abstract concepts.

◆ Include activities that utilize the four language skills—listening, speaking, reading, and writing (Crandall, 1987; Crandall, Jaramillo, Olsen, & Peyton, 2001; Short, 1991a, 1993).

Each academic discipline is written in a subject–specific style. History, for example, typically includes time references, sequences, and causes and effects. Science, on the other hand, often introduces specific vocabulary words that are followed by definitions and examples. English language learners need to master academic English, if they are to be successful in school (Echevarria, Vogt, & Short, 2004).

Because the time allotted for teaching English language learners both English language skills and academic content is short, both English as a second language (ESL) and content teachers have started to integrate language and content instruction (Short, 1993). This may mean that ESL teachers use content topics as the basis for their instruction. It may also mean that ESL and content teachers collaborate to plan their instruction. The instructional techniques used in these classes often include the use of visual aids, realia, demonstrations, hands–on activities, and prereading activities to teach content and develop students' thinking and study skills (Crandall, 1993; Crandall, Jaramillo, Olsen, & Peyton, 2001; Short, 1991a, 1993).

Native English speakers

When skilled native English speakers read history, they encounter and expect to read past tense verbs. These readers also know that the beginnings of words contain more useful information than the middles or endings of words (Weaver, 1994, cited in Birch, 2002). This may at first seem to be incorrect, because the ends of words contain morphological units that affect meaning. But English is read from left to right, so readers come upon the beginnings of words first. For native English speakers, this means that the ends of words are predictable because of the context in which they occur. Thus, as native English speakers recognize the beginnings of verbs in a history text, they automatically think "past tense" and are likely to not look at the verb endings, because they expect the verbs to be past tense. Because native English speakers also have had many experiences reading past tense verbs, when they see the spelling patterns and remember how they sound, they recognize the meanings of the words almost instantaneously. As a result, many native English speakers are able to understand the meaning of the text quickly and efficiently (Birch, 2002).

English language learners

An examination of social studies textbooks revealed that this discipline contains key vocabulary and reading tasks that are specific to the field (Short, 1993). For example, when studying the Boston Tea Party, recognizing the names of important people (e.g., Samuel Adams and Paul Revere) and knowing how to read timelines will help students read and understand the text. Such concrete vocabulary words "can be taught directly to English language learners, often through visual aids, demonstrations, and movement" (Short, 1993, p. 6).

Recognizing and knowing how to use signal words, such as *three major events* or transition words, such as *however*, *because*, and *on the other hand*, enables English language learners to read and understand their social studies texts better. Also, if English language learners receive explicit instruction in reading strategies that enables them to use their linguistic knowledge of English (e.g., the *–ed* suffix to signal past tense verbs), then they can read more effectively. They also will be able to better understand material in other academic areas, because these same signal words appear in texts other than social studies (Short, 1993).

Ways to Adapt Text

Many teachers know that the textbooks their students are expected to read are too difficult for many of them to read. In response, they seek ways to make the task of reading the text more manageable. A number of ways to adapt reading texts have been recommended for first language students, and they are equally appropriate for use with second language readers (Echevarria, Vogt, & Short, 2004). The adaptations, listed below, may be used before, during, and after reading.

Graphic Organizers: These visual displays of information and vocabulary help students recognize key concepts and their relationships.

- Used *before* reading, they help students build the necessary background information to read the text.
- Used *during* reading, they can help students take notes, see relationships among ideas, and recognize how the text is organized.
- Used *after* reading, they can be used by students to note what they understand and their own responses to the meaning (Buehl, 2001; Macon, Buehl, & Vogt, 1991, cited in Echevarria, Vogt, & Short, 2004).

Examples of graphic organizers include story maps, Venn diagrams, timelines, semantic webs, and charts. (See Crandall, Jaramillo, Olsen, & Peyton, 2001.)

Outlines: Teacher–prepared outlines are designed with the students' needs and the main points of the content in mind.

- Used *before* reading, they provide a guide for what students will read.
- Used *during* reading, they help students take notes.
- Used *after* reading, they can serve as a review of the information.

Outlines that have some of the information on them serve as scaffolding to which students can attach additional information.

Study Guides: Teacher–prepared study guides are designed with students' needs in mind.

- Used *before* reading, they can give students a brief summary of the text and provide a guide for the reading task.
- Used *during* reading, they can provide needed information so students can understand new vocabulary and concepts.
- Used *after* reading, they can offer challenges and opportunities for students to deepen their understanding.

Highlighted Text: Teachers preview the material to be read and highlight key terms, concepts, and summaries or other important information.

- Used *before* reading, only the highlighted text is read. This reduces the amount of reading students are required to do.

• Used *during* reading, the highlighted text provides reminders of what is important.

• Used *after* reading, the text provides a review of the key information.

Jigsaw Reading: This cooperative learning activity helps students by reducing the amount of text that must be read. It also limits the amount of information students must understand.

• Used *before* reading, jigsaw reading can provide students with an overview of the text.

• Used *during* reading, it helps make the reading task more manageable for them, because they do not need to attend to all of the information in the text.

• Used *after* reading, it can provide a review of the information.

Scaffolding Techniques: Scaffolding occurs when teachers assist students in learning new concepts. This assistance, used before, during, or after instruction, may be delivered through the use of paraphrasing, modeling of "think–alouds," and carefully framed explanations that enable students to make connections with the new concept.

Scaffolding may also be provided through the use of a variety of grouping strategies. This may include whole–group instruction in which the teacher teaches, models, and structures student practice with others and then has students use the procedure independently. Or, it may refer to small–group or one–on–one instruction. In these latter instances, students practice applying the new strategy with another, more experienced student (Echevarria, Vogt, & Short, 2004, pp. 26–29).

Directions: Review the two charts below. List one or more reasons why these charts are beneficial to English language learners.

K–W–H–L Chart

Topic			
Know (K)	**Wonder (W)**	**How (H)**	**Learned (L)**
What we know…	What we wonder…	How we can find out…	What we learned or still have questions about…

Sources: Fisher, Frey, & Williams, 2002; Ogle, 1986; Olsen & Gee, 1991.

5–W Chart

Who	What	When	Where	Why

_____

_____

_____

_____

_____

Anticipation Guides

Anticipation guides are composed of lists of statements or phrases that are related to the text topic that students will read. Successful guides include statements that cause readers to activate their prior knowledge about the topic and provoke disagreements with or challenges to their beliefs. In turn, these guides help students set purposes for reading (Conner, 2004).

Anticipation guide: Style #1
The Early American Diet

Directions: Read each sentence. In the section labeled "I think," put a check mark (✔) if you think the information is true. Read the text. In the section labeled "In the text," put an arrow (➜) if the information is in the text. Then compare what you think with the information that is in the text.

I think   In the text

_____   _____   1. The early colonists worried more about whether they would eat than about what they would eat.

_____   _____   2. The Pilgrims eagerly tried new kinds of food.

_____   _____   3. Corn was considered proper food only for livestock.

_____   _____   4. Thomas Jefferson loved corn so much that he grew it in his Paris garden.

Anticipation guide: Style #2
The Early American Diet

Directions: Read each sentence. Write an **A** on the line in front of the number if you agree with the sentence. Write a **D** on the line if you disagree with the sentence.

_____ 1. The colonists' hunting skills served them well.

_____ 2. The thought of varmint stew whets your appetite.

_____ 3. The colonists discovered cranberries.

_____ 4. The settlers learned new ways to cook food.

Anticipation guide: Style #3
The Early American Diet

Directions: Read each sentence. Put a check mark (✔) next to the sentences you agree with in the **BEFORE** column. After reading, put a check mark (✔) next to the sentences you agree with in the **AFTER** column. Compare your Before and After check marks.

BEFORE AFTER

_____ _____   1. The varieties of meat available to the early colonists gave them energy and ambition.

_____ _____   2. The ocean provided the raw materials for the foods the colonists ate.

_____ _____   3. Many colonists died of hunger.

_____ _____   4. A Patuxet Indian taught the colonists how to fish and plant corn.

Anticipation guide: Style #4
The Early American Diet

Directions: Before reading the next chapter, read each statement. Write **OW** on the line, if you think the sentence describes life in the Old World. Write **NW** on the line, if you think the sentence describes life in the New World. Read the chapter. Review your answers and note the page number where you found information that changed or confirmed your answer.

_____   1. Only the very rich ate meat.   page _____

_____   2. A variety of meats were readily available.   page _____

_____   3. Cornmeal was a popular food item.   page _____

_____   4. Foods were often prepared with molasses instead of sugar.   page _____

How to Construct Anticipation Guides

1. Select a text.

2. Prepare statements that focus on the topic addressed in the text.
   The statements should—
   - highlight the important information that is in the text and the information you want students to think about;
   - generate reactions without students having read the text;
   - refer to information within the text that supports, confirms, or refutes them; and
   - challenge students' beliefs (Duffelmeyer, 1994, cited in Conner, 2004).

3. Have students complete the guide before reading the text.

4. Talk about students' responses before having them read the text.

5. Assign the reading of the text, and ask students to use sticky notes or coding to note places in the text that caused them to change their responses to or thinking about the statements.

6. Hold a discussion following the reading that features the changes students made in their responses and thinking. Ask students to refer back to the text to underscore the portions of the text that caused them to make these changes (Conner, 2004).

Expository Paragraph Frames

Expository paragraph frames are a kind of scaffold that can help readers review content and explore how the author organized the information (Cudd & Roberts, 1989, cited in Olsen & Gee, 1991). Using paragraph frames, or partially completed paragraphs, readers have the opportunity to restate the information that they read (Olsen & Gee, 1991). As writers completing these frames, students can practice the ways writers think about and organize topics.

Textbook authors select from a variety of paragraph structures to present their target topics. The way a paragraph is constructed reflects the way people think about and understand a topic. Fowler, Aaron, and Travers (1995) define 10 patterns of paragraph development:

Narration: A report of how events happened, often reported chronologically, in story form, such as encountering a skunk when star gazing

Description: The impression of how a person, place, event, or experience looked, sounded, smelled, tasted, or felt, such as a young child's first dance recital

Illustration: One or more examples or reasons for an action or event or for thinking or believing as one does; for example, what the colonists did to prepare for the Boston Tea Party or reasons for good dental hygiene

Definition: An explanation of what a topic is and what it is not, such as freedom, democracy, and happiness

Analysis: An explanation of the parts, elements, or features of a topic and how they are related, such as the parts of the body and how they work together

Classification: An explanation of how items in a topic can be arranged; for example, explaining how music can be separated into subcategories (classical, rock, easy listening, etc.)

Comparison and contrast: An explanation of the similarities and differences between two or more topics; for example, the similarities between two types of gas–efficient cars or the differences between two classes of animals, such as vertebrates and invertebrates

Analogy: An extended comparison of two or more topics, such as a lesson plan and a menu

Cause–and–effect analysis: An explanation of why something happened and a description of the results, or both; for example, the causes and effects of global warming or outsourcing jobs

Process analysis: An explanation of the sequence of how to do something or how something works; for example, how to build a birdhouse or how a wheel and axle work

To use paragraph frames with students, first examine the paragraph structure of the text and create an appropriate framework for students to use. Prepare students to read the text and have them complete the reading. Olsen and Gee (1991) recommend that following the reading, primary grade students should explain what they read to a partner. This retelling gives them an opportunity to review what they read. With English language learners, explaining what they read to a peer gives them a chance to rehearse the information aloud, thus providing an opportunity for oral practice before being asked to write the information. Finally, after modeling how to complete paragraph frames, have students complete them in pairs, small groups, or individually.

Sample expository paragraph frame: Classification

Rocks

Scientists divide rocks into three groups. They group the rocks by the way they form. The

first group _____. The second group

_____. The third group _____

_____.

Sample expository paragraph frame: Illustration

Inborn Behavior

Inborn behavior is _____. An example of inborn behavior

is _____. The mother duck

_____. The duckling

pecks _____.

Sample expository paragraph frame: Process analysis

How to Prepare Natural Dyes

Follow these six steps to make natural dyes.

1. Choose leaves, roots, fruits, bark, or nuts.
2. Chop _____
3. Soak _____
4. Heat _____
5. Simmer _____
6. Strain _____

Sample expository paragraph frame: Cause–and–effect analysis

Early American Scarecrows

Early American farmers used scarecrows to _____

_____. After a few days, however, _____

_____. So, the best–dressed scarecrows _____

_____.

Even though they were dressed in bright colors, the farmer had to _____

or _____ to keep the

crows from eating the seeds.

Directions: Using content that you are currently teaching, construct a sample expository paragraph frame like the ones above.

_____

_____

_____

_____

Scaffolding Students' Reading Experiences

Fitzgerald and Graves (2004) advocate that teachers scaffold reading instruction, especially for English language learners, so that they can "better understand, learn from, and enjoy each and every text they read" (p. 2). The researchers explain that scaffolded reading instruction helps students better use what they know from personal knowledge and experiences, learn new concepts, and feel that they are successful contributors in the classroom.

To put scaffolded reading instruction into practice, Fitzgerald and Graves (2004) suggest teachers consider each of these categories and these questions.

- Motivating

    What is students' goal for reading?

    Will they be informed, enlightened, inspired, or entertained?

    What can I do to make them really want to read?

- Relating to Students' Lives

    What background information and experiences do the students have?

    Is there anything in the reading that I can relate to their lives?

    How can I help them see these relationships?

- Building on or Activating Background Knowledge

    What might students need to know before they read?

    What concepts might be helpful?

    What vocabulary might be helpful?

    What text–specific features might be helpful?

- Prequestioning, Predicting, and Direction Setting

    How can I help them ask questions?

    How can I help them make predictions?

    How can I help them set purposes for reading?

- Suggesting Strategies

    What strategies do students already have that they can choose to use?

    What new strategy could be introduced and practiced?

    How might students use their native language(s)?

- Involving Students' Communities and Families

    How do the theme, concepts, or vocabulary relate to the students'

    world, and how can I help them make these connections?

Appropriate Teacher Talk

Directions: Read through the following suggestions and list others that you think are useful.

To help English language learners understand English, teachers can do the following:

- Use simple sentences that are familiar to students.

- Reduce or avoid using pronouns.

- Slow the rate of speech.

- Repeat information.

- Rephrase information.

- Enunciate clearly.

- Present information step–by–step using visuals to support the presentation, for example, use diagrams, charts, graphic organizers, pictures, and realia.

- Demonstrate activities without giving away the results.

- Ask students to summarize.

- Ask one or more students to paraphrase (Fathman & Crowther, 2006).

_____

_____

_____

_____

_____

_____

_____

_____

_____

Teaching Reading Strategies

◆ Identify the purpose for reading.

◆ Identify the strategy to be used.

◆ Explain how to use the strategy.

◆ Model how to use the strategy several times.

◆ Explain when and why the strategy is useful.

◆ Model your own thinking about how well the strategy is working.

◆ Model when and why changing strategies may be a good idea.

A Sample of Reading Strategies

Skim: Read the text quickly to get the gist.

Scan: Read the text to find specific, predetermined information.

Look for context clues: Read the text around an unknown word or concept to determine the meaning.

Reread: Go back and read the text again.

Analyze words: Look for word parts (e.g., roots, prefixes, suffixes) and cognates.

Sound words out: Use your knowledge of the sounds of the letters to pronounce words.

Use graphic organizers: Use visual diagrams to show relationships among ideas.

Use flashcards: Repeatedly practice words and phrases to commit them to memory.

Underline: Highlight important portions of the text.

Take notes: Write down the important information.

Ask someone: Get information from a knowledgeable person.

Source: Echevarria, Vogt, & Short, 2004.

Learning Strategies Lesson: Identifying and Evaluating Strategies to Unlock the Meaning of New Words

By Jennifer Delett, National Capital Language Resource Center (Georgetown University, George Washington University, Center for Applied Linguistics)

In explicitly teaching learning strategies, it is important to name the strategy, model it, and discuss it with the students. The goal is for students to be able to assess whether the strategy is useful for them, determine when it is useful, and use it at those times. The teacher facilitates students' gradual independent use of strategies. The following is a lesson that can be used to help students activate their knowledge of the strategies they currently use to unlock the meaning of new words.

Level/language: Can be used for any language and level

Objectives: To identify and evaluate the strategies students are currently using to unlock the meaning of new words. To share effective strategies with classmates.

Rationale: Building vocabulary is an essential feature of learning a second language. Learning to recognize unfamiliar words in a reading passage is often the first step in developing vocabulary. Students have knowledge about language (prefixes, suffixes, and roots) and learning (guessing and inferring) that they use to help them learn and remember new words. Teachers can help students build their second language vocabulary by encouraging them to identify and evaluate the strategies they are using to unlock the meaning of new words.

Materials: Student text

Procedure

Preparation: Students are often used to taking specific steps to solve a math or science problem, whereas they are less likely to use or be aware of a process for learning a language. Having students analyze these steps prompts them to think about their learning and transfer this awareness of a process to language learning. Give the students a math problem or other problem to be solved. Ask them to think about how they would solve the problem and write down the procedure. Discuss responses as a class. Ask students if they ever think or talk about how they figure out the meaning of unknown words when they are reading. Explain that they are going to practice finding the meaning of unknown words in a reading passage.

Presentation 1: Tell students that there are many ways to use what you already know about language and about reading to learn unknown words. "You have knowledge about language (prefixes, suffixes, and roots) and learning (guessing and inferring) that you can use to learn and remember new words. I am sure that you are currently using one or more strategies to do this." Tell them that they are going to read the passage you have given them and underline the words that they do not know. Explain that afterwards they are going to work with a partner to find the meaning of the words they underlined by using the text and what they already know and discuss how they found the meaning of the words.

Demonstrate the process. Read aloud a section from the text that the students are going to read or a text that they have recently read. Underline a few words that students may not know. Then, ask students to listen and watch as you think aloud how you would try to figure out the meaning of the word. (Thinking aloud is a technique in which a person verbalizes his or her thought process while working on a task.) Ask students to explain your process: What did you do to figure out the meaning of the words? Discuss with the class the different strategies you used—transfer of cognates, knowledge of prefixes, or re–reading the sentences and inferring from the context. During the lesson, emphasize the process with students and not the product—the right answer. Getting students to focus on how they learn new words is as important as having them get the correct answer.

Practice: Have students read part or all of the text and underline unknown words. Put students in pairs and ask them to use what they know (context, knowledge of the language, and cognates) to find the meaning of the words. (Students should not be given too much guidance here. The task is for the students to discover what strategies they are already using.) Students take turns using the think–aloud technique you modeled. While one student is working, the other is taking notes on the student's thinking process. Students should work through several words each as the think–aloud process is done.

After working on several words, allow the pairs time to review their strategies. Ask each pair to make a chart on paper with columns for cognates, word analysis (prefix and suffix), inference from context, combination of strategies, and other strategies. Ask students to try to categorize the strategies they used to find the meaning of each word. For example, if a student recognized the word because it looked similar to a word in her native language, then she would write the word she learned in the column for cognates. If her partner read and reread the paragraph to determine the meaning of a word, he would write the word in the column for inference. If a student has used several strategies to figure out a word, she or he would write the word in the column for combination and identify the different strategies she or he used. If a student used pictures, guessing, or another strategy not listed, the student would write the word and the strategy in the column for other.

Presentation 2: Model the evaluation of your strategies for the students. For example, you might say "I first tried to see if the word was a cognate because that was the easiest strategy for me to think of. However, the word was not a cognate. Then I read and re–read the word to see if I recognized any part of the word—the prefix or suffix—and tried to determine the part of speech. Finally, I re–read the sentences around the word to see if I could get the meaning from context. I came up with a meaning for the word that seemed to make sense, and I could go on reading. I used several strategies to unlock the meaning of the word. I think I was successful because I got an idea of what the word meant and I could continue reading for comprehension."

Evaluation: After your modeling, ask the pairs to evaluate the strategies they each used. As each student describes what she or he did (and gives the definition of the word), she or he should follow your model of describing and evaluating the strategy used. Students can note their evaluations in the evaluation column of their chart by indicating whether the strategy was successful, somewhat successful, or not too successful. They should also indicate why.

Once students have had a chance to review their strategies in pairs, discuss the strategies as a group. Have the class discuss each strategy and evaluate its effectiveness. Did it work? Why did it work? Ask students additional questions: "What new strategies did you learn? What, if anything, will you do differently when you encounter new words in a text? How do you know what strategy to use and when?" These questions encourage students to think more critically about what they learned and, more importantly, how they learn.

(As you discuss different strategies, be clear and consistent about strategy names and definitions. Two students could give the same strategic behavior different names.)

Expansion: For homework, ask students to continue reading the text and keep a log of the strategies they use when they encounter new words. After reading, ask them to evaluate the strategies—did they help them understand the text and learn new words?

Source: Delett, 1998.

Directions: Describe how you could use one or more of these suggestions with English language learners.

_____

_____

_____

_____

Think–Aloud Strategies

Monitors comprehension and self–correction

- The reader recognizes when comprehension breaks down and an error occurs.
- The reader asks, "Am I understanding what I'm reading?" or "Is this making sense to me?"
- The reader takes steps to repair the misunderstanding.

Monitors verification

- The reader reads on and notices when a prediction or inference made is correct.
- The reader uses selective attention to identify specific information
- The reader actively chooses to use the title, captions, pictures, or other print clues to make meaning of the text.

Makes inferences

- The reader uses known information to understand the text.

Makes predictions

- The reader uses print and pictures to gain an understanding of the text.

Makes elaborations

- The reader consciously uses text structure and genre and personal experiences to understand the text (Keatley, 1998).

What's Different About Teaching Reading to Students Learning English?
Study Guide

Strategies for Understanding, Producing, and Remembering Information

Directions: For each category, list one or more questions students might ask.

PLAN	REGULATE	PROBLEM SOLVE	EVALUATE	REMEMBER
Set goals *What is the goal of the assignment?*	Ask myself if it makes sense *Do I understand the topic?*	Infer/Substitute *Can I guess what this word means?*	Verify predictions and guesses *Did I find out what I thought I would?*	Manipulate/Act out *What can I do to help me remember this?*
Activate background knowledge	Use background knowledge	Ask questions to clarify	Summarize	Visualize
Predict/Brainstorm	Visualize	Use resources	Check goals	Imagine with a keyword
Selectively attend	Manipulate/Act out		Evaluate myself	Personalize
	Talk myself through it		Evaluate my strategies	Group
	Cooperate			Cooperate
				Transfer/Cognates
				Self-evaluate

Source : National Capital Language Resource Center, 1996.

What's Different About Teaching Reading to Students Learning English?
Study Guide

Summarize: The BIG 10

What readers do	Estimated time
1. Preview the text.	1–2 minutes
2. List two to three items that you and a partner think you will find out.	2–3 minutes
3. Listen and follow along as a reader reads aloud, or read it individually, and list the 10 most important words or ideas.	2–4 minutes
4. Compare your BIG 10 with a partner.	2–3 minutes
5. Work with a partner or individually and write one or two sentences using as many of the BIG 10 as possible.	2–3 minutes

~

SQP2RS

Survey: Read through the text quickly for 1–2 minutes. Get the big picture.

Question: Ask questions that are likely to be answered by reading the text.

Predict: State one to three ideas or key points that are likely to be learned based on the questions.

Read: Look for answers to the questions and confirm or refute predictions.

Respond: Answer the questions and ask new questions for the next section of the text.

Summarize: Explain the key points in writing.

Source: Echevarria, Vogt, & Short, 2004.

What's Different About Teaching Reading to Students Learning English?
Study Guide

Slice of Life

How to carve a turkey:

Assemble the following tools—carving knife, hot water, soap, wash cloth, two bath towels, barbells, and a meat cleaver.

If the house lacks a meat cleaver, an ax may be substituted. If it is, add bandages, sutures, and iodine to above list.

Begin by moving the turkey from the roasting pan to a suitable carving area. This is done by inserting the carving knife into the posterior stuffed area of the turkey and the knife–sharpening stone into the stuffed area under the neck.

Thus skewered, the turkey may be lifted out of the hot grease with relative safety. Should the turkey drop to the floor, however, remove the knife and stone, roll the turkey gingerly into the two bath towels, wrap them several times around it and lift the encased fowl to the carving place.

You are now ready to begin carving. Sharpen the knife on the stone and insert it where the thigh joins the torso. If you do this correctly, which is improbable, the knife will almost immediately encounter a barrier of bone and gristle.

This may very well be the joint. It could, however, be your thumb. If not, exercise a vigorous sawing motion until satisfied that the knife has been defeated.

Withdraw the knife and ask someone nearby, in as testy a manner as possible, why the knives in your house are not kept in better carving condition.

Exercise the biceps and forearms by lifting barbells until they are strong enough for you to tackle the leg joint with bare hands.

Wrapping one hand firmly around the thigh, seize the turkey's torso in the other and scream. Run cold water over hands to relieve pain of burns.

Now, take a bath towel in each hand and repeat the above maneuver. The entire leg should snap away from the chassis with a distinct crack, and the rest of the turkey, obedient to Newton's law about equal and opposite reactions, should roll in the opposite direction, which means that if you are carving at the table, the turkey will probably come to rest in someone's lap.

Get the turkey out of the lap with as little fuss as possible and concentrate on the leg. Use the meat cleaver to sever the sinewy leather that binds the thigh to the drumstick.

If using the alternate, ax method, this operation should be performed on a cement walk outside the house in order to preserve the table.

Repeat the above operation on the turkey's uncarved side. You now have two thighs and two drumsticks. Using the wash cloth, soap, and hot water, bathe thoroughly and, if possible, go to a movie.

Otherwise, look each person in the eye and say, "I don't suppose anyone wants white meat."

If compelled to carve the breast anyhow, sharpen the knife on the stone again with sufficient awkwardness to tip over the gravy bowl on the person who started the stampede for white meat.

Slice of Life *(continued)*

While everyone is rushing about to mop gravy off their slacks, hack at the turkey breast until it starts crumbling off the carcass in ugly chunks.

The alternative method for carving white meat is to visit around the neighborhood until you find someone who has a good carving knife and borrow it, if you find one, which is unlikely.

This method enables you to watch the football game on neighbors' television sets and also creates the possibility that somebody back at your table will grow tired of waiting and do the carving herself.

In this case, upon returning home, cast a pained stare upon the mound of chopped white meat that has been hacked out by the family carving knife and refuse to do any more carving that day. No one who cares about the artistry of carving can be expected to work upon the mutilations of amateurs, and it would be a betrayal of the carver's art to do so.

Source: Unknown.

From One Teacher's Perspective

The Classification System

This lesson was created and taught by Ana Oveido Healey, Mulchaey Middle School, Taunton, Massachusetts. Used with permission.

Students

Fifth Grade	Student A	Student B	Student C
Native Language	Bulgarian	Portuguese	Spanish
Native Language Proficiency	Early Intermediate	Early Intermediate	Intermediate
English Proficiency Level	Beginning	Beginning	Intermediate
English Reading Level	Beginning	Beginning	Beginning

Theme: The classification system

Content Objectives

Students will be able to achieve the following:

- Understand that living things are different but share similar structures.
- Use the Classification System to group organisms.
- Categorize information using a graphic organizer.

Language Objectives
Key Vocabulary

class	classify
family	genus
kingdom	order
phylum	species

Language Structures

Synonyms: classify = organize, group, categorize

Comparisons of two and three or more items using –er and –est

Language Functions

Orally describe how objects were classified.

Orally describe and compare sets of objects.

Reading Skills

Students will be able to achieve the following:

- Make predictions using prior knowledge, pictures, and text features (title, captions, and illustrations).
- Identify main ideas and supporting details.

Materials

Walsh, P. (n.d.). *Grouping Living Things*. Glenview, IL: Pearson Education.

Science: See Learning in a New Light. Glenview, IL: Scott Foresman/Pearson.

sets of colored pencils, crayons, and markers

soup mix beans

pictures

Before Reading: Build Background Information

- Have small groups of students identify attributes to group sets of colored pencils.
- Ask groups to share orally and compare their classification systems.
- Record students' responses on chart paper using a word splash.
- Repeat the activity using soup mix beans.
- Ask students to construct sentences using the words on the chart.

During Reading: Guide the Reading

- Conduct teacher read–think–aloud and model how to ask key questions to comprehend text.

    What are the most important words?

    Record the keywords on the word splash.

    What does the author want me to learn in this paragraph?

    Do I understand what I am reading?

    If I don't understand what I am reading, what can I do?

- Note key vocabulary and definitions in the text.
- Note main ideas in text.

After Reading: Review Main Ideas and Vocabulary
- Present and discuss how a mnemonic sentence for the Classification System can help students remember the main ideas.

    King Philip Came Over From Germany Singing

- Complete a word splash

    Students add words to the word splash begun during reading.

    Students use the words as a basis to make oral statements about the main
    ideas, adding details as needed.

- Answer the questions in the science textbook.

Reflections on Instruction

The Classification System lesson was one part of an assignment for teachers attending a reading workshop. The second part of the assignment was to reflect on how the instruction had gone by answering three questions (A, B, and C below). The following comments were those made by the teacher who planned and taught the Classification System lesson.

A. Which strategy seemed to work best and why do you think this happened?

The strategy that worked the best was Teach the Text Backwards. I think this happened because, first, I used the students' prior knowledge during the hands–on sorting activities. This in turn allowed me to include the new vocabulary as we discussed their comparisons. When the time to read the text came, the students had enough language to comprehend the content and answer the questions in the textbook.

B. How was doing what you did different from the way you usually teach reading?

While teaching this lesson, I was aware of using the planned reading strategy, and at the same time I was teaching academic content. I usually teach reading using the selection from the reading program without making connections with academic content.

C. What this experience tells me about teaching reading to students who are learning English is....

This experience has brought me to a refreshing start. English language learners require additional support by way of the use of their prior knowledge and experiences. By helping them make these connections, new content is much easier for them than going right into the reading. Even more, the English language learners stay engaged all the time during the development of the lesson when students' experiences are used. Using the hands–on activities first helped in the success of this lesson. These activities allowed us to develop and use oral language to make connections and construct meaning.

What's Different About Teaching Reading to Students Learning English?
Study Guide   235

The word splash strategy was fascinating for me. This is the first time I have used it. Before reading the lesson, I asked students to write sentences using the words on the chart paper. I was expecting to see correct answers related to the content of the lesson, but I didn't. So, I decided to stop and use it as an assessment tool instead. At the very end of the lesson, I asked the students to finish writing their sentences begun during the word splash. Later, beyond this, I realized that it is an excellent strategy to use at the beginning of a lesson to assess students' oral proficiency and content knowledge and to provide opportunities to introduce needed information for their language development.

After this experience, I plan to use as many reading strategies as possible to help my students not only succeed in English, but also to help them in their academic classes and, at the same time, improve my teaching.

Chapter Summary and Beyond the Workshop

Chapter 6: Content Area Reading and Study Skills
What's Different About Teaching Reading to Students Learning English?

Some native English speakers may

- not need to focus attention on the endings of the words they read because of the contexts in which they occur. The beginnings of words contain more useful information because the endings of the words are predictable (Birch, 2002).

Some English language learners may

- understand more of what they read when they have reading experiences that draw on their linguistic and cultural heritage (Fillmore & Snow, 2002, cited in Meltzer & Hamann, 2004);
- view their native language and English as separate and unrelated (Jimenez, 1997);
- consider their native language as less prestigious than English and lack a biliterate perspective (Jimenez, 1997; Walqui, 2000);
- Benefit from recognizing cognates (Jimenez, 1997; Singhal, 2001);
- transfer information from their native language to English (Jimenez, 1997; Singhal, 2001); and
- reflect on the meaning of the text in their native language or English or both languages (Cohen, 2006; Jimenez, 1997; Singhal, 2001).

Beyond the Workshop

1. Outside reading (1)

Read *Reading Next: A Vision for Action and Research in Middle and High School Literacy, A Report to Carnegie Corporation of New York*, a report that describes what is known based on current research and identifies strategies to improve adolescent literacy. After reading the article, respond to each of the following questions: What are the key points presented in the article? How does the information in this article reflect the four principles of instruction for English language learners—comprehensibility, interaction, thinking and study skills, and connections to students' lives and cultures? What are you doing already that is reflected here? How can you apply the information in the article to modify your current instructional practice? Be prepared to share your responses at the next session. The article is available at www.all4ed.org/publications/ReadingNext/.

2. Outside reading (2)

Read *Teaching Science to English Learners, Grades 4–8*, a guide to help teachers plan, design, and implement science activities that integrate language and content instruction for English learners. Drawing on the five learning principles and four teaching principles that are advocated by the American Association for the Advancement of Science, the guide also includes sample lessons and instructional activities. After reading the article, describe one or more ways you could incorporate these principles and activities in your teaching of science, and describe why the items you selected are beneficial for English learners. The article is available at www.ncela.gwu.edu/pubs/pigs/pig11.htm.

3. Content text review

Select a chapter from a content area textbook that is used at the grade level you teach. Review the chapter to identify what's provided that you could build on and what's missing that you might need to augment. Examine the language structures and conventions that are used in the chapter and describe what you would need to do to prepare students to handle them. Be prepared to share your analysis and suggestions at the next session.

4. Read with a student

Select a passage from a content textbook or content–related tradebook. Plan how to engage the student's prior knowledge and experiences. Identify any new vocabulary and language structures, and plan how to teach them. Plan how to set the purpose(s) for reading. Identify one or more reading strategies that the student will use and plan how you will verify that the student used them. Plan how to assess the student's comprehension of the content. After reading with the student, reflect on what happened during the reading session. Be prepared to share your experience with colleagues at the next session.

CHAPTER 7
Putting It All Together

Goal and Objectives

Goal
Participants will achieve the following:

- Reflect on the basic components of learning to read and consider what is the same and what is different about teaching reading to native English speakers and English language learners.

Objectives
Participants will be able to do the following:

- Describe ways to assess students' reading.

- Describe ways to use assessment results to plan reading instruction.

- Plan a reading lesson that integrates language and content instruction; increases comprehensibility, interaction, and thinking and study skills; and makes connections with students' lives and cultures.

- Describe what is the same and what is different about teaching reading to native English speakers and English language learners.

Assessing Students' Literacy

Best Practices in Literacy Assessment

Best practices in literacy assessment do the following:
- Address important goals and support student learning that is meaningful.
- Draw from the most current understandings about literacy and child development.
- Provide students with an awareness of their own learning and development.
- Draw upon standards and criteria that are made available to students, teachers, parents, and others so that all stakeholders know what's expected.
- Begin with what students know.
- Involve teachers (and often students) in their design and application.
- Empower teachers to trust their professional judgment about learning.
- Foster trust and cooperation between teachers and students.
- Focus on students' strengths rather than their weaknesses.
- Build on the principle that growth and excellence can be conveyed through a variety of forms.
- Treat assessment as an essential part of instruction.
- Collect multiple forms of data over time and through different contexts.
- Provide rich and fair information about students that is meaningful and useful to all stakeholders.
- Lead to a systemic approach for educational improvement in strengthened curriculum, professional development, and assistance for students who need it.
- Provide clear and useful information to all stakeholders.
- Undergo review, revision, and improvement continually.

Source: Winograd, Flores–Dueñas, & Arrington, 2003.

What's at Stake in High–Stakes Testing for English Language Learners?

Potential problems for English language learners in high–stakes testing

The No Child Left Behind Act (2001) mandates that all students in Grades 3–8 be tested annually in reading, science, and math. While the intention of this testing is to raise standards and improve education for all students, the results may be far different for English language learners. Almost all of the high–stakes tests, such as the Iowa Test of Basic Skills, the Stanford 9, or the individual state–constructed standardized tests are written and administered only in English. For English language learners, this means they must make sense of the test questions and demonstrate what they know about the content (Carrillo–Daniels, 2005). Sometimes the sense–making may require them to translate the test item into their native language and then translate the answer into English, a necessary and time– and energy–consuming task (Carrillo–Daniels, 2005; Cohen, 2006). Based on the considerations of these difficulties, students' English language proficiency may not accurately reflect their content knowledge or skills (Menken, 2000, cited in Coltrane, 2002).

Another problem involves the factor of a lack of cultural familiarity. Test items may contain references to events or information that are not familiar to English language learners. Because they come from other cultures and bring other experiences and background knowledge, they may not be familiar with what is typically known by their native English–speaking peers who have lived in the United States all of their lives. For example, a multiple choice question about nutrition and what constitutes a proper breakfast involves the concept of *breakfast* as a meal. For many Americans, the items bacon, eggs, toast, and juice come to mind, but for many Asian students, breakfast brings to mind such items as rice, soup, fried fish, and dried seaweed. Choosing the correct answer to such a question may require students to draw on cultural knowledge that they may not have, depending on how long they have lived in the United States (Coltrane, 2002).

Another problem with test questions is the matter of question type. In the nutrition multiple choice question format above, it is possible that students come from countries where they have been expected to write essay responses. They may not be familiar with the multiple choice format (Carrillo–Daniels, 2005) or how to respond to it.

Possible solutions to the problems

Teachers and administrators may consider a number of ways to accommodate English language learners when they are involved in high–stakes testing. These accommodations may include the following (if possible and they don't compromise the integrity of the test):

- Allow additional time for students to take the test and arrange for breaks during the test period.
- Administer the test to small groups of students or arrange to have it administered in a familiar setting.
- When administering the test repeat or explain the directions.
- Administer a translation of the test in the students' native language.

• Allow students to respond in their native languages or orally dictate their answers (Coltrane, 2002).

Beyond addressing the actual test–taking setting and test administration, teachers and administrators should also consider other factors, including the following:

• The tests reflect what has been taught in the content standards and the curriculum.

• Classroom instruction addresses the kinds of language used in tests and test formats.

• Classroom instruction addresses test–taking skills, for example, how to handle multiple choice, true–false, fill–in–the–blank, and open–book tests (Coltrane, 2002; Jameson, 1998).

Reading Tests for English Language Learners

Tests	Test Descriptions	Description of Test Items
Informal Reading Inventory (IRI) (Clay, 1993)	Composed of graded reading passages and comprehension questions, both literal and interpretive; may consist of both oral and silent reading tasks. Oral reading may include a "running record" (Clay, 1993).	Students read the passages and answer comprehension questions. Done orally, students may read aloud or read into a tape recorder. Independent Level: 100–98% words correct 90% comprehension Instructional Level: 94–91% words correct 60% comprehension Frustration Level: 90% words correct 50% or less comprehension (May, 1986)
Qualitative Reading Inventory (QRI) (Leslie & Caldwell, 1995)	Composed of graded reading narrative and expository reading passages, explicit and implicit comprehension questions, retelling, and miscue scoring	Before the oral reading, the student reads a list of words taken from the passage and answers questions about the topic. These prereading tasks help identify the proper level at which to begin the assessment. Scoring adheres to that of the IRI.
Group Reading Inventory (GRI) (Vacca & Vacca, 1989, cited in Peregoy & Boyle, 2001)	Created using narrative or content text similar to that which students will be required to read in terms of concepts, length, and complexity. May be preformed with groups or individuals.	Following the selection of the text, identify the key concepts students should know after reading it. Next, identify the reading skill(s) needed to accomplish the reading task. Design a comprehension check to assess students' understanding.

Strategies and Implementations Chart

Reading Strategies and Implementations in the Content Areas

EP = Early Production; **SE** = Speech Emergence; **I** = Intermediate

Phases of the Reading Process	Strategies	Actions	Implementation Modifications
Before	Identify background information	What is the topic? What do I know about the topic?	**EP** Draws one or more pictures. **SE** Explains orally. **I** Begins a K—W—L chart using words and phrases.
	Preview text, identify unfamiliar words, and make predictions	Skim, scan, ask questions, and use pictures to make predictions about the content of the text. Make guesses about and identify the meanings of unfamiliar vocabulary.	**EP** Uses keywords and pictures on a chart and matches them or groups them to make predictions about the content. **SE** Uses title, headings, print cues, and pictures to make oral predictions about the content. **I** Previews the text and uses a glossary or dictionary to find the meanings of unfamiliar words.
	Identify purposes for reading	What questions do I have? What does the author want me to understand, learn, or do?	**EP** Responds to Yes/No questions. **SE** Rephrases a teacher—formulated question about the purpose of the reading task. **I** Makes predictions about the topic of the reading.

Reading Strategies and Implementations in the Content Areas *(continued)*

EP = Early Production; SE = Speech Emergence; I = Intermediate

Phases of the Reading Process	Strategies	Actions	Implementation Modifications
During	Identify what I know and how I know it (metacognition)	Self—monitor and adjust reading to comprehend text.	**EP** Underlines, circles, or copies unknown words. **SE** Describes what happened during the reading and the strategies used. Highlights sentences that contain the important ideas. **I** Identifies the main idea and details orally or in writing. Re–reads text or uses other fix–up strategies when comprehension falters.
	Make inferences	Identify what is implied or not directly stated.	**EP** Makes a guess: What do the pictures tell you? **SE** Uses the title, headings, and pictures to make guesses about the content of the text. **I** Explains word meanings using context clues.
	Acquire vocabulary meanings	Determine the important unknown words in the reading and learn meanings.	**EP** Draws pictures to identify a few unknown words. **SE** Reads with a buddy to learn new words, perhaps using native language. **I** Lists unknown words and investigates their meanings through questioning, dictionary use, or native language. Takes notes while reading. Asks additional questions in response to what has been read.

© 2007 Center for Applied Linguistics. All rights reserved. May not be photocopied.

Reading Strategies and Implementations in the Content Areas *(continued)*

EP = Early Production; **SE** = Speech Emergence; **I** = Intermediate

Phases of the Reading Process	Strategies	Actions	Implementation Modifications
After	Summarize	Recall main ideas and details.	**EP** Makes flash cards of key terms. **SE** Illustrates and labels main ideas and details. **I** Creates a graphic organizer for the main idea(s).
	Analyze	Identify the logical argument of the text or the organization of the text.	**EP** Arranges pictures, symbols, or keywords in logical order. **SE** Retells the argument of the text using a graphic organizer or outline. **I** Creates an outline or graphic organizer of the text. Writes a summary of the major points.
	Draw conclusions	Seek additional information through the use of additional texts, experiments, or other related hands–on activities.	**EP** Identifies additional pictures that are related to the content. Draws one or more pictures to summarize the content. **SE** Completes a Venn diagram or other graphic organizer to summarize content. **I** Creates a poster or graphic organizer to summarize main points and details

What's Different About Teaching Reading to Students Learning English?
Study Guide

From One Teacher's Perspective

April Morning

This lesson plan was created and taught by Lori Veit, an eighth–grade teacher at North Attleborough Middle School, North Attleborough, Massachusetts. Used with permission.

Materials

April Morning, Howard Fast (1983). New York: Bantam Books.

Opinion poll

Historical fiction graphic organizer: Historical Figures/Events, Clothing/Fashion, Housing/Daily Activities, Food and Drink/Dishes, Cooking, and Language

Visuals: maps, posters of colonial militia and British redcoats, pictures from history textbook

CD player: *April Morning* CD, colonial marching music

Overview of the novel

Some people have compared Howard Fast's coming–of–age novel, *April Morning*, to Stephen Crane's *Red Badge of Courage*. The main character's journey from boyhood to manhood in a matter of hours is a powerful story that many adolescent students easily connect with. However, it is a difficult text for all eighth–grade students, not just English language learners. The novel requires a certain amount of background knowledge of American history and has demanding vocabulary. The opening lesson encourages students to make personal connections to the themes in the novel, and ultimately, students will be required to demonstrate their understanding of characterization and point of view by writing a multiparagraph essay.

General information

Lesson or Topic/Theme: Howard Fast's *April Morning*: Coming of Age during the
 American Revolution
Length of Lesson: 45 minutes
How the Lesson Fits into the Curriculum: Introduction to novels; identification of genres
Class Characteristics:
 Number of Students: 130 (total); class size ranges from 23–29 students,
 5 English language learners
 English Proficiency Levels: 1 Beginning, 1 Intermediate, 3 Transitioning
 Ethnic Mix: 1 Cambodian, 2 Indian, 1 Chinese, and 1 Kenyan

Other useful, general information

This middle school is organized into three academic teams per grade level. My 130 students have five core classes together each day that are taught by a team of five teachers. Our six–day, rotating schedule enables students to experience their classes at different times each day. The English language learners attend one ESL class per day, which does not shift with the rotating schedule. Therefore, these students miss one content class per day, but it is a different class each day.

I. Preparation before reading

Massachusetts English Language Arts (ELA) Curriculum Standards:

9.5   Making Connections: Relate a literary work to artifacts, artistic creations, or historical sites of the period of the setting.

10.4   Genre: Identify and analyze the characteristics of various genres as forms chosen by an author to accomplish a purpose.

English Language Proficiency Benchmarks and Outcomes (ELPBO):

R.4.8:   Compare and contrast various literary genres as forms selected by authors to accomplish their purposes (link to Massachusetts ELA Standard 10.4).

S.3.65: Participate in classroom discussions and other academic interactions, using basic and complex sentence structures and addressing abstract topics.

Objectives
Content Objectives

Students will be able to do the following:

1. Make connections to themes presented in other pieces of literature, as well as topics covered in other content area classes (in this case, history).
2. Identify the characteristics of a literary genre (historical fiction).
3. Summarize the main ideas in a literature selection.

Language Objectives

Students will be able to do the following:

1. Participate orally in a classroom discussion concerning opinions about abstract topics.
2. Participate in a discussion with a partner.
3. Complete a graphic organizer with a partner.
4. Listen to an oral reading of selected text.
5. Use a graphic organizer to summarize text (homework).

Learning Strategies

1. Topic Activator: Opinion Poll
2. Graphic Organizer
3. Partner Work

Key Vocabulary (from the first two chapters of April Morning)

genre	revolution	bastard	atheist	blackguard	crony
deacon	dissenter	Papist	yeoman	cozen	abomination
Fat George	manifesto	rancor	doggerel	slaver	yoke

Key Grammatical Structures/Uses of Language

1. Reading comprehension–difficult narrative text
2. Filling in graphic organizers
3. Summarizing (homework)
4. Identifying difficult vocabulary (homework)

II. Procedures in class

Motivation/Warm–Up

Before Reading

1. Ask students to recall ways other novels/stories have been introduced in class.
2. Distribute opinion polls. Instruct students to read silently and answer honestly.
3. Discuss topics in poll. For example, war is always wrong. Teenagers often rebel against authority. It is acceptable to break the law if you believe the law is morally wrong.

Note: The English language learners are encouraged to share perspectives unique to their cultures and experiences.

During Reading

4. Distribute the novel to students. Listen to the CD reading of the first four pages.
5. Ask two students to explain how they know the story does not take place in 2006. Students share a few examples orally.

After Reading

6. Distribute historical fiction graphic organizer (see attached student sample).
7. Instruct students to work with a partner and re–read the first four pages, recording evidence that the story does not take place in 2006. (Play colonial music in background while students work.) Intermediate to transitioning students would be expected to follow their partner's lead. Distribute history textbooks to groups with English language learners to serve as graphic representation of some of the topics discussed. As a class, develop a clear definition of historical fiction. Share answers in the different categories on the graphic organizer. Instruct students to record answers they were lacking. Examine posters of militia and redcoats together.

Assessment/Evaluation

(Informal) As students work with a partner, the teacher moves around the room and checks with each pair to determine if all students grasp the concept. Intermediate and transitioning English language learners should be able to use background knowledge from history class to discuss aspects of colonial American life and fill in the graphic organizer (perhaps with the assistance of a partner). Beginning to intermediate English language learners are encouraged to more closely examine posters of colonial militia and British redcoats. History textbooks should be used to point out some of the topics discussed in the first chapter. The novel *April Morning* lacks illustrations.

Review/Closure

Review general definition of genre in fiction. Ask students to identify the genres read previously in class. Use some well–known movies to help clarify the idea of genre.

Extension/Homework

Students will read 10 more pages for homework. Students will use a summary strategy introduced to them earlier in the school year.

Procedure

Fold a piece of notebook paper into eight squares. Number each square according to the 10 pages assigned for homework (use front and back). Using bullets, identify three important ideas per page (number may vary) and one or more difficult vocabulary words. Record one piece of evidence per square that shows the novel belongs to the genre of historical fiction. Intermediate to transitioning students are provided with photocopies of the reading assignment and encouraged to highlight important events and to circle difficult words to discuss in tomorrow's class.

250

Reflections on Instruction

The *April Morning* lesson was one part of an assignment for teachers attending a workshop. Another part of the assignment was to reflect on how the instruction had gone by answering five questions (1, 2, 3, 4, and 5 below).

1. How did the lesson increase comprehensibility?

Most students were very successful with the completion of the graphic organizer to categorize and clarify information with a partner. We then further clarified the information by bringing the subject back to a whole classroom discussion. Every student had the opportunity to add to his or her responses while listening to the responses of others. Both English language learners and students with Individualized Educational Programs (IEPs) were encouraged by my aide to self–assess their own answers and improve their responses. In my opinion, modeling is one of the best teaching techniques a teacher can use. Again, both students with IEPs and students learning to speak English benefited from watching me fill in the graphic organizer first. Highlighted photocopies of the text also assisted English language learners in their search for the four perspectives.

2. How did the lesson increase interaction?

All students communicated their thoughts aloud to another student or to the whole class. Partner work allowed students to initially discuss their ideas without taking the risk of volunteering information in front of the entire class. This is always helpful to English language learners. I find that students are far more apt to volunteer information orally when they have first shared information with a partner or a group.

3. How did the lesson increase thinking and study skills?

While working with partners, students questioned, explained, and clarified ideas in order to agree upon answers. For example, during the lesson, I heard students disagreeing about the definition of historical fiction. As they debated their answer, they unknowingly assisted English language learners (and others who needed guidance) by modeling aloud good analyzing strategies and other thinking skills.

4. How did the lesson develop academic language?

This lesson reinforced the use of academic language used in history texts as well as introduced vocabulary that is difficult for all eighth–grade students. Although the lesson presented here was not specifically a vocabulary lesson, students were required to pick out words or phrases that indicated the story was set in the past. Words like yoke and references to individuals like Fat George are difficult for English language learners who may possess less background knowledge of American history. The use of posters, maps, and history textbooks with illustrations was helpful.

5. How did the lesson make connections to students' lives and cultures?

This lesson allowed students to share opinions about some very touchy subjects—war, parents, authority, immoral laws, and so on. The conversation generated by these topics is always quite animated and even sometimes a bit heated. Because the topic activator is based on opinion, I never have a difficult time getting students to warm up to the subject. I find that English language learners are often quite willing to share during these types of discussions. As you might expect, my Asian students had some very interesting things to say about parents, respect, and authority.

The following comments (1, 2, 3, 4, 5, and 6 below) were also made by the teacher who planned and taught the *April Morning's* lesson.

1. Overall, how did the lesson work for your students?

Overall, I think the lesson went very well. All students, including IEP students and English language learners, were able to demonstrate their understanding of the historical fiction genre by the end of the lesson.

2. What part(s) of the lesson worked particularly well?

Graphic organizers are so helpful! Although I teach eighth grade now, I was once an elementary school teacher, and most of the time (without even thinking about it) I presented information in three ways: orally, visually, and on paper. Graphic organizers help students who are struggling with the abstract concepts—sequencing, categorizing, and summarizing to name a few.

3. Did any part(s) of the lesson work less well? Why?

Although the lesson went well as a whole, I think the difficult vocabulary in *April Morning* is always a challenge for me as a teacher. I do not have leveled classes, and some of my students are able to fly through the novel while others (including English language learners) are struggling to get through just a chapter. I need to improve my sheltered instruction activities for English language learners so that they can more easily access meaning.

4. How did you assess student learning of the academic language and content? How well did the students learn the language and content?

I assessed the students informally and through the use of a rubric. I always distribute rubrics to students ahead of time so they can also self–assess while they work on an assignment. I believe the majority of the students were quite successful.

5. What will you do differently the next time you teach these lessons?

I believe that I should alter my historical fiction genre assignment by giving beginning and transitioning students more support. These students could be provided with a word bank or pictures that they could cut and glue into appropriate categories. I would also like to try some new vocabulary strategies throughout the reading of this novel.

6. What did you learn from this experience that you can apply to other lessons?

I believe I learned to be even more visual and to demonstrate difficult ideas and instructions in a more concrete fashion. For example, we are finished with the novel, and right now students are working on the final assessment—a colonial newspaper. I presented my directions in a totally different way this year. I first started with a newspaper scavenger hunt. Students (working in groups of four) had to cut sample articles, banners, illustrations, political cartoons, and so on from actual newspapers and create a poster showing the major components of a newspaper. The students really enjoyed this activity. It was so visual and hands–on! The next day I asked students to chart everything they learned about the book. I gave them several categories: genre, characters, setting, plot, conflict, theme, tone/mood, vocabulary, and so on. I then asked them to place these two posters side by side. I told them I wasn't going to give them a final test on the novel. Instead they would be required to show me what they learned through the design of a colonial newspaper based on the book. It was like dozens of light bulbs were going off all over the room! I also distributed a typed list of project requirements, but the posters really did the trick. I even picked the best ones and created a question/answer bulletin board for students to refer to while working on their projects. We are currently in the finishing stages and I am very proud of their work! All students—mainstream, IEP, and English language learners—are enjoying great success.

A Call to Action: What We Know About Adolescent Literacy and Ways to Support Teachers in Meeting Students' Needs

A Position/Action Statement from the National Council of Teachers of English (NCTE) Commission on Reading, May 2004

Purpose

The purpose of this document is to provide a research–based resource for media, policy makers, and teachers that acknowledges the complexities of reading as a developmental process and addresses the needs of secondary readers and their teachers.

What is reading?

The NCTE Commission on Reading has produced a statement, "On Reading, Learning to Read, and Effective Reading Instruction," that synthesizes current research on reading. Reading is defined as a complex, purposeful, social, and cognitive process in which readers simultaneously use their knowledge of spoken and written language, their knowledge of the topic of the text, and their knowledge of their culture to construct meaning. Reading is not a technical skill acquired once and for all in the primary grades but rather a developmental process. A reader's competence continues to grow through engagement with various types of texts and wide reading for various purposes over a lifetime.

What is unique about adolescent literacy?

In middle and high schools, students encounter academic discourses and disciplinary concepts in such fields as science, mathematics, and the social sciences that require different reading approaches from those used with more familiar forms such as literary and personal narratives (Kucer, 2005). These new forms, purposes, and processing demands require that teachers show, demonstrate, and make visible to students how literacy operates within the academic disciplines (Keene & Zimmermann, 1997; Tovani, 2000).

Adolescents are already reading in multiple ways, using literacy as a social and political endeavor in which they engage to make meaning and act on their worlds. Their texts range from clothing logos to music to specialty magazines to Web sites to popular and classical literature. In the classroom, it is important for teachers to recognize and value the multiple literacy resources students bring to the acquisition of school literacy.

In effective schools, classroom conversations about how, why, and what we read are important parts of the literacy curriculum (Applebee, 1996: Schoenbach, Greenleaf, Cziko, & Hurwitz, 1999). In fact, discussion–based approaches to academic literacy content are strongly linked to student achievement (Applebee, Langer, Nystrand, & Gamoran, 2003). However, high–stakes testing, such as high school exit exams, is not only narrowing the content of the literacy curriculum but also constraining instructional approaches to reading (Amrein & Berliner, 2002; Madaus, 1998). Limited, "one right answer" or "main idea" models of reading run counter to recent research findings, which call for a richer, more engaged approach to literacy instruction (Campbell, Donahue, Reese, & Phillips, 1996; Taylor, Anderson, Au, & Raphael, 1999).

What current research is showing teachers

1) That literacy is a dynamic interaction of the social and cognitive realms, with textual understandings growing from students' knowledge of their worlds to knowledge of the external world (Langer, 2002). All students need to go beyond the study of discrete skills and strategies to understand how those skills and strategies are integrated with life experiences. Langer (2002) found that literacy programs that successfully teach at–risk students emphasize connections between students' lives, prior knowledge, and texts, and emphasize student conversations to make those connections.

2) That the majority of inexperienced adolescent readers need opportunities and instructional support to read many and diverse types of texts in order to gain experience, build fluency, and develop a range as readers (Greenleaf, Schoenbach, Cziko, & Mueller, 2001; Kuhn & Stahl, 2000). Through extensive reading of a range of texts, supported by strategy lessons and discussions, readers become familiar with written language structures and text features, develop their vocabularies, and read for meaning more efficiently and effectively. Conversations about their reading that focus on the strategies they use and their language knowledge help adolescents build confidence in their reading and become better readers (Goodman & Marek, 1996).

3) That most adolescents do not need further instruction in phonics or decoding skills[1] (Ivey & Baker, 2004). Research summarized in the National Reading Panel report noted that the benefits of phonics instruction are strongest in first grade, with diminished results for students in subsequent grades. Phonics instruction has not been seen to improve reading comprehension for older students (National Reading Panel, 2000). In cases in which older students need help to construct meaning with text, instruction should be targeted and embedded in authentic reading experiences.

4) That utilizing a model of reading instruction focused on basic skills can lead to the mislabeling of some secondary readers as struggling readers and nonreaders because they lack extensive reading experience, depend on different prior knowledge, and/or comprehend differently or in more complex ways. A large percentage of secondary readers who are so mislabeled are students of color and/or students from lower socioeconomic backgrounds. Abundant research suggests that the isolated skill instruction they receive may perpetuate low literacy achievement rather than improve their competence and engagement in complex reading tasks. (Allington, 2001; Alvermann & Moore, 1991; Brown, 1991; Hiebert, 1991; Hull & Rose, 1989; Knapp & Turnbull, 1991; Sizer, 1992). In addition, prescriptive, skills–based reading instruction mislocates the problem as the students' failure to learn, rather than the institution's failure to teach reading as the complex mental and social activity it is (Greenleaf, Schoenbach, Cziko, & Mueller, 2001).

---

[1] Adolescent English language learners may need phonics instruction, especially if they have little or no literacy in their native language.

---

5) That effective literacy programs move students to deeper understandings of texts and increase their ability to generate ideas and knowledge for their own uses (Newmann, King, & Rigdon, 1997).

6) That assessment should focus on underlying knowledge in the larger curriculum and on strategies for thinking during literacy acts (Darling–Hammond & Falk, 1997; Langer, 2000; Smith, 1991). Likewise, preparation for assessment (from ongoing classroom measures to high–stakes tests) should focus on the critical components above.

What adolescent readers need

- Sustained experiences with diverse texts in a variety of genres and offering multiple perspectives on real–life experiences. Although many of these texts will be required by the curriculum, others should be self–selected and of high interest to the reader. Wide independent reading develops fluency, builds vocabulary and knowledge of text structures, and offers readers the experiences they need to read and construct meaning with more challenging texts. The text should be broadly viewed to include print, electronic, and visual media.
- Conversations/discussions regarding texts that are authentic, student initiated, and teacher facilitated. Such discussion should lead to diverse interpretations of a text that deepen the conversation.
- Experience in thinking critically about how they engage with texts:
  When do I comprehend?
  What do I do to understand a text?
  When do I not understand a text?
  What can I do when meaning breaks down?
- Experience in critical examination of texts that helps them to achieve the following:
  Recognize how texts are organized in various disciplines and genres.
  Question and investigate various social, political, and historical content and purposes within texts.
  Make connections between texts, and between texts and personal experiences to act on and react to the world.
  Understand multiple meanings and richness of texts and layers of complexity.

What teachers of adolescents need

- Adequate and appropriate reading materials that tap students' diverse interests and represent a range of difficulty.
- Continued support and professional development that enable teachers to achieve the following:
  Bridge between adolescents' rich literate backgrounds and school literacy.
  Teach literacy in their disciplines as an essential way of learning in their disciplines.
  Recognize when students are not making meaning with text and provide appropriate, strategic assistance to read course content effectively.

Facilitate student–initiated conversations regarding texts that are authentic and relevant to real–life experiences.

Create environments that allow students to engage in critical examinations of texts as they dissect, deconstruct, and reconstruct in an effort to engage in meaning making and comprehension processes.

Available at www.ncte.org/about/over/positions/category/read/118622.htm.

Beyond the Workshop

1. Reading lesson

Using the Reading Lesson Plan and Reflections on Instruction in this chapter, plan and teach two or more lessons. Share the results of the instruction with a peer.

2. Assess a student

Select a student and administer one of the standardized and one of the informal assessments described in the chapter. Review the results and describe their usefulness in terms of planning for instruction.

References

Adams, M. J. (1990). *Beginning to read: Thinking and learning about print.* Cambridge, MA: MIT Press.

Adams, M. J., Foorman, B., Lundberg, I., & Beeler, T. (1998). *Phonemic awareness in young children.* Baltimore: Brookes.

Adger, C., Kalyanpur, M., Peterson, D., & Bridger, T. (1995). *Engaging students: Thinking, talking, cooperating.* Thousand Oaks, CA: Corwin.

Adler, C. R. (Ed.). (2001). *Put reading first: The research building blocks for teaching children to read.* Washington, DC: Partnership for Reading, National Institute for Literacy, National Institute of Child Health and Human Development, and U.S. Department of Education. Retrieved October 23, 2006, from http://www.nifl.gov/partnershipforreading/publications/PFRbooklet.pdf

Allen, C. (1992). *Japanese numerals from Japan: Traditions and trends.* Torrance, CA: Good Apple.

Allen, J. (2003). But they still can't (or won't) read! Helping children overcome roadblocks to reading. *Language Arts, 80,* 268–274.

Allen, T. (n.d.). *The taxonomy of educational objectives.* Retrieved October 23, 2006, from http://www.humboldt.edu/~tha1/bloomtax.html

Allington, R. L. (2001). *What really matters for struggling readers: Designing research–based programs.* New York: Addison Wesley Longman.

Alvermann, D., & Moore, D. (1991). Secondary school reading. In R. Barr, M. L. Kamil, P. Mosenthal, & P. D. Person (Eds.), *Handbook of reading research* (vol. 2, pp. 951–983). New York: Longman.

Amrein, A. L., & Berliner, D. C. (2002). High–stakes testing, uncertainty, and student learning. *Educational Policy Analysis Archives, 10*(18). Retrieved October 23, 2006, from http://epaa.asu.edu/epaa/v10n18

Anderson, N. J. (2002). *The role of metacognition in second language teaching and learning.* ERIC Digest. Washington, DC: Center for Applied Linguistics. Retrieved October 23, 2006, from http://www.cal.org/resources/digest/0110anderson.html

Anderson, R. C., Hiebert, E. H., Scott, J. A., & Wilkinson, I. A. G. (1985). *Becoming a nation of readers: The report of the commission on reading.* Washington, DC: National Institute of Education.

Anderson, V. A., & Roit, M. (1993). Planning and implementing collaborative strategy instruction for delayed readers in grades 6–10. *Elementary School Journal, 94,* 121–137.

Anstrom, K. (1997). *Academic achievement for secondary language minority students: Standards, measures, and promising practices.* Washington, DC: National Clearinghouse for Bilingual Education. Retrieved October 23, 2006, from http://www.ncela.gwu.edu/pubs/reports/acadach.htm

References

Antunez, B. (2002). *Implementing reading first with English language learners* (Directions in Language and Education #15). Washington, DC: National Clearinghouse for English Language Acquisition & Language Instruction Educational Programs.

Applebee, A. (1996). *Curriculum as conversation: Transforming traditions of teaching and learning.* Chicago: University of Chicago Press.

Applebee, A., Langer, J., Nystrand, M., & Gamoran, A. (2003). Discussion–based approaches to developing understanding: Classroom instruction and student performance in middle and high school English. *American Educational Research Journal, 40,* 685–730.

Appleton–Smith, L. (1998). *A book to remember.* Lyme, NH: Flyleaf. Available from http://www.flyleafpublishing.com

Au, K. H. (1993). *Literacy instruction in multicultural settings.* New York: Harcourt Brace Jovanovich.

August, D., & Shanahan, T. (Eds.). (2006). *Developing literacy in second–language learners: A report of the National Literacy Panel on Language–Minority Children and Youth.* Mahwah, NJ: Erlbaum.

Barnhardt, S. (1997, December). Development of strategies use and instruction across levels of language study. *NCLRC Readings: Newsletter. The NCLRC Language Resource.* Retrieved October 23, 2006, from http://nclrc.org/readings/caidlr11.htm#BM1

Beck, I. L. (2006). *Making sense of phonics: The how's and why's.* New York: Guilford.

Beck, I. L., & McKeown, M. G. (1991). Conditions of vocabulary acquisition. In R. Barr, M. Kamil, P. Mosenthal, & P. D. Pearson (Eds.), *Handbook of reading research* (vol. 2, pp. 789–814). New York: Longman.

Beck, I. L., & McKeown, M. G. (1997). *Questioning the author: An approach for enhancing student engagement with text.* Newark, DE: International Reading Association.

Beck, I. L., McKeown, M. G., & Kucan, L. (2002). *Bringing words to life: Robust vocabulary instruction.* New York: Guilford.

Beimiller, A., & Slonin, N. (2001). Estimating root word vocabulary growth in normative and advantaged populations: Evidence for a common sequence of vocabulary acquisition. *Journal of Educational Psychology, 93,* 498–520.

Bell, J. S. (1995). The relationship between L1 and L2 literacy: Some complicating factors. *TESOL Quarterly, 29,* 687–704.

Bernhardt, E. (2003). Challenges to reading research from a multilingual world. *Reading Research Quarterly, 38,* 112–119.

Bialystok, E. (1997). Effects of bilingualism and biliteracy on children's emerging concepts of print. *Developmental Psychology, 33,* 429–440.

Birch, B. M. (2002). *English L2 reading: Getting to the bottom*. Mahwah, NJ: Erlbaum.

Bloom, B. S. (1956). *Taxonomy of educational objectives. Handbook I: The cognitive domain*. New York: David McKay.

Bodrova, E., Leong, D. J., & Semenov, D. (1998). *100 most frequent words in books for beginning readers*. Denver, CO: Mid–Continent Research for Education and Learning.

Bond, G., & Dykstra, R. (1967). The cooperative research program in first–grade reading instruction. *Reading Research Quarterly, 2,* 5–142.

Brown, J. (1994). *Travels with Ted*. Oxford, MA: Wilson Reading System.

Brown, R. G. (1991). *Schools of thought: How the politics of literacy shape thinking in the classroom*. San Francisco: Jossey–Bass.

Buehl, D. (2001). *Classroom strategies for interactive learning* (2nd ed.). Newark, DE: International Reading Association.

Burns, M. S., Griffin, P., & Snow, C. (1999). *Starting out right*. Washington, DC: National Academy Press.

Burt, M., Peyton, J. K., & Adams, R. (2003). *Reading and adult English language learners: A review of the research*. Washington, DC: Center for Applied Linguistics.

Calderón, M. (2004). *Evidence–based program for ELLs*. Baltimore: Johns Hopkins University, Center for Data–Driven Reform.

Campbell, J., Donahue, P., Reese, C., & Phillips, G. (1996). *National Assessment of Educational Progress 1994 reading report card for the nation and the states*. Washington, DC: U.S. Department of Education, National Center for Education Statistics.

Campbell, K. (1998). *Great Leaps reading program*. Gainesville, FL: Diarmuid. Available from http://www.GreatLeaps.com

Capps, R., Fix, M., Murray, J., Ost, J., Passel, J., & Herwanton, S. (2005). *The new demography of America's schools: Immigration and the No Child Left Behind Act*. Washington, DC: The Urban Institute.

Carlisle, J. E. (2004). Morphological processes influencing literacy learning. In C. A. Stone, E. R. Stillman, B. J. Ehren, & K. Apel (Eds.), *Handbook on language and literacy: Development and disorders* (pp. 318–339). New York: Guilford.

Carlson, G. R. (1974). Literature is. *English Journal, 63,* 23–27.

Carnegie, D., Carnegie, D., & Prell, A. R. (1998). *How to win friends and influence people*. New York: Simon & Schuster.

Carrillo–Daniels, M. (2005, July). Accommodating linguistic diversity in testing. *Bilingual Basics*.

References

Celce–Murcia, M., & Goodwin, J. M. (1991). Teaching pronunciation. In M. Celce–Murcia (Ed.), *Teaching English as a second or foreign language* (pp. 136–153). Boston: Heinle & Heinle.

Center for Applied Linguistics. (2002). *Why reading is hard.* Washington, DC: Author.

Center for Research on Education, Diversity & Excellence. (2002, Summer). Five standards featured in new media. *Talking Leaves. 6*(2). Retrieved October 23, 2006, from htttp://www.cal.org/crede/pubs/tl–15.pdf

Center for the Improvement of Early Reading Achievement (CIERA). (2001). *Teaching every child to read: Frequently asked questions.* Ann Arbor, MI: Author. Available from htttp://www.ciera.org/library/instresrc/tecr/index.html

Chall, J. S. (1967). *Learning to read: The great debate.* New York: McGraw–Hill.

Chall, J. S. (1996). *Stages of reading development* (2nd ed.). Orlando, FL: Harcourt Brace.

Chamot, A., Barnhardt, S., El–Dinary, P., & Robbins, J. (1999). *The learning strategies handbook.* White Plains, NY: Addison Wesley Longman.

Chamot, A., & O'Malley, J. (1986). *A cognitive academic language learning approach: An ESL content–based curriculum.* Rosslyn, VA: National Clearinghouse for Bilingual Education.

Chamot, A., & O'Malley, J. (1994). *The CALLA handbook: Implementing the cognitive academic language learning approach.* Reading, MA: Addison Wesley.

Christian, D. (1996). Language development in two–way immersion: Trends and prospects. In J. E. Alatis, C. A. Straehle, M. Ronkin, & B. Gallenberger (Eds.), *Georgetown University Round Table 1996* (pp. 30–42). Washington, DC: Georgetown University Press.

Clair, N. (Ed.). (2001). *Why reading is hard: Viewers guide.* Washington, DC, and McHenry, IL: Center for Applied Linguistics and Delta Systems.

Clark, D. (1999). *Learning domains or Bloom's taxonomy: The three types of learning.* Retrieved October 23, 2006, from htttp://www.nwlink.com/~donclark/hrd/bloom.html

Clay, M. M. (1993). *Reading recovery: A guidebook for teachers in training.* Portsmouth, NH: Heinemann.

Cloud, N., Genesee, F., & Hamayan, E. (2000). *Dual language instruction: A handbook for enriched education.* Boston: Heinle & Heinle.

Cohen, A. D. (2006, March 15). *Translating in L2 reading? Exercising the inner voice.* PowerPoint presentation at the annual meeting of Teachers of English to Speakers of Other Languages, Tampa, Florida.

Collier, V. (1989). How long? A synthesis of research on academic achievement in a second language. *TESOL Quarterly, 23,* 617–641.

Collier, V. (1995a). Acquiring a second language for school. *Directions in Language and Education, 1*(4). Retrieved January 30, 2007, from htttp://www.ncela.gwu.edu/pubs/directions/04.htm

Collier, V. (1995b). *Promising academic success for ESL students: Understanding second language acquisition for school.* Woodside, NY: Bastos Educational Books.

Colorado Department of Education. (1997). *Handbook on planning for limited English proficient (LEP) student success.* Denver: Author. Retrieved January 30, 2007, from http://www.ncela.gwu.edu/policy/states/colorado/lephandbook.pdf

Colorado Department of Education. (2001). *Read for the fun of it: Teen read week.* Denver: Author. Retrieved October 23, 2006, from http://www.cde.state.co.us/cdelib/download/pdf/teenweek_pkt.pdf

Coltrane, B. (2002, November). *English language learners and high–stakes tests: An overview of the issues.* ERIC Digest. Washington, DC: Center for Applied Linguistics. Retrieved October 23, 2006, from http://www.cal.org/resources/digest/0207coltrane.html

Conner, J. (2004). *L517: Advanced teaching of secondary school reading. Instructional reading strategy: Anticipation guides.* Bloomington: Indiana University. Retrieved October 23, 2006, from http://www.indiana.edu/~l517/anticipation_guides.htm

Covey, S. R. (2005). *The 8th habit: From effectiveness to greatness.* New York: Simon & Schuster.

Coxhead, A. (2000). *The academic word list.* Victoria, New Zealand: University of Wellington. Retrieved October 23, 2006, from http://www.vuw.ac.nz/lals/research/awl/

Crandall, J. A. (Ed.). (1987). *ESL through content–area instruction: Mathematics, science, social studies.* Englewood Cliffs, NJ: Prentice Hall Regents.

Crandall, J. A. (1993). Content–centered learning in the United States. *Annual Review of Applied Linguistics, 13,* 111–126.

Crandall, J., Jaramillo, A., Olsen, L., & Peyton, J. K. (2001). Diverse teaching strategies for diverse learners: Immigrant children. In R. W. Cole (Ed.), *Educating everybody's children: More teaching strategies for diverse learners* (pp. 33–71). Alexandria, VA: Association for Supervision and Curriculum Development.

Crandall, J., Jaramillo, A., Olsen, L., & Peyton, J. K. (2002). *Using cognitive strategies to develop English language and literacy.* Washington, DC: ERIC Clearinghouse on Languages and Linguistics. Retrieved October 23, 2006, from http://www.cal.org/resources/digest/0205crandall.html

Crandall, J., Jaramillo, A., Olsen, L., Peyton, J. K., & Young, S. (2006). Diverse teaching strategies for immigrant children. In R. W. Cole (Ed.), *More strategies for educating everybody's children* (2nd ed.). Alexandria, VA: Association for Supervision and Curriculum Development.

Cummins, J. (1979). Linguistic interdependence and the educational development of bilingual children. *Review of Educational Research, 49,* 222–251.

References

Cummins, J. (1981). The role of primary language development in promoting educational success for language minority students. In California State Department of Education (Ed.), *Schooling and language minority students: A theoretical framework* (pp. 3–50). Los Angeles: California Sate University; Evaluation, Dissemination, and Assessment Center.

Cummins, J. (1991). The role of primary language development in promoting educational success for language minority students. In California Department of Education (Ed.), *Schooling and language minority students: A theoretical framework*. Los Angeles: California State University; Evaluation, Dissemination, and Assessment Center.

Darling–Hammond, L., & Falk, B. (1997). Using standards and assessments to support student learning. *Phi Delta Kappan, 79,* 190–199.

De la Colina, M. G., Parker, R. I., Hasbrouck, J. E., & Lara–Alecio, R. (2001). Intensive intervention in reading fluency for at–risk beginning Spanish readers. *Bilingual Research Journal, 25,* 503–538.

Deci, E. L., & Ryan, R. M. (1985). *Intrinsic motivation and self–determination in human behavior.* New York: Plenum.

Delett, J. (1998, January). A learning strategies lesson: Identifying and evaluating strategies to unlock the meaning of new words. *The Language Resource, 2*(1). Retrieved October 23, 2006, from http://nclrc.org/readings/caidlr21.htm

Denton, C. A. (2000). *The efficacy of two English reading interventions in a bilingual education program.* Unpublished doctoral dissertation, Texas A&M University, College Station.

Dochy, F., Segers, M., & Buelh, M. M. (1999). The relation between assessment practices and outcomes of studies: The case of research on prior knowledge. *Review of Educational Research, 69*(2), 145–185.

Doughty, C., & Pica, T. (1986). "Information gap" tasks: Do they facilitate second language acquisition? *TESOL Quarterly, 20,* 305–325.

Dubin, F., & Bycina, D. (1991). Academic reading and the ESL/EFL teacher. In M. Celle–Murcia (Ed.), *Teaching English as a second or foreign language* (2nd ed.). New York: Newbury House.

Durgunoglu, A., Nagy, W., & Hancin–Bhatt, B. J. (1991). *Cross–language transfer of phonemic awareness* (Technical Rep. No. 54). Urbana, IL: Center for the Study of Reading. (ERIC Document Reproduction Service No. ED334565)

Durgunoglu, A., Nagy, W., & Hancin–Bhatt, B. J. (1993). Cross–language transfer of phonological awareness. *Journal of Educational Psychology, 85,* 453–465.

Durrell, D. D. (1958). *Success in first–grade reading* (3rd ed.). Boston: Allyn & Bacon.

Echevarria, J., Vogt, M. E., & Short, D. J. (2000). *Making content comprehensible for English language learners: The SIOP model.* Boston: Allyn & Bacon.

Echevarria, J., Vogt, M. E., & Short, D. J. (2004). *Making content comprehensible for English learners: The SIOP model* (2nd ed.). Boston: Pearson Education.

Ellis, R. (1997). *Second language research and language teaching.* Oxford, UK: Oxford University Press.

Escamilla, K. (2000). Bilingual means two: Assessment issues, early literacy, and Spanish–speaking children. In *A research symposium on high standards in reading for students from diverse language groups: Research, Practice, & Policy* (pp. 100–128). Washington, DC: U.S. Department of Education, Office of Bilingual Education and Minority Languages Affairs. Retrieved October 23, 2006, from http://www.ncela.gwu.edu/pubs/symposia/reading/bilingual5.html

Eskey, D. E. (1997). Models of reading and the ESOL student: Implications and limitations. *Focus on Basics, 2*(A). Retrieved October 23, 2006, from http://www.ncsall.net/?id=459

Eskey, D. E. (2002). Reading and the teaching of L2 reading. *TESOL Journal, 11,* 5–9.

Fathman, A. K., & Crowther, D. T. (Eds.). (2006). *Science for English language learners.* Arlington, VA: National Science Teachers Association.

Fathman, A. K., Quinn, M. E., & Kessler, C. (1992, Summer). Teaching science to English learners, grades 4–8 (Program Information Guide Series, Number 11). Washington, DC: National Clearinghouse for Bilingual Education. Retrieved October 23, 2006, from http://www.ncela.gwu.edu/pubs/pigs/pig11.htm

Feelings, M. (1992). *Jambo means hello: Swahili alphabet book.* New York: Penguin Young Readers Group.

Feitelson, D. (1988). *Facts and fads in beginning reading: A cross–linguistic perspective.* Norwood, NJ: Ablex.

Fillmore, L. W., & Snow, C. E. (2000). *What teachers need to know about language.* Washington, DC: Center for Applied Linguistics.

Fisher, D., Frey, N., & Williams, D. (2002). Seven literacy strategies that work. *Educational Leadership, 60*(3), 70–73.

Fitzgerald, J., & Graves, M. F. (2004). *Scaffolding reading experiences for English–language learners.* Norwood, MA: Christopher–Gordon.

Fountas, I. C., & Pinnell, G. S. (2001). *Guiding readers and writers grades 3–6.* Portsmouth, NH: Hinemann.

Fowler, H. R., Aaron, J. E., & Travers, J. K. (1995). *The little, brown handbook: Instructor's annotated edition.* New York: HarperCollins.

References

Fradd, S. H. (1998). Literacy development for language enriched pupils through English language arts instruction. In S. H. Fradd & O. Lee (Eds.), *Creating Florida's multilingual global work force: Educational policies and practices for students learning English as a new language.* Tallahassee: Florida Department of Education. Retrieved October 23, 2006, from http://www.ncela.gwu.edu/pubs/florida/workforce98/fradd/literacy.htm

Francis, D. J. (2005). *Developing language and literacy in English language learners: Research, practice, and partnerships.* PowerPoint presentation to the Board of Education, Brownsville Independent School District, Brownsville, Texas. Retrieved October 23, 2006, from http://www.ncela.gwu.edu/resabout/curriculum/literacyDavidFrancis.pdf

Freeman, D., & Freeman, Y. (1998–1999, December/January). Checklist for effective practice with English language learners. *TESOL Matters.*

Fry, E. B., Kress, J. E., & Fountoukidis, D. (1993). *The reading teacher's book of lists.* Englewood Cliffs, NJ: Prentice Hall.

Garcia, G. E. (1999, Fall). Bilingual children's reading: An overview of recent research. *ERIC/CLL News Bulletin, 23.* Retrieved October 23, 2006, from http://www.cal.org/resources/archive/news/199909/main.html

Gardner, H. (1989). *To open minds: Chinese clues to the dilemma of contemporary education.* New York: Basic.

Genesee, F., Lindholm–Leary, K., Saunders, W., & Christian, D. (2006). *Educating English language learners: A synthesis of research evidence.* New York: Cambridge University Press.

Gibbons, P. (2002). *Scaffolding language, scaffolding learning: Teaching second language learners in the mainstream classroom.* Portsmouth, NH: Heinemann.

Goldberg, N. (1986). *Writing down the bones: Freeing the writer within.* Boston: Shambhala.

Goldenberg, C. (1992–1993). Instructional conversations: Promoting comprehension through discussion. *Reading Teacher, 46,* 316–326.

Gonzáles, N., Moll, L. C., Floyd–Tenery, M., Rivera, A., Rendón, P., Gonzales, R., & Amanti, C. (1994). *Funds of knowledge: Learning from language minority households.* Washington, DC: National Center for Research on Cultural Diversity and Second Language Learning. Retrieved October 23, 2006, from http://www.cal.org/resources/digest/ncrcds01.html

Good, R. H., & Kaminski, R. A. (2003). *Dynamic indicators of basic early literacy skills, DIBELS* (6th ed.). Longmont, CO: Sopris West. Available from http://www.soprishwest.com

Goodman, K., Goodman, Y., & Flores, B. (1979). *Reading in the bilingual classroom: Literacy and biliteracy.* Retrieved October 23, 2006, from http://www.ncela.gwu.edu/pubs/classics/reading/

Goodman, Y., & Marek, A. (1996). *Retrospective miscue analysis: Revaluing readers and reading.* Katonah, NY: R. C. Owens.

Grabe, W. (1991). Current developments in second language research. *TESOL Quarterly, 25*, 375–406.

Grabe, W., & Stoller, F. L. (2002). *Teaching and researching reading*. Harlow, UK: Pearson Education.

Graham, C. (1978). *Jazz chants*. New York: Oxford University Press.

Graham, C. (2000). *Children's jazz chants: Old and new*. Oxford, UK: Oxford University Press.

Gray Oral Reading Test Fourth Edition (GORT–4). (2002). Bloomington, MN: AGS. Available from http://ags.pearsonassessments.com

Green, J. F., & Woods, J. F. (2000). *J & J language readers.* Longmont, CO: Sopris West. Available from http://www.sopriswest.com

Greenleaf, C., Schoenbach, R., Cziko, C., & Mueller, F. (2001). Apprenticing adolescent readers to academic literacy. *Harvard Educational Review, 71,* 79–129.

Grognet, A., Jameson, J., Franco, L., & Derrick–Mescua, M. (2000). *Enhancing English language learning in elementary classrooms: Training manual*. McHenry, IL, and Washington, DC: Delta Systems and Center for Applied Linguistics.

Harris, A. J., & Jacobson, M. D. (1982). *Basic reading vocabularies*. New York: Macmillan.

Harvey, S. (1998). *Nonfiction matters: Reading, writing, and research in grades 3–8*. Portland, ME: Stenhouse.

Harvey, S., & Goudvis, A. (2000). *Strategies that work*. Portland, ME: Stenhouse.

Hasbrouck, J., & Tindal, G. (2005). *Oral reading fluency: 90 years of measurement* (Tech. Rep. No. 33). Eugene: University of Oregon, College of Education, Behavioral Research and Teaching. Retrieved October 23, 2006, from http://brt.uoregon.edu/techreports/ORF_90Yrs_Intro_TechRpt33.pdf

Heilman, A. W. (1968). *Phonics in proper perspective* (2nd ed.). Columbus, OH: Charles E. Merrill.

Heilman, A. W. (1972). *Principles and practices of teaching reading* (3rd ed.). Columbus, OH: Charles E. Merrill.

Hiebert, E. H. (1991). *Literacy for a diverse society: Perspectives,policies, and practices*. New York: Teachers College Press.

Hiebert, E. H., Pearson, P. D., Taylor, B. M., Richardson, V., & Paris, S. G. (1998). *Every child a reader: Applying reading research to the classroom*. Ann Arbor: University of Michigan, School of Education, Center for the Improvement of Early Reading Achievement.

Hirsch, E. D., Jr., (2006). *The knowledge deficit: Closing the shocking gap for American children*. Boston: Houghton Mifflin.

Holt, D. (1993). *Cooperative learning: A response to linguistic and cultural diversity*. Washington, DC, and McHenry, IL: Center for Applied Linguistics and Delta Systems.

References

Holt, D., Chips, B., & Wallace, D. (1991). *Cooperative learning in the secondary school: Maximizing language acquisition, academic achievement, and social development* (NCBE Program Information Guide Series No. 12). Retrieved January 30, 2007, from http://www.ncela.gwu.edu/pubs/pigs/pig12.htm

Hudelson, S. (1984). Kan yu ret an rayt en ingles: Children become literate in English as a second language. *TESOL Quarterly, 18,* 221–238.

Hudson, R. F., Lane, H. B., & Pullen, P. C. (2005). Reading fluency instruction and assessment: What, why, and how? *Reading Teacher, 58,* 702–714. Retrieved October 23, 2006, from http://www.fcrr.org/publications/publicationspdffiles/hudson_lane_pullen_readingfluency_2005.pdf

Hull, G. A., & Rose, M. (1989). Rethinking remediation: Toward a social–cognitive understanding of problematic reading and writing. *Written Communication, 8,* 139–154.

Humphreys, J. (1996). *Find your optimum rate of speech.* Retrieved October 23, 2006, from http://www.telemarketingsuccess.com/predictive_dialer/optimum_speach_rate.htm

International Reading Association. (1998a). Learning to read and write: Developmentally appropriate practices for young children. A joint position statement of the International Reading Association and the National Association for the Education of Young Children (NAEYC). *The Reading Teacher, 52,* 193–216.

International Reading Association. (1998b). *Resolution on initial literacy instruction in a first language.* Newark, DE: Author.

International Reading Association. (1999). *Using multiple methods of beginning reading instruction: A position statement of the International Reading Association.* Newark, DE: Author.

International Reading Association. (2001). *Second language literacy instruction: A position statement of the International Reading Association.* Newark: DE: Author. Retrieved October 26, 2006, from http://www.reading.org/downloads/positions/ps1046_second_language.pdf

Ivey, G. (2006). *Interview with Gay Ivey.* Alexandria, VA: Association for Supervision and Curriculum Development. Retrieved October 23, 2006, from http://www.ascd.org/portal/site/ascd/menuitem

Ivey, G., & Baker, M. I. (2004). Phonics instruction for older students? Just say no. *Educational Leadership, 61,* 35–39.

Jacob, E. (1999). *Cooperative learning in context.* Albany: State University of New York Press.

Jaeneung Educational Institute. (2000). *JEI self–learning English program.* (2000). Seoul, Korea: Author.

Jameson, J. (1998). *Enriching content classes for secondary ESOL students: Training manual.* McHenry, IL, and Washington, DC: Delta Systems and Center for Applied Linguistics.

What's Different About Teaching Reading to Students Learning English?
Study Guide

Jimenez, R. T. (1997). The strategies reading abilities and potential of five low–literacy Latina/o readers in middle school. *Reading Research Quarterly, 32*(3) 224–243.

Joftus, S. (2002). *Every child a graduate: A framework for an excellent education for all middle and high school students.* Washington, DC: Alliance for Excellent Education. Retrieved October 23, 2006, from http://www.all4ed.org/publications/EveryChildAGraduate/every.pdf

Johnson, D. D., & Pearson, P. D. (1984). *Teaching reading vocabulary* (2nd ed.). New York: Holt, Rinehart, & Winston.

Just, M. A., & Carpenter, P. A. (1987). *The psychology of reading and language comprehension.* Boston: Allyn & Bacon.

Kagan, S. (1986). Cooperative learning and sociocultural factors in schooling. In Bilingual Education Office, California Department of Education (Ed.), *Beyond language: Social and cultural factors in schooling language minority students.* Los Angeles: California State University; Evaluation, Dissemination and Assessment Center.

Kamil, M. L. (2003). *Adolescents and literacy: Reading for the 21st century.* Washington, DC: Alliance for Excellent Education.

Kamil, M. L., & Hiebert, E. H. (2005).The teaching and learning of vocabulary: Perspectives and persistent issues. In E. H. Hiebert & M. L. Kamil (Eds.), *Teaching and learning vocabulary: Bringing scientific research to practice.* Mahwah, NJ: Erlbaum.

Kauffman, D. (1992, 1997, 1999). *Critical thinking with literature.* Elizabethtown, PA: Continental.

Kauffman, D. (1994). Getting to know Theresa. In J. A. Bennett et al. (Eds.), *Tapir* (p. 76). Benque Viejo, Belize: Cubola.

Keatley, C. (1998, January). Learning strategies research and teaching implications: Helping elementary language immersion students read in a foreign language. *The Language Resource, 2*(1). Retrieved October 23, 2006, from http://nclrc.org/readings/caidlr21.htm

Keatley, C. (2002). *Elementary language immersion students: Changes in reading comprehension strategies across grades.* Retrieved October 23, 2006, from http://www.nclrc.org/readings/hottopics/elemlangimmersion.html

Keene, E. O., & Zimmerman, S. (1997). *Mosaic of thought: Teaching comprehension in a reader's workshop.* Portsmouth, NH: Heinemann.

King, K., & Fogle, L. (2006). *Raising bilingual children: Common parental concerns and current research.* Washington, DC: Center for Applied Linguistics. Retrieved October 23, 2006, from http://www.cal.org/resources/digest/RaiseBilingChild.html

Kintch, W., & Van Dijk, T. A. (1978). Toward a model of text comprehension and production. *Psychological Review, 85,* 363–394.

References

Klinger, J. K., & Vaughn, S. (1996). Reciprocal teaching of reading comprehension strategies for students with learning disabilities who use English as a second language. *Elementary School Journal, 96,* 275–293.

Klinger, J. K., Vaughn, S., Dimino, J. A., Bryant, D. P., & Schumm, J. S. (2001). *Collaborative strategic reading.* Longmont, CO: Sopris West.

Knapp, M. S., & Turnbull, B. (1991). *Better schools for the children in poverty: Alternatives to conventional wisdom.* Berkeley, CA: McCutchan.

Knutson, E. K. (1998). *Reading with purpose: Communicative reading tasks for the foreign language classroom.* ERIC Digest. Washington, DC: Center for Applied Linguistics. Retrieved October 23, 2006, from http://www.cal.org/resources/digest/reading_digest.html

Krashen, S. D. (1981). *Second language acquisition and second language learning.* Oxford, UK: Pergamon.

Krashen, S. D. (1982). *Principles and practice in second language acquisition.* Oxford, UK: Pergamon.

Krashen, S. D. (1985). *The input hypothesis: Issues and implications.* New York: Longman.

Krashen, S., & Terrell, T. (1983). *The natural approach.* San Francisco: Pergamon/Alemany.

Krathwohl, D. R., Bloom, B. S., & Bertram, B. M. (1973). *Taxonomy of educational objectives, the classification of educational goals. Handbook II: Affective domain.* New York: David McKay.

Kucer, S. (2005). *Dimensions of literacy: A conceptual base for teaching reading and writing in school settings* (2nd ed.). Mahwah, NJ: Erlbaum.

Kuhn, M. R., & Stahl, S. A. (2000). *Fluency: A review of developmental and remedial practices* (Report No. 2–008). Ann Arbor, MI: Center for the Improvement of Early Reading Achievement.

Kuhn, M. R., & Stahl, S. A. (2003). Fluency: A review of developmental and remedial practices. *Journal of Educational Psychology, 95,* 3–21.

Langer, J. (2000). *Teaching middle and high school students to read and write well: Six features of effective instruction.* Albany, NY: National Research Center on English Learning and Achievement.

Langer, J. (2002). *Effective literacy instruction: Building successful reading and writing programs.* Urbana: National Council of Teachers of English.

Larrick, N. (1969). The ALL white world of children's books. *Saturday Review, 48,* 63–65, 84–85.

Lehr, F., Osborn, J., & Hiebert, E. H. (2004). *A focus on vocabulary. Research–based practices in early reading series.* Honolulu, HI: Regional Educational Laboratory at Pacific Resources for Education and Learning. Retrieved October 23, 2006, from http://survey.prel.org/cs/rel/create/rvb?x–template=html.form

Leslie, L., & Caldwell, J. (1995). *Qualitative reading inventory II.* New York: Addison–Wesley.

Levine, L. N. (1995). Outline of topics and skills covered in teaching ESL K–12. In S. Hudelson, (Ed.), *English as a second language teacher resource handbook: A practical guide for K–12 ESL programs* (pp. 75–78). Thousand Oaks, CA: Corwin.

Li, D., & Nes, S. H. (2001). Using paired reading to help ESL students become fluent and accurate readers. *Reading Improvement, 38,* 50–61.

Long, M. (1983). Native speaker/non–native speaker conversation in the second language classroom. In M. Clarke & J. Handscombe (Eds.), *On TESOL '82 Pacific perspectives on language learning* (pp. 207–225). Washington, DC: Teachers of English to Speakers of Other Languages.

Long, M., & Porter, P. (1985). Group work, interlanguage talk, and second language acquisition. *TESOL Quarterly, 19,* 207–228.

Madaus, G. (1998). The distortion of teaching and testing: High–stakes testing and instruction, *Peabody Journal of Education, 65,* 29–46.

Maine Department of Education, Division of Curriculum, Federal Projects for Language Minorities. (1991). *Practical practices for ESL te*achers. Augusta: Author.

Maney, E. S. (n.d.[a]). *Directed reading–thinking activity.* Unpublished materials. East Petersburg, PA: Reading Center.

Maney, E. S. (n.d.[b]). Workshop activities for visual discrimination. Unpublished materials. East Petersburg, PA: Reading Center.

Martens, C. (2006). *Cueing systems.* Retrieved October 26, 2006, from http://www.saskwest.ca/teacher/martenschad/

Maryland Department of Education. (n.d.[a]). *Cueing bookmark.* Baltimore: Division of Instruction, Language and Learning Improvement Branch.

Maryland Department of Education. (n.d.[b]). *Teaching thinking skills.* Baltimore: Division of Instruction, Language and Learning Improvement Branch.

Marzano, R., Pickering, D., & Pollack, J. (2001). *Classroom instruction that works: Research–based strategies for increasing student achievement.* Alexandria, VA: Association for Supervision and Curriculum Development.

May, F. B. (1986). *Reading as communication: An interactive approach* (2nd ed.). Columbus, OH: Merrill.

McGee, L. M., & Richgels, D. J. (2003). *Designing early literacy programs: Strategies for at–risk preschool and kindergarten children.* New York: Guilford.

McKenna, B. (2002, Spring). Teacher works magic with CREDE's five standards and Harry Potter. *Talking Leaves.* 6(1). Retrieved October 23, 2006, from http://www.cal.org/crede/pubs/tl–14.pdf

References

McKeown, M. G., Beck, I. L., Omanson, R. C., & Pople, M. T. (1985). Some effects of the nature and frequency of vocabulary instruction on the knowledge and use of words. *Reading Research Quarterly, 20,* 522–535.

McLaughlin, B. (1995). *Fostering second language development in young children: Principles and practices.* Washington, DC: U.S. Department of Education, Office of Educational Research and Improvement. Retrieved October 26, 2006, from http://www.ncela.gwu.edu/pubs/ncrcdsll/epr14.htm

McLaughlin, B., August, D., Snow, C., Carlo, M., Dressler, C., White, C., Lively, T., & Lippman, D. (2000). Vocabulary improvement and reading in English language learners: An intervention study. In *A research symposium on high standards in reading for students from diverse language groups: Research, practice, & policy. Proceedings* (pp. 129–143). Washington, DC: U.S. Department of Education, Office of Bilingual Education and Minority Languages Affairs. Retrieved October 26, 2006, from http://www.ncela.gwu.edu/pubs/symposia/reading/index.htm

McLaughlin, M., & Devoogd, G. L. (2004). *Critical literacy: Enhancing students' comprehension of text.* New York: Scholastic.

Meltzer, J., & Hamann, E. T. (2004). *Meeting the literacy development needs of adolescent English language learners through content area learning. Part one: Focus on motivation and engagement.* Providence, RI: Brown University. Retrieved October 26, 2006, from http://www.alliance.brown.edu/pubs/adlit/adell_litdv1.pdf

Meltzer, J., & Hamann, E. T. (2005). *Meeting the literacy development needs of adolescent English language learners through content area learning. Part two: Focus on classroom teaching and learning strategies.* Providence, RI: Brown University. Retrieved October 26, 2006, from http://www.alliance.brown.edu/pubs/adlit/adell_litdv2.pdf

Menkart, D. (1993). *Multicultural education: Strategies for linguistically diverse schools and classrooms* (NCBE Program Information Guide Series, No. 16). Washington, DC: National Clearinghouse for Bilingual Education. Retrieved October 26, 2006, from http://www.ncela.gwu.edu/pubs/pigs/pig16.htm

Mesmer, H. A., & Griffith, P. L. (2005–2006, December/January). Everybody's selling it—but just what is explicit, systematic phonics instruction? *Reading Teacher, 59,* 366–376.

Mikulecky, B. S. (1985). Reading skills instruction in ESL. In P. Larson, E. L. Judd, & D. S. Messerschmitt (Eds.), *On TESOL '84: A brave new world for TESOL* (pp. 261–277). Washington, DC: Teachers of English to Speakers of Other Languages.

Moats, L. C. (1999). *Teaching reading IS rocket science: What expert teachers of reading should know and be able to do.* Washington, DC: American Federation of Teachers.

Moats, L. C. (2000). *Speech to print: Language essentials for teachers.* Baltimore: Paul H. Brookes.

Moll, L., Amanti, C., Neff, D., & Gonzalez, N. (1992). Funds of knowledge for teaching: Using a qualitative approach to connect homes and classrooms. *Theory Into Practice, 31*(1), 132–141.

Montes, F. (2002, Fall). Enhancing content areas through a cognitive academic language learning based collaborative in south Texas: CAPE Program in South Texas. *Bilingual Research Journal Online, 26(3)*. Retrieved January 30, 2007, from http://brj.asu.edu/content/vol26_no3/pdf/art12.pdf

Nagy, W. E., & Anderson, R. C. (1984). How many words are there in printed school English? *Reading Research Quarterly, 19,* 304–330.

Nagy, W. E., & Herman, P. A. (1987). Breadth and depth of vocabulary knowledge: Implications for acquisition and instruction. In M. McKeown & M. Curtis (Eds.), *The nature of vocabulary acquisition* (pp. 19–35). Hillsdale, NJ: Erlbaum.

Nagy, W. E., & Scott, J. A. (2000). Vocabulary processes. In M. Kamil, P. Mosenthal, P. D. Pearson, & R. Barr (Eds.), *Handbook of reading research* (vol. 3, pp. 269–284). Mahwah, NJ: Erlbaum.

Nash, R. (1997). *NTC's dictionary of Spanish cognates: Thematically organized.* Lincolnwood, IL: National Textbook.

National Assessment of Educational Progress. (1995). *Oral reading fluency scale.* Retrieved October 31, 2006, from http://nces.ed.gov/pubs95/web/95762.asp

National Capital Language Resource Center. (1996). *Teacher resource cards. Model of strategic comprehension and production.* Washington, DC: Author. Retrieved February 2, 2007, from http://nclrc.org/teaching_materials/assessment/assessment_tools/strategy_cards.pdf

National Council of Teachers of English. (2004). *A call to action: What we know about adolescent literacy and ways to support teachers in meeting students' needs.* Retrieved October 31, 2006, from http://www.ncte.org/about/over/positions/category/read/118622.htm?source=gs

National Reading Panel. (2000). *Teaching children to read: An evidence–based assessment of the scientific research literature on reading and its implications for reading instruction. Reports of the subgroups.* Washington, DC: National Institute for Literacy and U.S. Department of Health and Human Services.

Newmann, F., King, B., & Rigdon, M. (1997). Accountability and school performance: Implications from restructuring schools. *Harvard Educational Review, 67,* 41–74.

No Child Left Behind Act of 2001. Pub. L. No. 107–110. Retrieved October 31, 2006, from http://www.ed.gov/legislation/ESEA02/107–110.pdf

Northwest Regional Educational Laboratory. (n.d.). *K–3 developmental continuum oral reading rubric for fluency, rate, expression, and self–monitoring.* Portland, OR: Author. Retrieved October 31, 2006, from http://www.nwrel.org/assessment/scoring.php

Ogle, D. M. (1986). KWL: A teaching model that develops active reading of expository text. *Reading Teacher, 39,* 564–570.

Olsen, M., & Gee, T. (1991). Content reading instruction in the primary grades: Perceptions and strategies. *Reading Teacher, 45,* 298–307.

References

O'Malley, J., & Valdez–Pierce, L. (1996). *Authentic assessment for English language learners: Practical approaches for teachers*. Reading, MA: Addison Wesley.

Padolsky, D. (2002, December). *How many school–aged English language learners (ELLs) are there in the U.S.?* Retrieved October 31, 2006, from http://www.ncela.gwu.edu/expert/faq/01leps.html

Padrón, Y. N. (1992). The effect of strategy instruction on bilingual students' cognitive strategy use in reading. *Bilingual Research Journal, 16,* 35–51.

Padrón, Y. N., Waxman, H., & Rivera, H. (2002). *Educating Hispanic students: Obstacles and avenues to improved academic achievement* (Educational Practice Rep. No. 8). Santa Cruz, CA: Center for Research on Education, Diversity & Excellence.

Palincsar, A. S., & Brown, A. L. (1985). Reciprocal teaching: Activities to promote read(ing) with your mind. In T. L. Harris & E. J. Cooper (Eds.), *Reading, thinking, and concept development: Strategies for the classroom* (pp. 19–20). New York: College Board.

Partnership for Reading. (2001). *Put reading first: The research building blocks for teaching children to read.* Washington, DC: Author. Retrieved October 31, 2006, from http://www.nifl.gov/partnershipforreading/publications/reading_first_print.html

Peregoy, S. F., & Boyle, O. F. (2000). English learners reading English: What we know, what we need to know. *Theory Into Practice, 39,* 237–247.

Peregoy, S. F., & Boyle, O. F. (2001). *Reading, writing, and learning in ESL.* New York: Longman.

Peters, L. W. (1994). *When the fly flew in.* New York: Penguin Books.

Quindlen, A. (2005). *Being perfect.* New York: Random House.

Ramirez, J. D. (2000). Bilingualism and literacy: Problem or opportunity? A synthesis of reading research on bilingual students. In *Proceedings. A research symposium on high standards in reading for students from diverse language groups: Research, practice, & policy.* Washington, DC: U.S. Department of Education, Office of Bilingual Education and Minority Languages Affairs.

Raphael, T. E. (1982). Teaching children question–answering strategies. *Reading Teacher, 36,* 186–191.

Raphael, T. E. (1984). Teaching learners about sources of information for answering comprehension questions. *Journal of Reading, 28,* 303–11.

Rasmussen, K. (2000). *Give me shelter: Reading and limited English proficiency learners.* Alexandria, VA: Association for Supervision and Curriculum Development.

Rasinski, T. V. (2003). *The fluent reader: Oral reading strategies for building word recognition, fluency, and comprehension.* New York: Scholastic Professional Books.

Read Naturally. (n.d.). *Reading fluency benchmark assessor.* Retrieved October 31, 2006, from http://www.readnaturally.com/products/rfmInfo.htm

What's Different About Teaching Reading to Students Learning English?
Study Guide

Richard–Amato, P. A., & Snow, M. A. (1992). *The multicultural classroom: Readings for content–area teachers.* White Plains, NY: Longman.

Rigg, P., & Enright, D. (1986). *Children & ESL: Integrating perspectives.* Alexandria, VA: Teachers of English to Speakers of Other Languages.

Rodriguez, R. (1982). *Hunger of memory: The education of Richard Rodriguez, an autobiography.* Toronto, Canada: Bantam.

Rosenshine, B. (1997). Advanced research in instruction. In J. W. Lloyd, E. J. Kameanui, & D. Chard (Eds.), *Issues in educating students with disabilitie.* Mahwah, NJ: Erlbaum.

Rowling, J. K. (1999). *Harry Potter and the chamber of secrets.* New York: Scholastic.

Sakiey, E., & Fry, E. (1993). Sakiey–Fry 3000 Instant Words. In E. B. Fry, J. E. Kress, & D. Fountoukidis (Eds.), *The reading teacher's book of lists.* Englewood Cliffs, NJ: Prentice–Hall. Available from http://www.thinkquest.org

Schleppegrell, M., & Achugar, M. (2003, Summer). Learning language and learning history: A functional linguistics approach. *TESOL Journal, 12,* 21–27.

Schoenbach, R., Greenleaf, C., Cziko, C., & Hurwitz, L. (1999). *Reading for understanding: A guide to improving reading in middle and high school classrooms.* San Francisco: Jossey–Bass.

Shanahan, T. (2006). Ask the experts Q & A. *Expanding the Reach of Scientifically Based Research in Title I Schools, 1(2),* 2.

Shanker, J., & Ekwall, E. (1998). *Locating and correcting reading difficulties.* Columbus, OH: Merrill. Retrieved October 23, 2006, from http://www.nifl.gov/readingprofiles/Dolch_Basic.pdf

Short, D. (1991a). *How to integrate language and content instruction: A training manual.* Washington, DC: Center for Applied Linguistics.

Short, D. (1991b). *Integrating language and content instruction: Strategies and techniques* (NCBE Program Information Guide Series No. 7). Washington, DC: National Clearinghouse for Bilingual Education. Retrieved January 30, 2007, from http://www.ncela.gwu.edu/pubs/pigs/pig7.htm

Short, D. (1993). *Integrating language and culture in middle school American history classes.* Retrieved October 31, 2006, from http://www.ncela.gwu/pubs/ncrcdsll/epr8.htm

Short, D. (1994). Expanding middle school horizons: Integrating language, culture, and social studies. *TESOL Quarterly, 28,* 581–608.

Silverstein, S. (1985). The twistable, turnable man. In *A light in the attic.* New York: Harper & Row.

Singhal, M. (2001). Reading proficiency, reading strategies, metacognitive awareness, and L2 readers. *The Reading Matrix, 1*(1). Retrieved October 31, 2006, from http://www.readingmatrix.com/articles/singhal/

References

Sizer, T. (1992). *Horace's compromise: The dilemma of the American high school.* Boston: Houghton Mifflin.

Skehan, P. (1989). *Individual differences in second–language learning.* London: Edward Arnold.

Smith, F. (1978). *Understanding reading: A psycholinguistic analysis of reading and learning to read* (2nd ed.). New York: Holt, Rinehart, & Winston.

Smith, M. I. (1991). Put to the test: The effects of external testing on teachers. *Educational Researcher 20*(5), 8–11.

Snow, C. E. (2002, November). *The role of literacy in teaching English to younger learners.* Paper presented at a workshop for Teachers of English to Speakers of Other Languages, San Diego, CA.

Snow, C. E., Burns, M. S., & Griffin, P. (Eds.). (1998). *Preventing reading difficulties in young children.* Washington, DC: National Academy Press.

Snow, C. E., Tabors, P., Nicholson, P., & Kurland, B. (1995). SHELL: Oral language and early literacy skills in kindergarten and first–grade children. *Journal of Research in Childhood Education, 10,* 37–48.

Spangenberg–Urbschat, K., & Pritchard, R. (Eds.). (1994). *Kids come in all languages: Reading instruction for ESL students.* Newark, DE: International Reading Association.

Stahl, S. A., & Fairbanks, M. M. (1986). The effects of vocabulary instruction: A model–based meta–analysis. *Review of Educational Research, 56,* 72–110.

Stahl, S. A., & McKenna, M. C. (2000, April). *The concurrent development of phonological awareness, word recognition, and spelling.* Paper presented at the annual meeting of the American Educational Research Association, New Orleans, LA.

Stanovich, K. E. (1986). Matthew effects on reading: Some consequences of individual differences in the acquisition of literacy. *Reading Research Quarterly, 21,* 360–407.

Stauffer, R. G. (1969). *Directing reading maturity as a cognitive process.* New York: Harper & Row.

Sun, P. Y. (n.d.). *Graphic organizers—Elementary.* Retrieved October 31, 2006, from http://www.indiana.edu/~reading/ieo/bibs/graphele.html

Swain, M. (1995). Three functions of output in second language learning. In G. Cook & B. Seidhofer (Eds.), *Principle and practice in applied linguistics: Studies in honour of H. G. Widdowson* (pp. 125–144). Oxford, UK: Oxford University Press.

Swan, M., & Smith, B. (Eds.). (1988). *Learner English: A teacher's guide to interference and other problems.* New York: Cambridge University Press.

Taler, J. (1995). *In search of heroes.* Baltimore: Gateway.

Tang, G. M. (1992/1993). Teaching content knowledge and ESOL in multicultural classrooms. *TESOL Journal, 2,* 8–12.

Tankersley, K. T. (2005). *Literacy strategies for grades 4–12: Reinforcing the threads of reading.* Alexandria, VA: Association for Supervision and Curriculum Development. Retrieved October 31, 2006, from http://www.ascd.org/portal/site/ascd/template.chapter/menuitem

Taylor, B. M., Anderson, R. C., Au, K. H., & Raphael, T. E. (1999). *Discretion in the translation of reading research to policy* (Report No. 3–006). Ann Arbor, MI: Center for the Improvement of Early Reading Achievement.

Teachers of English to Speakers of Other Languages. (1997). *ESL standards for preK–12 students.* Alexandria, VA: Author.

Teachers of English to Speakers of Other Languages. (2000a). *Family involvement in the education of ESOL students.* Alexandria, VA: Author.

Teachers of English to Speakers of Other Languages (TESOL). (2000b). *Scenarios for ESL standards–based assessment.* Alexandria, VA: Author.

Teachers of English to Speakers of Other Languages (TESOL). (2006). *PreK–12 English language proficiency standards.* Alexandria, VA: Author.

Texas Education Agency. (n.d.). Examining phonics and word recognition instruction in early reading programs. In *Professional development guide: Phonological awareness. Principles for instruction and progress monitoring.* Austin: Region XIII Education Service Center.

Tharp, R. G., & Gallimore, R. (1988). *Rousing minds to life: Teaching, learning, and school in social context.* New York: Cambridge University Press.

Thomas, W., & Collier, V. (2002). *A national study of school effectiveness for language minority students' long–term academic achievement.* Santa Cruz, CA and Washington, DC: Center for Research on Education, Diversity, & Excellence. Retrieved January 30, 2007, from http://crede.berkeley.edu/research/llaa/1.1_final.html

Torgeson, J. (2004). *The right answer is the hard answer.* Retrieved October 31, 2006, from http://education.byu.edu/news/2004_features/joe_torgeson.html

Tovani, C. (2000). *I read it, but I don't get it: Comprehension strategies for adolescent readers.* Portland, ME: Stenhouse.

Ulanoff, S. H., & Pucci, S. L. (1999, Fall). Learning words from books: The effects of reading aloud on second language vocabulary acquisition. *Bilingual Research Journal, 23,* 319–332. Retrieved October 31, 2006, from http://brj.asu.edu/v234/articles/art6.html

Unsworth, L. (2001). *Teaching multiliteracies across the curriculum: Changing contexts of texts and image in classroom practice.* Maidenhead, UK: Open University Press.

U.S. Department of Education. (2002, October). *No Child Left Behind: A desktop reference. Reading First (I–B–1).* Washington, DC: Author. Retrieved October 31, 2006, from http://www.ed.gov/admins/lead/account/nclbreference/index.html

References

Vacca, J. A., Vacca, R. T., & Gove, M. K. (1987). *Reading and learning to read.* Boston: Little, Brown.

Valdés, G. (2003). *Expanding definitions of giftedness: The case of young interpreters from immigrant communities.* Mahwah, NJ: Erlbaum.

Valdez–Pierce, L. (2002, Fall). Performance–based assessment: Promoting achievement for English language learners. *ERIC/CLL News Bulletin, 26,* 1–3. Washington, DC: Center for Applied Linguistics. Retrieved October 31, 2006, from http://www.cal.org/resources/archive/news/2002fall/performance.html

Valdez–Pierce, L., & O'Malley, J. M. (1992). *Performance and portfolio assessment for language minority students.* Washington, DC: National Clearinghouse for Bilingual Education.

Vela, L. (2005, July). *Highlighting instruction in the core reading program that aligns with research–based guidelines for instruction for English language learners.* Presented at the second annual Reading First Conference, New Orleans, LA. Retrieved October 31, 2006, from http://www.centeroninstruction.org/files/HighlightingInstructionCoreReadingProgram.ppt

Violand-Sanchez, E., Sutton, C., & Ware, H. (1991). *Fostering home-school cooperation: Involving language minority families as partners in education* (NCBE Program Information Guide Series, No. 6). Washington, DC: National Clearinghouse for Bilingual Education. Retrieved January 29, 2007, from http://www.ncela.gwu.edu/pubs/pigs/pig6.htm

Walker, A. (n.d.). *Questioning: The science and the art.* Unpublished manuscript. Upper Marlboro, MD: Prince George's County Public Schools.

Walqui, A. (2000). *Contextual factors in second language acquisition.* ERIC Digest. Washington, DC: Center for Applied Linguistics. Retrieved October 31, 2006, from http://www.cal.org/resources/digest/0005contextual.html

West, M. (1953). *The general service list of English words.* London: Longman.

Whitehurst, G. J., & Lonigan, C. J. (2001). Emergent literacy: Development from prereaders to readers. In S. B. Neuman, & D. K. Dickinson (Eds.), *Handbook of early literacy research.* New York: Guilford.

Winograd, P., Flores–Dueñas, L., & Arrington, H. (2003). Best practices in literacy assessment. In L. M. Morrow, L. B. Gambrell, & M. Pressley (Eds.), *Best practices in literacy instruction* (2nd ed., pp. 209–209). New York: Guilford.

Wu, N. (1997). *Fish faces.* New York: Holt.

Wylie, R. E., & Durrell, D. D. (1970). Teaching vowels through phonograms. *Elementary English, 47,* 787–791.